CREATING A HOOSIER
SELF-PORTRAIT

CREATING A HOOSIER SELF-PORTRAIT

THE FEDERAL WRITERS' PROJECT IN INDIANA, 1935–1942

George T. Blakey

INDIANA UNIVERSITY PRESS
BLOOMINGTON & INDIANAPOLIS

This book is a publication of

Indiana University Press
601 North Morton Street
Bloomington, IN 47404-3797 USA

http://iupress.indiana.edu

Telephone orders   800-842-6796
Fax orders   812-855-7931
Orders by e-mail   iuporder@indiana.edu

Manufactured in the United States of America

Library of Congress Cataloging-in-Publication Data

Blakey, George T.
Creating a Hoosier self-portrait : the Federal Writers' Project in
Indiana, 1935–1942 / George T. Blakey.
p. cm.
Includes bibliographical references and index.
ISBN 0-253-34569-3 (cloth : alk. paper)
1. Indiana—Historiography.   2. Federal Writers' Project—
History.   3. Writers' Program (Ind.)—History.   4. Indiana—
Guidebooks—Authorship—History.   I. Title.
F525.2.B57 2005
977.2'0072'2—dc22
2004019206

1 2 3 4 5 10 09 08 07 06 05

CONTENTS

ACKNOWLEDGMENTS / VII

Introduction / 1

ONE
The National Context
6

TWO
The Hoosier Situation
28

THREE
The Indiana Guide
49

FOUR
Other Publications
80

FIVE
Oral History
107

· SIX
Almost Finished Projects
130

Contents

SEVEN

Incomplete Projects

151

EIGHT

Research Inventories

174

NINE

Conclusions and Legacy

197

NOTES / 213

BIBLIOGRAPHY / 241

INDEX / 251

Illustrations follow page 54

ACKNOWLEDGMENTS

I am indebted to the following for their assistance:

Librarians and archivists at many institutions, but especially at

   Library of Congress, Manuscript Division
   National Archives
   Indiana Historical Society
   Indiana State Library
   Cunningham Library, Indiana State University
   New Albany Public library
   Gary Public Library
   Indiana University East
   Miami University
   Ball State University

Indiana Historical Society for travel/research grants

Indiana University East for sabbatical support and office space

Dr. Joanne Passet, an anonymous reviewer, and Indiana University Press for astute criticism and suggestions. The book is better for their contributions, but its interpretations and shortcomings are mine.

CREATING A HOOSIER
SELF-PORTRAIT

Introduction

As the United States entered the Second World War in 1942 and left the Great Depression behind, literary critic Alfred Kazin published a study entitled *On Native Grounds*. Kazin recalled how the economic collapse of the 1930s had forced Americans to question their traditions and to search for insights into the country's character. Aiding in this national self-analysis was the Federal Writers' Project (FWP), a small part of President Roosevelt's Works Progress Administration, which created jobs for the unemployed. One of the most enduring products of the FWP was the American Guide series, which reviewed the past, described the present situation, and outlined tours in each of the forty-eight states. Kazin applauded these displaced writers who "went hunting through darkest America with notebook and camera" to "search out the land, to compile records, to explain America to itself."[1] Almost fifty years later, historian Bernard Weisberger revisited the American Guide series and once again applauded the writers who had probed the national past and psyche. According to Weisberger, their research had uncovered invaluable treasures and their publications were an exercise in "national self-portraiture."[2] This analogy of introspection and self-depiction mentioned by two scholars a half-century apart poses a fruitful way of assessing the work and the legacy of the Federal Writers' Project.

Approximately three hundred Hoosiers participated in this quest to search out and delineate the distinctive qualities of their state's heritage and character. When *Indiana: A Guide to the Hoosier State* appeared in late 1941, a national critic referred to it as one of the finest of the series. Since then, it has prevailed as an indispensable source of factual information and an invaluable mirror reflecting the attitudes of the writers who produced it. To pursue the Kazin-Weisberger analogy, it was a self-portrait of a state during a decade of transition from poverty to prosperity and from peace to military conflict. These writers became unofficial historians of the Indiana past and impromptu anthropologists of the contemporary scene. As tour guides, they charted the way through fascinating ephemera and idiosyncratic sites that dotted the landscape before it was homogenized by interstate highways, chain motels, and franchise restaurants. They also produced several other publications that fleshed out the portrait and made it a fuller portrayal than the singular guide could accomplish. A regional guide of the Calumet area, a collection of folklore, a recreational guide, and a series of newspaper columns all documented and publicized aspects of the state's historical activity and current conditions.

These publications featured only a small portion of the material that the FWP writers uncovered during their research. They compiled valuable information concerning such topics as racial and ethnic minorities, local histories, natural disasters, poet James Whitcomb Riley, witchcraft, indigenous foods, folklore, and gravestone inscriptions. Much of this material was the result of writers digging through local newspapers, most of which are not indexed; visiting sites, many of which no longer exist; and interviewing elderly Hoosiers, all of whom are now departed. This research in obscure sources on arcane subjects produced rich details, not available elsewhere. The bulk of their findings, unfortunately, remain in storage, unpublished and unappreciated. The Indiana self-portrait that emerges from the few official publications is a complimentary one that was edited and polished into a pleasing yet limited visage. If

2

only the information gleaned from the unpublished materials had been utilized in the published guide. Few scholars have delved into these manuscripts since the Second World War, but their findings have enriched the state's history.

As a child of the New Deal, the FWP experienced some of the same ideological criticism that was aimed at its parent. Roosevelt's administration introduced various programs to combat the economic depression, and some of them frightened conservatives who felt that the federal government was drifting dangerously toward socialism. The New Deal sided with organized labor, imposed new regulations on banks and business, competed with private utilities in the Tennessee valley, and introduced "welfare state" programs with its relief agencies and Social Security. These same conservative critics suspected that American writers who flirted with Marxist philosophy had infiltrated the New Deal. In particular, they could be found in the Federal Writers' Project. Congressional investigations in the late 1930s to ferret out radicals in the government damaged and diminished the FWP in the same manner that the Red Scare would do in the 1950s with its blacklists of political and literary radicals. These ideological purges in the 1930s can be seen less as an exposure of specific individuals and more as a general attack on the New Deal as a symbol of a federal government that had grown too large and posed too much of a threat to individualism, states' rights, and free enterprise.

Although several books have chronicled the Federal Writers' Project from its creation in 1935 to its demise in 1942, they have approached it only as a national or regional phenomenon. Jerre Mangione was an editor in the FWP, and his memoir, *The Dream and the Deal*, covers the subject with an insider's knowledge. Monty Penkower's *The Federal Writers' Project* brings a historian's sense of balance and context to the enterprise. Paul Sporn's *Against Itself: The Federal Theater and Writers' Projects in the Midwest* narrows the geographical field, but devotes half of its attention to another program, which dilutes the focus. Jerrold Hirsch's *Portrait of America* analyzes the cultural context and intellectual goals of the national FWP.[3] All of these authors consulted appropriate sources, and their books make valuable contributions to understanding the work and legacy of the program. So why another book on the subject? Because no one has yet approached the subject from the point of view of an individual state. If the major product of the FWP was a self-portrait, then an intimate analysis of one state, Indiana, could reveal much more about the Hoosier condition than would a distant glimpse at a group portrait of forty-eight.

The major goals of this work, therefore, are to survey the Indiana situation during the Depression and determine what this one New Deal program attempted as a remedy. Who were the Indiana administrators and writers who spent roughly seven years putting together this portrait of their state? As federally subsidized artists, what experiences, attitudes, and priorities did they bring to this enterprise? Did the Indiana project harbor any of the so-called radicals who caused such controversy for other states? Did they follow rigid New Deal guidelines and produce a generic product similar to the other forty-eight, or did they assert their state's individuality and render a portrait that was indigenous and unique? This book will depart from previous books on the subject in trying to answer these questions by focusing, as much as is possible, on the employees who were largely anonymous but who made significant contributions to the program. For example, the first state director, Ross Lockridge, shaped the direction of the Indiana project with his visions and enthusiasms, although he often clashed with federal administrators. Rebecca Pitts was a tireless editor whose skill as a writer elevated the state publications beyond the norm and won praise from Washington officials. And such fieldworkers as Emery Turner and Iris Cook, journalist and musician, respectively, supplied raw data for the state's self-portrait with their research and interviews. Another important departure from previous books on the FWP is the attention this one gives to the unfinished projects and unpublished research material. This massive body of information, stored in archival boxes at the Library of Congress, the National Archives, and Indiana State University, presents a more complex portrait of Indiana than do the few finished publications. It might not be as complimentary, but it would probably be more authentic. The unpublished materials conform to what historian John Bodnar calls the "public memory," which recalled various "local and personal" pasts rather than one government-endorsed version.[4] We owe these previously anonymous Hoosiers due credit for uncovering and preserving large portions of the state's heritage, even though their efforts were being ignored at the time. To paraphrase Alfred Kazin, they went hunting through darkest Indiana to explain Indiana to itself. It is time to pay attention to them.

ONE

The National Context

In 1935, the Great Depression still plagued the United States despite the best efforts of President Franklin D. Roosevelt and his New Deal. Since March 1933, the new administration had tried several experiments to revitalize American capitalism and to get the nation's economy back on its feet. The new Federal Deposit Insurance Corporation (FDIC) had helped to end the crippling banking crisis of 1929–32, and Americans began to trust their banks again. Emergency programs devised by the federal government also had smoothed the rough edges of hunger and homelessness. The Federal Emergency Relief Administration (FERA) had distributed millions of dollars in direct relief to the destitute, and the Home Owners Loan Corporation (HOLC) had rescued thousands of homeowners from eviction by renegotiating delinquent mortgages. The Civil Works Administration (CWA) had created temporary public works jobs for thousands of the unemployed until it expired in 1934, and the Civilian Conservation Corps (CCC) continued to hire young men to work in parks and forests. These and many other "alphabet soup" programs and agencies of the New Deal attempted to get the free enterprise system functioning again with unprecedented assistance from Washington.

Yet these measures that we now call the Welfare State had not been enough. Unemployment rates in 1935 hovered around 20 percent, certainly an improvement from the 25 percent of 1933, but still unacceptable.[1] Consequently, several charismatic leaders accused the New Deal of doing too little to assist the downtrodden. Their proposals to alleviate the poverty and suffering suggested that the federal government should be offering much more. For instance, Dr. Francis Townsend, a retired dentist in California, contrived a startling solution that attracted millions of followers, especially among the elderly. His revolutionary Old-Age Revolving Pensions, Ltd., would have the federal government give to each person over the age of 60 the sum of $200 per month. This would keep those individuals off the job market and, at the same time, pump huge sums of money into general circulation. Senator Huey Long from Louisiana stirred up another wave of support for an equally radical program. He proposed a program that would commit the government to a guaranteed minimum income for all. By taxing the incomes of the wealthy and redistributing the revenue among the poor, class divisions would be diminished and a decent standard of living would be federally mandated. Long's Share-the-Wealth movement gathered such rapid momentum that the Democratic Party feared it could have damaging effects on Roosevelt's reelection campaign in 1936. But Long's assassination and the passage of the Social Security Act, both in 1935, reduced some of this momentum. Nevertheless, these utopian schemes, regardless of their practicality, were popular and made the New Deal look conservative by comparison. They certainly gave testimony that the economic woes of the Depression were still very much present and that many Americans, perhaps a majority, wanted more and better solutions than their government had tried so far. Unemployment ranked as the most pressing problem in America, according to a Gallup Poll taken in the autumn of 1935; the allure of the Townsend Recovery Plan was not far behind in this tapping of public opinion.[2]

Additional testimony that many Americans wanted more government solutions to the lingering Great Depression was the dramatic rise in radical alternatives to democratic capitalism. Politics in America had traditionally supported a two-party system, with occasional third parties representing new national crises or challenges. They lasted briefly but seldom won elections. A few such parties introduced new concepts that were absorbed into the major parties. For instance, the Liberty Party of the 1850s urged abolition of slavery, and the Populist Party of the 1890s advocated government regulation of the railroads. Both concepts later became reality, although the two parties vanished. As historian Richard Hofstadter pointed out, "Third parties are like bees; once they have stung, they die."[3] The crisis of the Great Depression and the apparent inability of either the Democratic or the Republican Party to rise adequately to its challenges led many Americans to flirt with alternative political solutions. The Social Democratic Party, the champion of government intervention into the economy to benefit the working classes, had been a part of the American political scene since 1897 but had never attracted many voters. Its most popular leader for many years, Eugene V. Debs, could not get even its benign proposal of an eight-hour workday enacted. But following the collapse of the economy in 1929 and the rising concerns about capitalism's future, two alternative parties waved the flag of socialism for voter consideration in 1932: the Socialist Party polled 881,951 votes, and the Socialist Labor Party polled 33,276. Their combined total was insignificant with respect to affecting the outcome, but it was nearly a record for socialism in American elections and a fourfold increase over the total for 1928. Likewise, the tiny Communist Party, with its more radical proposals for converting capitalism into a classless society, had doubled its 1928 votes to 102,785 in 1932. With these votes, nearly a million Americans were in essence rejecting traditional solutions and urging their government to think of more radical answers.[4]

Two years later, one Democrat politician in California offered voters a very nontraditional option to the Depression, and his brief success revealed much about public receptiveness to radical alternatives. Upton Sinclair, the famous muckraking author of *The Jungle*, ran for governor of California in the Democratic primary. He startled the public and the Democratic Party with his proposal for taking idle farms and factories and turning them over to the unemployed, who would operate them as self-sustaining cooperatives. This utopian plan, which borrowed ideas from both socialism and communism, came to be known as End Poverty in California (EPIC). Sinclair defeated three candidates for the Democratic nomination. During the subsequent general campaign, the business community, the Republican Party, and the official neutrality of President Roosevelt all combined to defeat Sinclair and his radical EPIC crusade.[5]

Other American writers in the early 1930s joined Sinclair in questioning traditional capitalism and urging government to experiment with alternatives. Whereas Sinclair took his activism into the actual political arena, most of his colleagues confined their radicalism to the printed page. Their impact, less immediate and measurable than his, did, however, run parallel in spreading a revolutionary message and shaping public opinion. This literary march toward the ideological left included several notable figures and has been called by some historians the Red Romance. Lincoln Steffens was another muckraking journalist who had gained fame in the early twentieth century. His exposure of urban political graft appeared in a series of articles and a book, *The Shame of the Cities*. Later he drifted toward radicalism and visited the new communist government in Russia, about which he wrote, "I have seen the future and it works."[6] His popular *Autobiography*, published in 1931, and his public lectures expounded this philosophy. John Dos Passos used his personal experiences during the First World War in his novel *Three Soldiers* (1921), then began to question the status quo in articles that appeared in radical magazines. His popular *USA* trilogy in the early 1930s used a stream-of-consciousness style and romanticized figures such as socialist reformers Eugene Debs and Emma Goldman. Dos Passos also supported the Communist Party in the 1932 election. *An American Tragedy* in 1925 solidified the reputation of Hoosier Theodore Dreiser as a major novelist who was willing to criticize his country's economic environment. He used his high profile during the early Depression to publicize the positive accomplishments and economic stability of Russia in *Tragic America,* a book published in 1932. He also endorsed Sinclair's EPIC campaign in 1934.[7] Clifford Odets's message was similar, but he aimed it at Broadway audiences rather than readers of

books. He has been called the "official stage historian of the proletariat."[8] His *Awake and Sing* in 1935 ended with a call for revolution,
and that same year his *Waiting for Lefty* symbolized the radicalism of
the literary left wing. Therein his thespian taxi drivers agitate the
audience with a rousing cry to strike.

In light of the lingering Depression and the rising calls for radical
action, the New Deal responded with additional programs such as
Social Security to address some of these concerns. One response,
especially to the persistently elevated unemployment figure, was the
creation of the Works Progress Administration (WPA). The New
Deal introduced this public works program in 1935, and it endured
until 1943, when the massive defense spending of the Second World
War made it unnecessary. During its nearly eight years of existence,
the WPA hired approximately 9 million jobless Americans for part-
time temporary positions and pumped nearly $12 billion into the
nation's economy.[9] Among its diverse activities, construction workers
built or repaired thousands of miles of roads and sidewalks, "book-
women" on horseback delivered reading materials to remote communities in the Kentucky mountains that had no libraries, and students remained in high school and college with assistance from
part-time jobs in the National Youth Administration (NYA), a subsid-
iary of the WPA for young people. As one of the largest peacetime
efforts ever mounted by the federal government, it solidified the
concept of economic pump-priming and created thousands of public
facilities, such as city parks, sidewalks, bridges, and municipal airports, that are still in use today. The WPA also became one of the
most obvious targets for critics of government waste and profligate
spending. The term *boondoggling* was frequently used in reference to
WPA workers, who sometimes appeared to be leaning on shovels
more than doing meaningful work.

A very small subdivision of the WPA that hired writers, artists,
musicians, and theater people was known at Federal One. This somewhat rarefied section of the program constituted only a tiny percentage of the WPA personnel and expenditures, but assumed a public profile that was much larger than its numbers. Federal One was,
by the very nature of its artistic employees, the most creative of the

public works agencies. And it drew much criticism from conservatives at the time due to its perceived radicalism. In the end, it produced a legacy of artworks, theatrical and musical productions, and literary publications that endure today as nothing short of extraordinary. Compared to the millions of WPA employees who dug ditches, repaired sewers, and canned vegetables, these thousands of white-collar personnel who acted, sculpted, sang, and wrote appear to be an ephemeral minority, worthy of no special treatment or of more than a footnote to the larger welfare text. WPA administrator Harry Hopkins knew of this distinction and the dilemma faced by the unemployed arts community. His much-quoted assessment of the situation became famous. "Hell," he is supposed to have said, "they've got to eat just like other people."[10] In other words, the primary purpose of public works jobs was to provide sustenance for people; the end product of their efforts was secondary.

The end product of Federal One was in part ephemeral, as is frequently the case with the arts. The theater project staged hundreds of productions and thousands of performances in thirty-one states,[11] but once the curtain fell and the project ended, little remained of the experience. A few innovative productions such as *The Living Newspaper,* which commented on current events, and the Orson Welles production of *Macbeth* with an all-black cast made an impact on theater history, but most of the projects were just for actors and stagehands.[12] Likewise, the music project employed musicians who practiced and performed in live concerts and on special radio broadcasts. Opportunities ranged from opera to dance bands, symphony orchestras to choral units. These performers, composers, and conductors also collected folk music, gave classes, and repaired instruments. A few original compositions emerged from the FMP, such as William Schumann's, and a few premieres of American works, such as those by Virgil Thompson. But for the majority of the ensemble, it was a temporary job until the Depression ended.[13] More enduring was the end product of the Federal Art Project. Thousands of artists painted, sculpted, etched, lithographed, wove, and taught. Some of the tangible product was primitive and without real intrinsic worth. But some of it sold, generated controversy, entered museums.

Artists such as Jackson Pollock and Ben Shahn continued their careers through projects and classes of the FAP. Its murals and posters in public spaces were ubiquitous. One of the most enduring legacies was the Index of American Design, which hired artists to sketch and paint realistic replications of antiques, quilts, pottery, and folk art from the American past. These documentations of the nation's aesthetic heritage were deposited in the Library of Congress, and some appeared in published books.[14]

Writers created both transitory and permanent products as a result of their employment in the Federal Writers' Project. Several book-length studies document and analyze its activities.[15] Historians have long appreciated its most famous product, the American Guides. These were glorified travel guides filled with local history from each state, most of which are still in circulation today, having been reissued due to public demand. And historians continue to value the "ex-slave narratives," a collection of interviews with 2,300 elderly blacks who had survived slavery and shared their memories with the writers on relief. Only a small amount of the FWP research and writing saw the light of the printed page, however. Most of their efforts went into storage when the WPA ended in 1943. This lode of raw material offers a rich opportunity to uncover the hidden history begun in another era. More than any of the other Federal One components, the Federal Writers' Project provides researchers today a tantalizing challenge to complete the unfinished projects or to speculate as to what they might have become, and at the very least to more fully appreciate the attitudes and visions that their efforts reveal about the 1930s and early 1940s.

The Federal Writers' Project, small in numbers but prolific in productivity, served a particular need among the unemployed during the Great Depression. It rescued a portion of the population that was educated, middle-class, professional, and accustomed to white-collar work. They had previously been employed as journalists, freelance writers, editors, teachers, and clerical workers. Their product fell into the intangible category of writing rather than the more tangible categories of manufactured automobiles, harvested corn, and other visible commodities. Prior to the Great Depression, these writers had produced words and ideas that appeared on the printed page as books and articles. When the market for their product dried up, so did their jobs.

The decline in publishing outlets for writers is as easy to trace during the early Depression as is the closing of banks and the firing of workers from factories. In 1929, 5,000 periodicals were published in the United States, ranging from the popular *Saturday Evening Post* to the esoteric *Gospel Messenger;* four years later that number had shrunk to 3,500. Large daily papers remained relatively stable, but the smaller weekly press suffered. There were 7,000 weeklies before the Depression began, and in 1933 there were only 4,000. Between 1930 and 1935, at least five book publishers went bankrupt and other publishers cut back on the number of titles they issued each year, knowing that their market fell as the number of unemployed readers rose. In 1929, nearly 10,000 new titles appeared, and in 1933, that number declined to 8,000.[16] Sales of fiction titles dropped 55 percent, biographies fell 47 percent, and children's books were down 38 percent. Overall book purchasing dropped 50 percent in the first four years of the Depression. Some publishers began issuing titles in cheaper paperbound editions to counter the loss of sales; this may have helped somewhat, but it also meant a 50 percent cut in royalties for the authors. Some bookstores, in desperation, began lending books for a small fee, becoming inexpensive surrogate libraries. This, too, although it bolstered the income of the stores, did nothing for the authors.[17]

The appetite for literature had not slacked during the Depression, but America's ability or willingness to pay scarce money to feed that appetite had. The American Library Association estimated that as many as 5 million new patrons began to frequent libraries during this period, and the resulting increase in book circulation was nearly 40 percent.[18] The *Saturday Review of Literature* conducted a poll of its readers about this situation, and 1,417 of them responded, representing all forty-eight states. This was admittedly not a scientific questionnaire, but the results were still revealing. The data confirmed the worst fears of publishers and authors. More than 900 admitted that they were purchasing fewer books than previously, 749 admitted that cost was a factor, and 554 were resorting to their libraries with greater frequency than previously.[19]

In the face of these conditions, how were writers supposed to sustain themselves and their families? An article in the *Atlantic Monthly* shortly before the birth of the FWP in 1935 indicated that only about 13 percent of the authors in America earned enough from their writing to live comfortably; the other 87 percent had to rely on outside income. One writer asked a gathering of struggling colleagues in New York how they survived and was greeted with the answer, "We marry schoolteachers."[20] When the federal government began distributing relief and creating jobs for the unemployed in 1933 through the FERA and CWA, several journalists and organizations encouraged the director of these two agencies, Harry Hopkins, to establish projects specific to the needs of unemployed writers. After a few states, such as California and Connecticut, created temporary programs for writers,[21] the president of the newly established Newspaper Guild asked Hopkins to expand these temporary state experiments to a national program.[22] Numerous established authors, however, including Theodore Dreiser, Marianne Moore, Sinclair Lewis, and Booth Tarkington, expressed their opinions about the federal government's ability to hire and employ writers for productive work. While they did not agree on the means by which this could be achieved,[23] by 1935 it was obvious that many writers were looking to Washington for assistance.

When Congress established the WPA in 1935 to create federal public works jobs, the small Federal One section specifically addressed the issue of writers in need of work. Like the others to be employed in fields of theater, music, and art, these white-collar writers were to have jobs suitable to their skills. Harry Hopkins said earlier that it did not make good sense to take these people and "put them to work with pick and shovel."[24] These jobs were not to be considered a new career. These were temporary positions that were to last only until the Depression lifted and the writers could be absorbed back into the private sector. As one conservative editor put it at the time, FWP and Federal One were not to become "a kind of artistic old soldiers' home."[25] Neither were these to be full-time jobs that could be considered a new career at government expense. Only administrative staff worked full time; the bulk of the writers put in twenty to thirty hours per week and were paid accordingly. Salaries varied depending on regional wage scales. For instance, in New York a writer could take home roughly $100 per month, whereas in Mississippi, where the cost of living was considerably lower, the normal pay was around $40 per month.[26]

The demand for these jobs was quick and plentiful, despite their transient nature and less than munificent salaries. Ten thousand writers spent time on the federal payroll with this new form of welfare. Employee turnover was frequent, so precise statistics are difficult to determine. The whims of Congress and the concerns about government budgets also forced the rosters to rise and fall frequently. The peak year was 1936, with 6,600 listed on the FWP payroll.[27] This number declined as the war approached, and just before the attack on Pearl Harbor in December 1941, the number of writers on relief had fallen to 2,200.[28] The program expired early in 1943, since it was no longer necessary. In its brief duration, the FWP never constituted more than 1 percent of the total WPA personnel, and its expenditures of $27 million amounted to less than 1 percent of the WPA costs.[29]

To qualify for jobs in the FWP, writers had to be on the official relief rolls of the state where they lived. The act of getting registered on that list was, to many, a last resort and a demeaning admission of failure. The regular WPA offered other employment options such as construction and sewing, so applicants to the FWP had to possess some writing experience. These FWP employees represented a broad spectrum of writers. One contemporary questionnaire covering thirty-five states revealed that the largest number of FWP personnel were newspaper workers, followed by freelance writers, editors, and educators.[30] A later scholar added that the roster included many lawyers, ministers, and librarians.[31] One Pulitzer Prize–winning author from Massachusetts, Conrad Aiken, joined the ranks and for one year took home approximately $25 per week for his efforts as a researcher and writer.[32] Studs Terkel from Chicago did similar duty; this was prior to his fame as a radio interviewer and author.

The FWP sustained Ralph Ellison, Nelson Algren, Saul Bellow, and Zora Neale Hurston until they could establish their careers as novelists. Some of these writers regarded this welfare period of their lives as "a stigma of the lowest order" and rarely mentioned it in their autobiographies or résumés. Others, such as Jerre Mangione, wore it as a badge of honor. Later, as a professor of English at the University of Pennsylvania, he wrote that some of the FWP employees felt they had been part of a noble experiment in government support of the arts.[33]

Hired to administer the Federal Writers' Project was Henry Alsberg, a writer of varied background and an administrator of limited experience. A New Yorker of German Jewish parentage, he entered Columbia University at age 15 and graduated several years later from its school of law. He also studied literature at Harvard before pursing a career in journalism. Between 1913 and 1928 he worked for a variety of publications, including the *New York Evening Post,* the magazine *Nation,* and the *London Daily Journal.* Among his many assignments was foreign correspondent in Europe and Russia after the First World War. Following his journalism career, he served in at least two administrative capacities: director of the Provincetown Playhouse in New York City's Greenwich Village, and then editor with Harry Hopkins's FERA in the early New Deal. At the time of his appointment in 1935 he was 57, still a bachelor, a constant smoker, tall and portly with a craggy face and a short mustache.[34]

There is general agreement among scholars about Alsberg's less than stellar record as the chief executive of this WPA division. He seemed well intentioned but naive, more interested in being an editor than an administrator.[35] One contemporary recalled years later: "He was probably not the world's worst administrator, but he might have won an Olympic bronze medal for inspired fumbling."[36] Working from a series of offices in Washington that ranged from a renovated theater to an elegant old mansion with chandeliers and fireplaces, he devised projects, developed guidelines, hired directors for five regional offices, and selected and supervised directors for all forty-eight states. His roster of employees rose and fell in harmony with the budget that Congress supplemented and sliced with regularity. As the tone of Congress shifted toward conservatism after 1938, Federal One received more criticism for being both frivolous and radical. Even a seasoned and expert administrator would have had difficulty under these circumstances, and Alsberg was neither.

Alsberg's successor in 1939, the journalist and freelance writer John Newsom, had been the state director in Michigan. Newsom was an army veteran who had been educated in France and England, and in addition to his journalism career he had published one novel.[37] With most of the direction of the FWP set by 1939, Newsom administered it with greater efficiency and less creative volatility than his predecessor. *Time* quoted him as saying he regarded his job as one of production, not of supporting "art for art's sake."[38] His task was to complete as many as possible of the many pending projects, to locate and delegate to local sponsors, and to phase out much of the operation in the early days of the Second World War. As chief administrator, his emphasis was "not upon innovation but upon consummation."[39]

The largest project undertaken by the FWP, and the one best known by the general public, was the American Guide series. Each state produced a guide, and they received much publicity and wide circulation. A combination of state history, encyclopedia, and travel guide, these books generally followed a three-part format. Part 1 was a series of essays on distinctive aspects of each state's history such as geography, literature, architecture, and folklore. Part 2 surveyed the principal cities within the state. Part 3 was a detailed set of tours to lead visitors down the roadways and through museums, parks, churches, and local attractions. The guides employed dozens of writers in every state to research local heritage, to write stand-alone essays on distinctive aspects of the state, to recommend sites for illustrative photographs, and to travel mile by mile over suggested travel routes, citing what was worthy of a visitor's time. The intended result of these efforts was a uniform series of volumes for the general public to inform, entertain, and reintroduce the states' population to their past accomplishments and current features.

Guidelines from Washington dictated a uniformity in format, and these guidelines changed frequently in the early months of the FWP.

The constant changes that occurred in these guidelines were as frustrating as the guidelines themselves. Manuals mandated style, length of essays, types of tours, sources to consult, and a multitude of other regulations that intimidated some of the state editors and threatened to homogenize the results into cookie-cutter conformity. In addition to these restrictions, copy written by local writers was edited at the state headquarters, then edited again in the regional offices and once more in Washington, ensuring a standardized final product. One state editor expressed his frustrations in a transparent mocking of the familiar Joyce Kilmer poem:

> I think that I have never tried
> A job as painful as the Guide,
> A guide which changes every day
> Because our betters feel that way.[40]

Gradually the guidelines became more flexible, so regional and state differences could emerge. Generally positive in tone, the guides presented an upbeat overview of the states that would generate pride among the local citizenry and possibly encourage tourism. Yet they did not turn into boosterish propaganda that glossed over obvious flaws and undeniable problems. The Massachusetts guide, for example, angered the state governor, who felt that the book gave undue attention to the controversial Sacco and Vanzetti trial of the 1920s.[41] Wisconsin's conservative Republican state legislature took offense at what it considered an overly positive treatment of their "radical" governor, Robert La Follette.[42] Idaho's guide was the first one to be published, in 1937, and the others appeared sporadically until the last one, Oklahoma, which came out in late 1941.

The guides were several hundred pages long, in hardbound covers, and were contracted out to fifteen commercial publishers, including Oxford, Viking, and Hastings House. They sold surprisingly well, considering the Depression and war economies. Some went into third and fourth printings, and the forty-eight state guides sold approximately 100,000 by 1943.[43] Critics were won over by the immensity of the task, the generally high level of the writing, the thoroughness of the research, and the practical application of the past to the present. They were instantly recognized as compendia of fact and memory, trivia and substance, anecdotes and analysis. Even before the series was complete, the *New Republic* concluded that "it is doubtful if there has ever been assembled anywhere such a portrait so laboriously and carefully documented."[44] Together they captured a kaleidoscopic nation in all its diversity. The most thorough scholarly assessment of these guides said, "Behind their covers lay the story of many dedicated, albeit anonymous, individuals who accomplished a demanding and often boring task. These project employees overcame numerous difficulties to portray collectively the patchwork quilt of the country in informed and interesting prose. Through their resolve, they charted a nation."[45]

After the demise of the FWP, the American Guide series lived on in bookstores and libraries. Some books have since been reprinted as historical period pieces, and others have been revised and brought up to date. In 1949, Henry Alsberg combined and severely condensed the entire series into a massive 1,300-page version called *The American Guide*. The Book of the Month Club featured this volume as an alternative selection, which guaranteed a wide circulation.[46] In his 1961 *Travels with Charley,* John Steinbeck argued that the original guides comprised "the most comprehensive account of the United States ever got together," and that he would have taken all forty-eight of them on his tour of America if he had had room in his vehicle.[47] Other writers and travelers have since lauded the series and put them to innovative use. Geoffrey O'Gara, for example, toured several parts of the United States fifty years after the publication of the guides, but used them in a search "for eccentric places, odd conjunctions of history and landscape."[48] The result was *A Long Road Home,* which charts the changes and continuities that he encountered at the same sites discussed by the FWP writers. Archie Hobson, again a half-century later, gleaned from the original guides items that fascinated him. He stitched together pages and paragraphs from the series that fell into logical groups, such as religion, animals, monuments, and famous and unknown people. Hobson called this collection *Remembering America: A Sampler of the WPA Amer-*

ican Guide Series.[49] One thousand publications, besides the America Guide series, occupied the writers and generated considerable publicity for the FWP. There were approximately thirty guides to specific cities, such as New Orleans and Washington, D.C., which followed a format similar to that of the state guides. Then there were regional books such as *The Oregon Trail,* which traveled over a large territory from the Mississippi River to the Pacific Ocean and reprinted diaries and journals from pioneers who made the trek in the nineteenth century. There were also topical studies such as *The Negro in Virginia,* compiled and written by an all-black staff, which researched through newspaper files, records, and memoirs for local history and folklore. In addition to the almost 300 books, the FWP issued roughly 700 pamphlets on a wide variety of topics, such as *Immigrant Settlements in Connecticut* and the *Alabama Health Almanac,* and 340 brief "issuances" such as leaflets and articles. Included in the latter would be such wartime materials as bomb squad training manuals and recreation guides for military personnel.[50]

Two subgroups within the FWP were ostensibly to gather sociological information for inclusion within the state, local, and regional guide series. They did this so well that the material they gathered took on a life of its own and a separate and valuable reputation. These two groups were the Folklore Unit and the Social-Ethnic Studies Unit. John Lomax became the national advisor on folklore and helped to devise guidelines for state offices in gathering information and fashioning essays. Benjamin Botkin replaced Lomax in 1938 and expanded and refined the procedures to include additional subjects and more urban emphasis. Sociologist Morton Royse directed the latter group in its quest to document minority and immigrant groups and their manifestations in neighborhoods, churches, and foreign-language newspapers. Both units encouraged their writers to go beyond traditional research in printed records and to develop systematic oral interviews with individuals and groups. Botkin was interested in "history from the bottom up," and this was not always easy to accomplish, since portable tape recorders were not yet widely available. Nevertheless, these two units produced a flood of material well beyond the needs of the guide series, most of which was later deposited in the Library of Congress.[51] These interviews unearthed arcane local lore ranging from songs and recipes to gravestone epitaphs. One of the FWP administrators concluded that these efforts salvaged "for posterity a rich and significant part of the American past that was in imminent danger of being lost."[52] This new material became the basis for additional publications.

One segment of this material which has seen frequent publication is the group of interviews know as the Life History series. Begun as a collection of biographies of working-class people in North Carolina, the project spread to six other southern states. FWP employees were given lengthy guidelines for interviewing and techniques to elicit as much material as possible from the subjects. For instance, the instructions suggested that the writers gather material on standard items such as family, education, politics, and religion, plus less standard items such as diet, medical needs, use of time, and attitudes toward work and life.[53] W. T. Couch, the FWP regional director for the Southeast, published thirty-five of these interviews from three states in a collection entitled *These Are Our Lives*. The instructions had encouraged the writers to quote the interviewees as much as possible because, in Couch's words, "With all our talk about democracy it seems not inappropriate to let the people speak for themselves."[54] A white farm owner, a black sharecropper, a CCC boy, and a truck driver, among the thirty-five, all shared their histories, hopes, and daily routines with the writers, who assembled, edited, and presented their stories, with their names changed to protect their anonymity. The book appeared in 1939, received immediate and positive praise, and became an instant classic of its genre.

Plans for other books of the life histories failed to materialize when the WPA changed its focus in 1939, but subsequent collections of the interviews have continued to appear with some regularity. Although not a compilation of life histories, Benjamin Botkin's *Treasury of American Folklore*, published in 1944, included much anecdotal material gleaned from the FWP interviews, especially folktales. *Such as Us* was an anthology of southern lives, similar to *These Are Our Lives*, that appeared in 1978, edited by Tom Terrill and Jerrold Hirsch. Ann Banks expanded the geographical scope in 1980 in her collection of eighty interviews, *First-Person America*. It included many life stories from outside the South, as far north as New Hampshire, and as far west as Oregon. Virginia interviews were featured in 1996 in *Talk about Trouble,* edited by Nancy Martin-Perdue and Charles Perdue Jr. They supplemented their life histories from the Old Dominion state with photographs taken by the New Deal's Farm Security Administration. Former FWP employee Studs Terkel published several volumes of interviews, such as *Hard Times* (1970) and *Working* (1974), which replicated the life history format, but updated to contemporary times and themes.[55]

Historians have long appreciated the FWP interviews with former slaves, another by-product of the attempt to gather folklore and life histories. They have welcomed the wealth of information that this enterprise generated, since it was the first systematic attempt to gather memories concerning slavery. Lawrence D. Reddick from Kentucky State College in Frankfort had suggested this project to Harry Hopkins during the FERA days and had argued that the history of slavery would "never be complete until we get the view as presented through the slave himself."[56] John Lomax, once again, devised questionnaires to guide the writers in their interviews with the elderly former slaves. The questionnaires listed topics and techniques "to get the Negro to thinking and talking about the days of slavery." Such topics were biographical data, labor conditions, food, religion, education, runaways, freedom, and social customs.[57] Benjamin Botkin later revised the questionnaire to elicit more and different kinds of responses. When the project was complete in 1939, the FWP employees had conducted more than 2,300 interviews with blacks residing in seventeen states. These interviews produced the narratives, most of which now reside in the Library of Congress. They became an aggregate autobiography of these former slaves and their lives during bondage, the Civil War, and the years of freedom that followed emancipation. Lomax published excerpts of some of the narratives as early as 1938; Botkin published many others in his book *Lay My Burden Down* in 1945, and collections have appeared in numerous articles and books since then. George Rawick's massive compilation of the interview typescripts known as *The American Slave* finally made the narratives accessible to a wider audience in the 1970s. Since then other anthologies have appeared, such as *Weevils in the Wheat* (1976) from the Virginia interviews.[58]

Scholars have also been ambivalent about these interviews and narratives. Beyond their appreciation for the raw data newly available, they have lamented the missed opportunities that characterized this enterprise.[59] Even though these narratives added many layers of primary information to that previously known about slave life, the information was suspect on several levels. The former slaves being interviewed were, by necessity, elderly; two-thirds of them were over 80 in the mid-1930s. This meant that most of the interviewees were children during their bondage and knew of adult slave life only by secondhand reference to their relatives and acquaintances. It also meant that a time lapse of roughly seven decades had separated them from their pre-emancipation days. Memory is tricky under the best of circumstances, and those decades could have substantially altered reality through loss of detail, romanticized events, and changing contexts and circumstances. Compounding the problems associated with memory was that of the interviewers. The FWP employees were amateurs in this new field of oral history; they were not trained anthropologists, historians, or interviewers for the most part. The overwhelming number of FWP employees were also white, and the racial differences between them and their subjects might well have intimidated or at the least inhibited the open sharing of sensitive personal memories regarding master-slave relations. One former slave summed up this problem aptly: "Everything I tells you am the truth, but they's plenty I can't tell you."[60] This problem was embarrassingly evident on at least one occasion in South Carolina. One former slave was interviewed twice, once by a white woman and once by a black male. The former narrative emerged in a cautious presentation of slave life as a benign, even positive experience, almost as if the interviewee had offered what she thought the white interviewer wanted to hear. On the other hand, the narrative given to the black interviewer was filled with unvarnished tales of suffering and the negative aspects of life in bondage.[61] Dialect and speech patterns also created many problems for historians. Very few of the

FWP workers were equipped with tape recorders; they took notes by hand and later typed their interviews. Some tried to replicate the sound and rhythm of the interviews; others did not. Some transcribed the oral exchanges in first-person prose as if the interviewee were telling the story; others used third-person style, with the interviewer telling the story secondhand. None of these problems posed fatal barriers to accepting the FWP narratives as authentic voices from the past, but they did present serious caveats for scholars searching for reliability. Southern historian C. Vann Woodward summed up the problem and the potential of the narratives by admitting that, although they were flawed, incomplete, and suspect, they "still remain the daily bread on which historians feed."[62]

Perhaps the most singularly creative publication of the FWP employees was *American Stuff,* which was issued by Viking Press in 1937. It was an anthology of writings done by project employees on their own time. They contributed short stories, essays, and poems that proved they were, in fact, writers, not just people doing clerical work for the government. FWP director Henry Alsberg sent out a call for manuscripts from the FWP employees, and he commented in his foreword to the book that there were hundreds of submissions.[63] Jerre Mangione edited the compilation, which represented more supervisors than employees and was heavily dominated by entries from New York and California. Richard Wright contributed a noteworthy piece about Jim Crow life that later developed into his autobiographical books.[64] *American Stuff* received favorable reviews, with the *New York Times* commenting on the realism with which the authors portrayed life in the 1930s.[65] An attempt to continue this sort of public outlet for their creativity never developed, but a few poems and writings by FWP employees were featured occasionally in other magazines such as *Poetry* and the *New Republic.*

Perceived radicalism in the WPA and other government agencies led to congressional hearings in 1938; these hearings produced enough ill will on Capitol Hill to destroy one part of Federal One and to reduce support for the other three. The Dies Committee, the common name for the House Committee on Un-American Activities, headed by Democratic congressman Martin Dies from Texas, capitalized on a growing conservatism across America and an eagerness among some politicians to curtail New Deal spending.[66] The WPA did not have an official political stance on hiring, so there had been no ideological litmus test for prospective employees. But it was public knowledge that a vocal minority of FWP and FTP workers were perhaps overly sensitive to class issues and the struggle of the proletariat, and some of them had joined the Communist Party. This was particularly true in New York and Massachusetts. The Dies Committee sought to publicize this subversive situation and to deny further government aid to those who advocated left-wing causes. The hearings generated a massive amount of newspaper coverage, and some Gallup polls indicated that the public regarded the work being done by the committee as patriotic and effective.[67] Chairman Dies alleged that the FWP and FTP were "doing more to spread communist propaganda than the Communist party itself."[68] One committee member was especially critical of Richard Wright's writing in *American Stuff*. Even though this anthology was a collection of works written during the writers' free time, it appeared to some committee members to reflect a dangerous anti-Americanism within the FWP.[69]

Federal One found itself especially vulnerable to this criticism due to its small size and ephemeral nature. Hallie Flanagan, director of the theater project, had to defend her productions against charges that they were too critical of capitalism and fostered class hatred. And Henry Alsberg had to convince the committee that a few communist employees in a few metropolitan centers did not typify the FWP and did not influence its research or publications. Harry Hopkins sensed that the hearings were a political witch hunt to damage the New Deal and was reported to have given Flanagan and Alsberg permission to "spit in the faces of the Dies Committee."[70] Their appearances there helped to polarize issues rather than to protect their own interests. Flanagan's testimony at the hearings was defensive, maybe even adversarial, but Alsberg's was more conciliatory and deferential.[71] Whether the Dies Committee was the catalyst or just a publicist, Congress followed this new fiscal and ideological conservatism in 1939. It jettisoned the FTP and forced the other three arts projects to find local sponsors within the individual states to underwrite 25 percent of their budgets. Alsberg's administrative efficiency was already under attack, and this negative publicity from the congressional hearings probably offered the incentive to replace him with someone less politically suspect. The liberal magazine *Nation* at the time intimated that Alsberg was sacrificed on the altar of anti-communism. Using several decades of hindsight, historian Jerrold Hirsch takes a less simplistic stand on this episode. He views the Dies Committee's attack on the FWP as more than an exposure of left-wing subversion; it was, instead, a rejection of the New Deal championship of racial and ethnic minorities, labor unions, and the common man that the FWP reflected in its publications.[72]

Both the WPA and the FWP assumed new direction in 1939, and their programs reflected the new political atmosphere. The Works Progress Administration received a cosmetic name change to the Works Projects Administration, and the FWP officially became known as the Writers' Program. Harry Hopkins left the WPA that year for a variety of political and health reasons, and he was replaced by Colonel Francis Harrington, who had helped establish the early CCC program and was an engineer for the WPA. A career military man, Harrington was not nearly as supportive of the arts programs as Hopkins had been.[73] Likewise, John Newsom, the new leader of FWP, was reluctant to undertake major new departures and instead focused on completing the multitude of unfinished projects. Somewhat chastened by the publicity from the Dies hearings and the conservative gains in the 1938 elections, the WPA and Writers' Program walked a more cautious path politically.

International pressures also affected the activities of the WPA and Writers' Program after 1939. As the flames of war began to spread throughout Europe and Asia, fewer public works were necessary in the United States, and some of the writers' activities were channeled into military training manuals and service personnel recreational guides. Many of the early proposals were abandoned, and several of the projects already in midcourse were never finished. For instance, Nelson Algren's *America Eats,* an anecdotal history of regional foods, remained unpublished until 1992. Another victim of the personnel changes and the war atmosphere was the project "Hands That Built

America," a book which would have been illustrated with plates from the Federal Art Project's Index of American Design. It was never published.[74] In the spring of 1943, the WPA went out of existence. Some of the official records from the Writers' Program went to the Library of Congress and others to the National Archives. Most of the state records found homes in various libraries and universities around the country.

The major assessments of the FWP generally concur regarding its goals and accomplishments. It succeeded as an employment agency for the white-collar workers who were listed under the broad grouping called writers. Ten thousand writers or aspiring writers were able to sustain themselves during the Depression by working at their craft. They did not have to dig ditches or do other work for which they had no experience or aptitude. The FWP was welfare, but it recognized the recipient's professional calling. It failed as an agency to stimulate and produce memorable literature. Few people really felt it could do this from its inception. Harry Hopkins had indicated that jobs were the first priority and anything else that resulted was "gravy."[75] Nonetheless, it succeeded in researching and compiling a massive amount of data about America's past heritage and present diversity. The life histories, the ex-slave narratives, and the folklore all constitute a rich, albeit flawed, body of raw material for historians. As historian William McDonald concluded, all of this held up a "mirror to America" in the 1930s and early 1940s.[76] And it succeeded brilliantly with the publication of its American Guide series. Never before had the nation been described so thoroughly and systematically. As early as 1938, when many of the state guides were still in the research phase, a columnist for the *New York Times* stated that the guides constituted "one of the most valuable series of books ever issued in the United States."[77] The FWP also served as a precedent for government subsidy of the arts. Brief and fleeting, it established a model that announced that the literary arts were worthy of public underwriting. Not until 1965 with the creation of the National Endowment for the Arts would the federal government once again take this position and generate the same kind of social and ideological controversies that had occurred during the Great Depression.

TWO

The Hoosier Situation

The Great Depression plagued Indiana no less than it did the rest of America, because the Hoosier state typified the rest of the nation in a variety of ways. Both Americans and Hoosiers postponed marriages in the early days of the economic decline, and birthrates fell accordingly. People were understandably reluctant to start new families under such uncertain conditions.[1] Suicide rates went in the opposite direction, moving erratically upward, as more people chose to take their own lives in the face of sustained adversity.[2] And Indiana also paralleled the nation in the deferred hopes of its young adults to pursue professional careers. Aspiring teachers, lawyers, and physicians found it difficult, if not impossible, to find the necessary tuition for higher education. This can be seen in the drop in college enrollments. In 1930 there were 26,893 students matriculating at campuses across Indiana. That number fell to 23,374 in 1933.[3]

Before 1929, the state had a typically mixed economic base with a few urban-industrial centers dominated by iron, steel, and automobile manufacturing, and it still hosted major agricultural activity, led by hogs and corn. The federal census of 1920 revealed that Indiana had officially joined the American norm in having an urban majority. By 1930, Indianapolis with its 365,000 population constituted the only genuine metropolitan center, but four other cities tallied around 100,000 each: Fort Wayne, Gary, South Bend, and Evansville.[4] The rest of the state was rural, with many small towns and modest cities. Although the rural part of the state was now a minority, it still dominated the Hoosier character in the 1930s; sycamores reflecting in the waters of the Wabash more nearly described the self-image of the state than did Fort Wayne's Lincoln National Bank building. At twenty-two stories of Indiana limestone, it was the state's tallest building. Indiana was also typical in that, although usually Republican in politics, it elected a Democratic state legislature in 1932 and Governor Paul V. McNutt, who matched, if not exceeded, President Roosevelt in his ambitions, popularity, and experimental zeal. Indiana, like America, found itself in 1933 questioning old traditions of self-reliance and individualism in the face of the prolonged unemployment that had proven too much for private charities and local relief efforts. State government, similar to the federal counterpart, had made only a few provisions for assisting the destitute, elderly, and jobless, and these had proven inadequate to the task. This enduring depression served as a catalyst for a variety of Welfare State experiments that originated in both Washington and Indianapolis as Hoosiers, like other Americans, demanded that their governments offer more assistance to their distressed citizenry.

To get a full picture of the impact of the Great Depression on Indiana, you must combine economic statistics that are scattered among disparate areas. Together they portray a state in rapid transition from the comfortable traditions of the 1920s to the disturbing insecurities of the 1930s. The collapsing banking system can serve as a barometer of the general economic decline. During the late 1920s it was not unusual to have 20 or so Hoosier banks fail each year. Following the Wall Street crash in 1929, that number tripled to 62 in 1930, and then quadrupled the next year to 82, and in 1932 quintupled to 117.[5] With no depositors insurance available, these failures had a devastating ripple effect on industry, business, and family savings. As desperate bankers called in loans and mortgages, many businesses and families faced foreclosures and eviction. Factories and retail firms retrenched as a result of the financial crisis and released many of their employees. The Hoosier unemployment rate began to climb rapidly, from 6.9 percent in 1930 to 12.8 percent in early 1933. That latter percentage represented roughly 115,000 members of the workforce, seeking jobs that no longer existed.[6] Industrial employment was more condensed in the Calumet region, and with the Gary steel mills operating at less than 30 percent of capacity, the unemployment rates there were much higher than the state average.[7] According to one survey by state officials, some counties reported that as many as 33 percent of the families were receiving some kind of relief.[8] Hoosier farmers suffered less from joblessness than they did from falling farm prices. Hogs and corn, the two largest sources of agricultural revenue in the state, began to decline in market value even before the Crash of 1929, but accelerated their fall thereafter. Farmers received $10.91 per hundredweight for pork in 1925, $8.84 in 1930, and $3.34 in 1932. Statistical ratios for corn were similar, and because hogs consumed a major portion of the corn, their values naturally merged. The immediate result of this decline was reduced consumer spending for roughly 25 percent of the state's workforce and the possibility of foreclosure and eviction from their farms and homes.[9]

By digging beneath the statistical review of the state to an anecdotal portrait of human experience, you get a broader view of Indiana's reaction to the Great Depression. In hard-hit Lake County, community leaders organized a program to send recent Mexican immigrants back to their home country. This repatriation effort lessened the number of local job applicants and relief recipients by approximately three thousand.[10] Robert and Helen Lynd, who had published the classic and controversial sociological study of Muncie in the 1920s, returned in the 1930s to gauge the impact of the Depression on this supposedly typical small city. There they found that the city now provided vacant lots for more than twenty-five hundred unemployed citizens to raise vegetables, that the Community Fund in 1932 had failed for the first time to meet its goal, and that there was a boom in the sale of home sewing machines as more families resorted to self-sufficiency for their family clothing needs.[11] The annual State Fair took place as usual, but with crowds and attitudes considerably diminished. To help farmers cope with their economic plight, State Fair officials permitted them to exchange sacks of grain for admission tickets.[12] And while not typical of the entire state, one experience from Wayne County reflected the desperation and ingenuity that characterized many Hoosiers in the early 1930s. One man recalled years later that his family was in such need of extra funds that he captured stray cats and took them to the Eli Lilly research labs, which paid a small bounty per animal.[13]

In the face of this statistical and anecdotal evidence of economic insecurity, it is not surprising that Roosevelt's New Deal would find Indiana receptive to its experiments in government aid to the needy. By 1933, Indiana's township trustees, who oversaw care of the poor through an antiquated system of poor farms and minimal relief, could no longer cope with the severity of the unemployment crisis. The state welcomed Harry Hopkins's infusion of monetary "handouts" through the new Federal Emergency Relief Administration (FERA). During its first year, this program dispensed roughly $12 million in Indiana.[14] Likewise, the Civil Works Administration (CWA), also under the direction of Harry Hopkins, created temporary jobs at public works projects for 104,000 Hoosiers during the winter of 1933–34.[15] The Federal Deposit Insurance Corporation (FDIC) brought stability and trust to the shaky banking system, and to stanch the flood of home foreclosures, the Home Owners Loan Corporation (HOLC) refinanced 48,824 Indiana mortgages within its first three years. One grateful father in South Bend displayed his appreciation by naming his new son Homer Oscar Louis Clemens.[16] Another small but very popular attack on unemployment was the Civilian Conservation Corps (CCC), which employed 3,500 young men in firefighting, erosion control, and reforestation work around the state.[17] In 1935, the new Social Security system initiated a permanent program of pensions for the elderly, care for the disabled, and unemployment compensation. All of this, plus many other national New Deal programs, established precedents for federal aid to the needy and also established new priorities and loyalties among the citizenry about where to seek assistance. It was now primarily Washington and secondarily local and state governments.

Governor McNutt and his newly elected Democratic General Assembly not only worked in tandem with but, in some cases, paved the way for the New Deal in Indiana. Meeting from January to March 1933, before Roosevelt began his Welfare State experiments, they passed legislation that foreshadowed the federal programs, reorganized the state for greater administrative efficiency, and set up partnerships to expedite the flow of national revenues into the state. McNutt had been national commander of the American Legion and a dynamic dean of Indiana University's School of Law before his election to the governorship in 1932. He was uncommonly handsome, was openly ambitious for higher office, and lost little time establishing a record as the most powerful governor Indiana had seen since the Civil War days of Oliver P. Morton.[18] In March 1933, he created the Governor's Commission on Unemployment Relief (GCUR) to coordinate state activities and expedite the flow of federal funds. The new legislature also enacted a very limited pension program for the elderly. McNutt's major reorganization plan included the establishment of a Department of Public Welfare to replace the outdated Board of Charities and Corrections. All of these transformed the state's relief apparatus from its unwieldy local trustee network throughout ninety-two counties into a more streamlined state system that ran parallel with the federal government. Then the passage of the Public Welfare Act created the framework for a state-federal partnership of Social Security. Conservatives and the state Republican Party could not help but realize that all this activity lessened the traditional local responsibilities, diminished some of the state autonomy, and increased the political power of the chief executive. Roosevelt's coattails and the popularity of the New Deal among state voters assisted Hoosier Democrats in winning several subsequent elections. In 1936 Lieutenant Governor Clifford Townsend won the race for chief executive and enjoyed a Democratic majority in the General Assembly. Four years later, despite Republican Wendell Willkie carrying his home state in the presidential race, Democrat Henry Schricker won the governor's contest. Not since before the Civil War had there been three Democrat governors elected in succession.

Despite the extraordinary measures taken by both federal and state governments, many Hoosiers felt that these actions were inadequate responses to the economic crisis, and they demanded more radical solutions. Indiana had hosted radical dreamers since the utopian community of New Harmony in the 1820s, although their visions had little tangible effect on the state. Terre Haute socialist Eugene V. Debs had the same negligible impact at the turn of the twentieth century. But by 1932 the Great Depression had convinced some Hoosiers that neither the New Deal promised by Roosevelt nor four more years of President Herbert Hoover was equal to the task. They demanded more than either major party offered. Hapgood Powers, a native son, offered more far-reaching proposals in his Socialist candidacy for the Indiana governorship. This Harvard-educated labor organizer advocated unemployment insurance and demanded pensions for the elderly in the face of the Depression's challenges. To the surprise of most observers, Powers tallied 18,735 votes.[19] In the next few years of Welfare State experimentation by the Democrats, the popularity of the Townsend Recovery Plan demonstrated that many Americans wanted their governments to endorse this radical proposal for pensions to the elderly. The movement was especially popular in the Midwest, and in Indiana its appeal was a phenomenon. Precise membership in the Townsend clubs is difficult to determine, but when Dr. Francis Townsend spoke at the state fairgrounds in September 1935, he attracted a crowd of ten thousand. The Indiana lieutenant governor, the mayor of Indianapolis, and other political dignitaries formed a welcoming party suitable for a visiting head of state. Townsend drew sustained cheers when he charged that Roosevelt and his advisors did not understand poverty or the solutions for it.[20] Senator Huey Long and his Share-the-Wealth organization found equally eager Indiana audiences for his promise of guaranteed annual incomes. Thousands of Hoosiers joined the clubs, and in the spring of 1935 Long's wife, Rose, drew front-page coverage in the Indianapolis press, which called attention to her roots in Decatur County. That same spring the Democratic National Committee commissioned a presidential preference poll to gauge voters' attitudes. It revealed that in Indianapolis 7.5 percent of the respondents preferred Long as a presidential candidate.[21] As a collective group, the Powers, Townsend, and Long supporters were a minority, but a very vocal one that knew what they wanted: more government assistance during the Depression. Their combined demands, no matter how unrealistic, made the New Deal and the Mc-Nutt administration look cautious and conservative by comparison.

The Works Progress Administration in 1935 sought to tackle the lingering unemployment problem with a more radical approach than previous temporary experiments. It was a hybrid program of jobs, financed by the federal government and administered by supervisors within the state governments. In Indiana this hybrid experiment worked better than in some more conservative states that distrusted or fought the New Deal. McNutt's administration, followed by those of Townsend and Schricker, worked in a complementary way with Washington, in part because of their Democratic ties, and in part because a cordial partnership could produce greater financial benefits for the state than would a reluctant relationship. To direct the Indiana WPA, Harry Hopkins wanted an experienced administrator with political connections and a sympathetic attitude toward work relief. McNutt handed him just such a person in Wayne Coy, a former journalist from Franklin and Delphi who was an insider in the McNutt administration. Coy had worked with the Governor's Commission on Unemployment Relief since its inception in 1933 and had organized and administered the state's first Department of Public Welfare. One Washington correspondent described him as a "level-headed Liberal without an axe to grind." Coy quickly became a protégé of Harry Hopkins. He directed Indiana's WPA and coordinated relief activities in six midwestern states until 1937, when he left to fill a series of political, diplomatic, and broadcasting positions.[22] His successor was John K. Jennings, another active Indiana Democrat who had managed several mining and milling enterprises in Evansville and had run unsuccessfully to become its mayor. During the early Depression, Jennings had helped to organize the local relief organization and personally raised $130,000 to support its work relief efforts. In 1935 Coy and Hopkins appointed him to be the administrator of WPA operations for ten counties in southwestern Indiana.[23] After his ascent to the state WPA post in 1937, he continued through the governorships of Clifford Townsend and Henry Schricker until the demise of the program in 1943.

As the top WPA administrators in Indiana for almost eight years, Coy and Jennings oversaw the Hoosier portion of America's most ambitious peacetime humanitarian operation, in both size and cost. They were responsible for hiring a multitude of Hoosiers for temporary, part-time jobs; in its peak month, September 1938, WPA had roughly 100,000 on the payroll. And during these years they channeled into the state $302 million in federal funds.[24] This was a major attack on the lingering unemployment crisis and an equally major boost to local economies. WPA workers in Indiana did the typical highway, sewing, canning, and construction projects found elsewhere. Its junior component, the National Youth Administration (NYA), also found part-time jobs for college and high school students, almost 10,000 in its first academic year, 1935–36.[25] Despite the standard complaints that many of these jobs were trivial and that boondogglers leaned on their shovels most of the time, many Indiana WPA projects were distinctive and of enduring worth. In Fort Wayne, workers constructed fifty experimental prefabricated homes that sold for $900 to low-income families. These unique Art Deco dwellings received national attention in *Architectural Record* and the *Reader's Digest*.[26] Just east of Evansville, WPA employees participated in an archaeological dig of ancient Native American mounds under the supervision of geologist Glenn Black from Indiana University. This site later became Angel Mounds State Park.[27] During the devastating flood of the Ohio River in 1937, John Jennings mobilized his WPA personnel and equipment in rescue and reconstruction work.[28] And rural Indiana, especially its small county schools, received a monumental gift to sanitation, 100,000 outdoor privies, thanks to the WPA.[29]

Politically the WPA was supposed to be nonpartisan, but Republicans argued that Democrats got preferential treatment in hiring for relief jobs, and logically they voted their appreciation on election day. Relief and politics became a major issue in the 1938 elections, which produced a Senate investigation and a Pulitzer prize for one journalist who proved just how pervasive politics was in the WPA.[30] Indiana was not central to these scandals, but neither was it exempt from frequent charges of mixing welfare with ballot boxes, particularly when the top WPA administrators were all Democrats.[31] Anti–New Deal politicians in Indiana insisted that WPA relief rolls increased just before elections and that traditionally Democratic counties received more benefits than did Republican counties. Following the victories by conservatives in 1938, seven of Indiana's Republican congressmen called for an investigation of WPA's involvement in politics in their state. John Jennings called their charges "ridiculous," saying that the state organization had been investigated three times and cleared of political coercion three times.[32]

The WPA's Federal One section offered jobs for hundreds of Hoosiers in the fields of theater and music. Wayne Coy selected Indiana University professor Lee Norvelle to head the state Federal Theatre Project, and from 1935 until 1937 Norvelle supervised an ambitious program of plays in the Keith Theater in Indianapolis. Of special note were four plays by Hoosier playwrights. There was also an active children's performance group in Gary.[33] The state Federal Music Project probably reached a wider audience in Indiana than did all the other components of Federal One, due to the fact that orchestras, bands, and choral societies performed frequently to large groups and sometimes over radio broadcasts. Led by William Pelz, a recent graduate of Indiana University, the FMP produced 177 free summer concerts in 1937 alone to an audience of 55,000. In addition to the Indianapolis Federal Orchestra, there were concert bands in Evansville and Fort Wayne and a folk music ensemble in Terre Haute that featured both choral and string music. Indianapolis also hosted a black dance band, and there were folk groups in South Bend and Hammond as well. By 1940 the WPA estimated that a million Hoosiers had heard performances by these varied groups.[34] Although some unemployed Hoosier artists found work through New Deal programs, the state never did organize an official unit of the Federal Art Project and therefore did not participate fully in that program's most famous activity, the Index of American Design. Hence very few replications of antiques, quilts, and folk arts from

Indiana were included in the massive collection of national artistic folklore.[35] Nevertheless, many state artists did paint murals for post offices and other public facilities. The WPA's recreation and education projects also hired many artists. For example, sculptor John Q. Adams constructed a diorama depicting canal boats for the Indianapolis Children's Museum, painter Charles Bauerley installed a multi-panel mural in the Indianapolis Naval Armory, and William Kaeser instructed art classes, the products of which were exhibited in several galleries.[36]

The final component of WPA's Federal One, the Writers' Project, offered jobs to several hundred Hoosier writers. Indiana's literacy rate at this time, 98.3 percent, exceeded the national norm and was far ahead of all the bordering states.[37] Hoosiers had a long tradition of not only reading voraciously but writing prolifically. The state in 1935 was in the middle of its Golden Age of Literature, which had begun in the late nineteenth century; this generation had seen an extraordinary number of writers gain fame and fortune. Established authors such as Booth Tarkington and George Ade were comfortably retired by 1935 and did not need WPA assistance; others, such as Theodore Dreiser and Ernie Pyle, no longer lived in the state and were gainfully employed at their craft. Still others, such as Claude Bowers and Meredith Nicholson, had shifted emphasis into international diplomacy while pursuing writing as a sideline. Those who needed the Writers' Project in Indiana were the same as in other states: unemployed journalists, teachers, librarians, ministers, secretaries, or, in the words of one contemporary observer, "anybody who could write English."[38] They were not famous authors down on their luck at the time, and unlike a few in other states such as Richard Wright, Studs Terkel, and Zora Neale Hurston, they did not become famous following their stint in the FWP. They were, for the most part, educated, middle-class professionals who had been displaced by the economy and harbored aspirations to return to writing or to begin writing as an occupation. The Depression had diminished the opportunities for their talents, and the FWP could revitalize them.

The Depression had, in fact, closed many doors for writers in Indiana, just as it had across America. The steady decline in the number of newspapers from 1920 through the 1930s, combined with the rise of radio listeners during that same period, resulted in fewer jobs for researchers, writers, editors, and advertising personnel in the print media. The number of cities in Indiana with daily newspapers declined from 112 in 1929 to 103 in 1935. For example, Kokomo lost its *Dispatch,* Greencastle lost its *Herald,* and Terre Haute lost its *Post.* The number of smaller weekly papers, which were the social and political heart of many communities, shrank from 319 to 292 during this same four years. Aurora no longer had its *Dearborn Independent,* New Harmony's *Register* failed, and Rushville said goodbye to its *American.*[39] Conforming to the national trend, public libraries, just like unemployed workers, had less revenue to spend on new books and magazines. In Muncie, for example, the expenditures for new books and periodicals fell by at least 10 percent every year from 1930 to 1934, and the library also reduced its professional staff correspondingly. At the same time, new patrons of the library increased, as did the circulation of materials. A review of annual statistics from other libraries, such as those in Gary, Terre Haute, and Shelbyville, reveals the same pattern of increased demand and decreased services during the Depression.[40] A cruel logic fueled this sequence: as unemployment rose, the purchase of books, newspapers, and magazines fell; as jobless people increased their use of public libraries, those facilities reduced their staffs and purchases.

The man selected by the WPA to head Indiana's FWP wore many hats, and most of them fit the writers' situation in 1935. Ross Lockridge was a writer, a book salesman, a teacher, and a civil servant. A native of Miami County and a history major at Indiana University, Lockridge excelled at speech and debate. Following his graduation he taught history at Peru High School and organized a debate team there. He completed law school in 1907 and practiced law in Oklahoma until 1913, when he returned to Indiana for the rest of his life. His later career encompassed teaching for Indiana University, selling books for the World Book Company, and writing popular history for young audiences in such books as *George Rogers Clark* (1927), *Abraham Lincoln* (1930), and *LaSalle* (1931). Personally he was dynamic and colorful, with a stocky frame and deep voice. His son remembered him as a person of "almost terrifying energy."[41] During the 1920s he developed a series of pageants or historic site recitals in which he dramatized events and persons from the past. He focused on the heroic, pulling in songs, poetry, and populist traditions to reunite Hoosiers with their roots. These traveling exercises, or "History on Wheels," continued into the 1940s. His grandson recalled from his childhood seeing Lockridge exhuming the past for present audiences. "He was both evangelical preacher and traveling salesman. . . . I remember some of his performances—this resolute orator silhouetted against a bonfire, gesticulating grandly."[42] His wife, Elsie, was at one time a Socialist who voted for Norman Thomas for president, but Ross was a Democrat.[43] He had become friends with Paul McNutt, since both lived in Bloomington and both worked for Indiana University.

When McNutt became governor, he appointed Lockridge to his Commission on Unemployment Relief, an appointment that permitted Lockridge to pursue his writing and historical enthusiasms. His official title was state supervisor of correlated programs for the emergency education division, and its amorphous description gave Lockridge almost carte blanche to travel the state, working on projects with schools, libraries, historical societies, museums, and county trustees, many of which received federal relief funds through GCUR. Lockridge used this position to present more of his fireside pageants. One was a pilgrimage to twelve sites located along the route of the Wabash and Erie Canal, which evoked memories of the 1830s and 1840s, and another was the Civil War raid through southeastern Indiana by Confederate general John Hunt Morgan in July 1863. Lockridge wrote these scripts, directed the pageants, often played major roles in them, and arranged for local musicians to dance, play, and sing period pieces. He generated much publicity and coverage from the local newspapers and later wrote fulsome and glowing reports of the activities.[44]

Federal FWP officials, in their typical fashion, conferred with state WPA administrators and leading Democrats to find a suitable person to lead the state FWP. They decided that Lockridge could fill the position and offered it to him when he returned to Indianapolis from one of his historic site pilgrimages. According to one Washington administrator, Lockridge was somewhat dazed at this sudden change in jobs, but he agreed to rise to the challenge.[45] For roughly two years, he would oversee the hiring of writers through the WPA system, supervise their research and writing through FWP guidelines, and pursue his own projects at the same time. It was a tumultuous task that he undertook with his usual energy and flamboyance. During weekdays in Indianapolis he stayed at the English Hotel and worked out of the WPA offices, which were located at 217 North Senate Avenue until 1937 when they moved to 1200 Kentucky Avenue, once the site of the Marmon Motor Car Company. On weekends he returned home to Bloomington, burning up the highway at 80 mph in his Plymouth, according to his grandson.[46] He was paid $200 per month for his administrative and editorial work, which was average pay for FWP state directors.[47]

Lockridge received much assistance in the state headquarters from a small group of full-time editors who provided expertise and continuity in the production of the guide and other publications. These assistants and editors did not come from the usual WPA relief rolls; they filled a non-relief quota, originally set at 10 percent of total personnel, but later raised to 25 percent as the magnitude of their task became apparent. A native New Yorker, Gordon F. Briggs held one of these editorial posts and later assumed the state director's job when Lockridge departed in 1937. Briggs had earlier worked as a journalist in New York and Washington for United Press International. Following the First World War he served as an assistant to Congressman Andrew Hickey from La Porte, Indiana. Briggs moved to Indianapolis in the mid-1920s, where he held a variety of positions, the most recent of which was publicity director for the Indianapolis Chamber of Commerce. He brought to this FWP position a passion for folklore and a steady competence, especially needed during Lockridge's frequent absences.[48] Another editor was Quaker activist Rebecca Pitts. She had earned an English degree from Butler University and also received a master's degree in English from the University of Chicago. Her career included several years of teaching in Indiana schools, reading manuscripts for the Bobbs-

Merrill publishing company in Indianapolis, and publishing occasional articles in such magazines as the *New Republic*. As an aspiring writer and latent radical, she attended a conference in 1932 at which John Dos Passos transformed her Quaker idealism into political activism. Her productivity in the state office and the regional office in Chicago impressed national administrators, and at one point there was some discussion of transferring her to the Washington headquarters to work with FWP director Henry Alsberg.[49] Clay Stearley was an enterprising and unemployed writer who had written to Alsberg in 1935 seeking employment. He had previously attended Indiana State Teachers College and served in the U.S. Cavalry during the war. For eight years he had worked for the *Terre Haute Post*, but when that paper went defunct, so did his job. A series of temporary positions had not lasted, and he told Alsberg, "I really need a job badly."[50] Stearley began work at the state headquarters in the first year of the operation and was particularly valuable in editing the tours for the guide.

The FWP writers in Indiana were typical of those in most states. They had to come from the ranks of the unemployed and be certified as eligible by their township trustees and WPA officials. Until the hiring procedures were clear and publicized, many unemployed writers contacted the WPA or the national FWP headquarters in Washington. Others contacted their congressmen or senators hoping to get appointed. One even wrote to First Lady Eleanor Roosevelt, who forwarded the letter ultimately to Lockridge.[51] These writers were generally referred to as "fieldworkers," since few of them were professional writers, and their work consisted primarily of research rather than writing. Most of them worked only a few months and departed for other positions as the economy improved or the WPA periodically reduced its hiring quotas. Lockridge reported that at the end of the first year, twenty-five of his fieldworkers had returned to private employment, including one to the *Indianapolis Times*, one to the *Evansville Courier*, and one to the ministry, and one student had found a scholarship for further study.[52] Urban centers had little difficulty providing enough personnel to fill the quotas, but rural areas as often as not had no one on the relief rolls who could qualify. Lockridge explained that he did what other state directors did under these circumstances. He convinced WPA officials to transfer unemployed teachers, ministers, and secretaries over to the FWP, so he could pursue the research and writing projects outlined from Washington.[53] Indiana seldom had more than 150 so-called writers employed at any given time, and when the program ended in 1942, the number was down to approximately 25. It is difficult to assess the ratio according to gender and race because of the constant shifting of employees, but according to the roster for December 1, 1936, Indiana employed 53 male fieldworkers and 48 female.[54] This ratio of women was much higher than the normal hiring pattern for the WPA in general, which limited female employment to a few specific categories such as sewing and canning projects. On the other hand, black fieldworkers were scarce in Indiana. Apparently there were very few on the relief rolls who claimed literary expertise in the 1930s, so the FWP had few to choose from. There were rarely more than one or two on the payroll, and those were usually from Marion County. Consequently, Indiana ranked behind all its surrounding states in the number of racial minorities in the FWP.[55] During the initial months of the program, Lockridge set up district offices in the larger cities around the state, staffed with supervisors who would distribute assignments and guidelines for research and writing, collect the written manuscripts, and forward them to the state headquarters for editing. Most of the fieldworkers received around $80 per month, clocked twenty to thirty hours per week, and at times were required to submit a weekly account of their productivity, usually within a range of 1,200 to 2,000 words.[56]

Among the hundreds of fieldworkers who passed through the Indiana FWP revolving doors, a few with little or no formal writing experience distinguished themselves for either the quality or the quantity of their work. Albert Strope is a good example. Born and raised on a farm in southeastern St. Joseph County, he briefly attended Manchester College and taught grade school until the First World War erupted. He served in the army in England and France for more than a year, then returned to teaching in Mishawaka until he lost his job in 1931. Thereafter, to support his wife and five children, he went "on the dole" with FERA, worked under the CWA, and as a white-collar unemployed, joined the FWP at its inception.[57] James Clarence Godfroy was another fieldworker of distinction. A native of Miami County, and a direct descendent of both the legendary Frances Slocum and Chief Francis Godfroy of the Miami Indians, Clarence frequently signed his FWP manuscripts with this genealogical information, of which he was obviously proud. Erratically educated and sporadically employed as a factory worker, vaudeville performer, and farmer, Clarence took a position with FWP and specialized in gathering folklore and Native American customs. He researched local newspapers, visited cemeteries, and conducted interviews to gather information previously unpublished.[58] Iris Cook was a fieldworker of tenacity and longevity. Her independence and resourcefulness could be witnessed early in her life, when, at the young age of 16, she worked as a musician at the Kerrigan Theater in her hometown of New Albany. When the Kerrigan closed during the Depression, she was left single, without a job or an education. When the FWP began hiring in 1935, she was 27 and quickly became one of its most versatile employees.[59] Lauana Creel from Evansville nearly matched Iris Cook in her versatility and longevity. Creel's family had moved from Alabama and Kentucky to southwestern Indiana, where she taught music. During the early 1930s, she and her mother lived in her brother's home with his wife and children, a situation not too uncommon for families who were combining incomes during the Depression. Similar to Cook, Creel was unmarried when the FWP began. At age 50 she became an energetic, prolific long-term fieldworker.[60]

Reflecting the national norm, a few of the fieldworkers had some professional writing experience. Emery C. Turner was one well suited to the mission of the FWP. A graduate of Oolitic High School in Lawrence County, he attended Indiana University and taught school and sold insurance before settling down to a career in journalism. He covered the police beat for the *Louisville Herald-Post* until the Depression hit and he was let go in 1930. In his mid-forties, married with six children, Turner went through rough times until the New Deal created jobs. In 1935 he transferred from a WPA sanitation crew to the FWP, where he excelled at research, writing, and assisting other fieldworkers in southern Indiana.[61] William W. Tuttle from Muncie was one of the older Indiana fieldworkers, but one who proved capable of generating more than his weekly quota of prose. Aged 65 at the inception of the Writers' Project, Tuttle had already retired from his full-time jobs of teaching and operating a grocery store. As an avocation he had written columns on nature topics for the *Muncie Star* for twenty-five years, so he considered himself a writer, although not professionally.[62] One of the few FWP employees who had pursued a career as a creative writer was Charles Bruce Millholland of Indianapolis. He had attended Indiana University, where he was active in the Jordan River Revue, and later held a variety of jobs involving film, ballet, and theater. While working for an impresario in 1929, he traveled by rail from New York to Chicago on the Twentieth Century Ltd. He wrote a play script about this experience, which eventually became a Broadway show by Ben Hecht and Charles McArthur, *Twentieth Century*, in 1932 and a Hollywood movie of the same name in 1934. He returned to Indianapolis in 1935 for a production of his play *Faun* by the Indianapolis Civic Theater and began working for the FWP.[63]

Although the vast majority of the Indiana fieldworkers were not professional writers, many of them harbored literary aspirations. Some of these individuals took their extracurricular writing seriously, considered their work worthy of public notice, and had published verse and songs before joining the FWP. William Tuttle, for example, wrote a large number of poems and published a collection in 1933 entitled *Memories of White Oak School Days* about his earlier teaching experiences.[64] Likewise, Emery C. Turner had written and submitted for publication several poems and lyrics for songs. One of the latter, "If You're Irish, It Don't Matter Where You Are," had been published in 1924 by a New York music firm.[65] When the national FWP solicited manuscripts for its creative writing anthology, *American Stuff*, several Hoosier fieldworkers submitted some of their work for consideration. Ross Lockridge forwarded them to the Washington headquarters and endorsed them as "worthy," but none were accepted.[66] Tuttle and Turner were among those who sought the validation that this publication would bring to their literary aspirations, as were Elizabeth Kargacos from Bicknell and Merton Knowles from Warren County. Most of their poems were in rhymed format and dealt with Hoosier subject matter. One of Tuttle's, for example, was a tribute to a statue recently installed in Muncie called Appeal to the Great Spirit; two of Turner's were homages to James Whitcomb Riley and Eugene V. Debs; and Kargacos's lengthy verse covered the recent visit of President Roosevelt to Vincennes to dedicate the George Rogers Clark Memorial.[67]

Lockridge's leadership of the Indiana FWP lasted only two years, from late 1935 to late 1937. The major problem appeared to be a basic incompatibility between his personal enthusiasms and the official goals established in Washington. The primary goal for state directors was to see that the state guide was researched, written, and published. Other goals such as gathering folklore, interviewing former slaves, and compiling local histories were secondary and not to interfere with the accomplishment of the first. Lockridge had some difficulty adhering to these priorities, and he became the subject of several private reprimands and public investigations. His proposal to use FWP fieldworkers to assist the Indiana Historical Society in surveying pioneer cemeteries around the state met with disapproval in Washington because it would slow down work on the guide.[68] In a similar manner, his suggestion that Indiana personnel could provide local newspapers with historical materials for their columns went nowhere, since this too would interfere with the progress of the primary goal.[69] Federal officials considered Lockridge's work on another book of his own an impediment to his job. He and his son, Ross Jr., were collaborating on a volume about the Fauntleroy house in New Harmony. The time and travel involved in this enterprise raised considerable ire among Washington FWP administrators.[70]

Probably the factor that most damaged Lockridge's position as director was his passion for his "History on Wheels" pilgrimages. He insisted that they were closely related to researching local history for the guide and that they generated positive publicity for the Indiana FWP.[71] Consequently, he and some of the fieldworkers launched several of his historical site recitals, including one in lime-stone country at Bedford, one tracing William H. Harrison's 1811 march from Vincennes to the Tippecanoe battleground, and one under the state capitol dome commemorating pioneer lore, com-plete with cider and parched corn, all of which Lockridge enthusi-astically documented and described in his official reports. An un-impressed FWP field supervisor estimated that each of these "goodwill tours" cost approximately $100 in travel and expenses.[72] FWP investigators from Ohio and Illinois concurred with Indiana WPA director Wayne Coy and Henry Alsberg that Lockridge had been "careless, indiscreet, negligent of his responsibilities as Direc-tor, and abusive of his travel authority"; also, he apparently had "never made a real effort to understand either administrative or ed-itorial procedure."[73] FWP leaders reprimanded him, then supervised him more closely in 1937, but they were never convinced that the guide would make sufficient or timely progress under his leadership. Despite his popularity and his friendly contacts within the state gov-ernment, they consequently encouraged him to terminate his direc-torship.[74] His forced resignation in July 1937 ushered him into a rather large company of former state FWP directors; 75 percent of the initial appointees around the nation did not complete their terms. Most of them resigned, and a few were fired.[75] Lockridge's departure appears to have been a little of both.

Gordon Briggs's leadership of the Indiana FWP from late 1937 to its completion in early 1942 was less public, not as colorful, more in harmony with federal goals, and ultimately more productive than Lockridge's two years. He presided over the completion and publi-cation of the guide and several smaller projects. His tenure ran par-allel with the conservative shift in Congress, one consequence of which was reduced funding for the WPA. The rise of Indiana's Ho-mer Capehart as a new force in the state's Republican Party char-acterized this move against big and expensive government.[76] Briggs also survived the Dies Committee investigations in 1938 about un-American activities in the FWP. These ideological charges focused mainly on New York and other urban centers, so Indiana was not centrally involved in the investigations. As early as 1936, FWP field

46

supervisor James Dunton had checked out a criticism that some rough drafts of the Indiana guide might be too favorable toward such radicals as Eugene V. Debs. Dunton dismissed the criticism and concluded that "if all the communists in Indiana were laid end-to-end and stretched across the steps of the state house it would still be possible to leave the building without having to step over any-one."[77] His dismissal of Hoosier radicalism was perhaps a bit too glib and not altogether correct. The Townsend and Huey Long movements had attracted thousands of supporters in Indiana, and several Hoosier FWP employees were open in their advocacy of left-wing movements. Emery C. Turner submitted a poem to the *American Stuff* anthology entitled "Why I Am a Socialist," in which he sided with laborers shackled by poverty. Editor Rebecca Pitts went even further to the left. In the 1930s she had published in the communist magazine *New Masses* several articles that denounced capitalism and praised Lenin's revolution for the workers.[78] These literary polemics did not make Turner or Pitts dangerous subversives, and their ideological predilections did not seem to overtly affect their work for the FWP. But their political leanings could have proven embarrassing if they had been exposed during the polarized investigations of the late 1930s.

One result of this new conservative mood in Washington was the restructuring of WPA in 1939, which forced the FWP to find local sponsors for its activities. The public relations department of Indiana State Teachers College became the Indiana sponsor, consequently paid a quarter of the bills, acted as an advisory body, and made some proposals such as producing educational materials for schools. Despite the location of the new sponsoring institution in Terre Haute, state FWP headquarters, with Briggs and his editorial staff, remained in Indianapolis. In the summer of 1940, Indiana's WPA offices moved once again, this time to 429 North Pennsylvania, the former home of an insurance company. Its four tall Corinthian columns and imposing stone façade gave the new headquarters of the recently renamed Writers' Program an appearance of the dignity and stability that it was gradually losing.[79]

The election of Henry Schricker as governor in 1940 perpetuated

Democratic control of the Indiana statehouse, but Schricker had never been close to the McNutt and Townsend administrations, and his relationship with the New Deal was more grudging than admiring. Schricker's term coincided with the coming of war, which diminished the importance of the WPA to the national economy, and employment quotas for the Writers' Program shrank commensurately. A few fieldworkers undertook small defense-related projects; several long-term plans never got under way, and some projects were never completed. In early 1942, with only a handful of employees, most of whom were elderly, the Hoosier Writers' Program quietly expired.[80] At its demise, seven years' worth of office correspondence, fieldworker reports, manuscripts, printed guidelines, and photographs were hastily piled into boxes and divided among national and state archives.[81] This small but unique portion of the New Deal soon disappeared from view, with the exception of its most public product, the Indiana guide. Its years of research, interviewing, compiling data, and writing rough drafts on historical topics from the Hoosier past would now be stored away, largely inaccessible and mostly forgotten.

THREE

The Indiana Guide

When *Indiana: A Guide to the Hoosier State* appeared in September 1941, it was the forty-seventh of the forty-eight state guides. In November Oklahoma's guide appeared, completing the long project of research, writing, and publishing begun in 1935. To mark the occasion, a consortium of book publishers and sellers arranged for the week of November 10–16 to be celebrated as American Guide Week. President Franklin D. Roosevelt endorsed the celebration with a public letter that took the opportunity to

> commend this splendidly written and illustrated series of books about the United States to the attention of readers not yet familiar with them. Through these guides, citizens and visitors to our country now have at their finger-tips for the first time in our history a series of volumes that ably illustrate our national way of life, yet at the same time portray the variants in local patterns of living and regional development. . . . Several volumes of the American Guide Series are among the books in the White House library and the Hyde Park Library. I urge the American reading public to take advantage of AMERICAN GUIDE WEEK to refresh their knowledge of their own land.[1]

These books were the major undertaking of the national FWP and its forty-eight state offices. From the beginning, the Washington administrators of the Federal Writers' Project decreed that each state would produce a volume according to national guidelines. There was a certain inevitability about them; state directors who could not conform to the system departed sooner or later and were replaced by directors who could generate words and photographs on schedule. In microcosm this situation reflected a trend that characterized the New Deal; more authority accumulated in Washington as the separate states abdicated or lost responsibility.

When Ross Lockridge assumed the Indiana FWP directorship in late 1935, Henry Alsberg and the national FWP officials had already determined the primacy and scope of the guide series. Not since 1909 had there been a comprehensive tour guide of the United States—the famous Baedeker series that instructed travelers about what was worthy of seeing and doing in their treks across the countryside. The Baedekers were woefully outdated by 1935, due especially to the presence of automobiles and good highways that were not present in 1909.[2] Katherine Kellock of the FWP staff was the major inspiration for an American Baedeker, a new United States tour guide, whether in the form of one comprehensive national guide, several regional ones, or forty-eight separate state volumes.[3] Prior to the establishment of the WPA, one state, Connecticut, had already produced a modest tourist guide, using unemployed white-collar workers in the state.[4] The FWP guides, therefore, were not completely original in concept or in means of production. Precedents existed for both the idea and the execution. What was distinctive was the magnitude of the enterprise. Forty-eight states, thousands of workers, government subsidies, private publishers, and conservative critics all added up to an enormous public works experiment.

The basic format for the guides was a hybrid compilation that fell somewhere between a tour guide and a state encyclopedia. Three major sections within the books would give readers a grand overview of the state. Part 1 would consist of essays on the state's history and culture; part 2 would describe each of the major cities, and part 3 would be a series of guided tours to all corners of the state. Maps, photographs, and a timeline would supplement the three sections, and a selected bibliography would direct readers to additional information. All state guides were to adhere to the same format unless some major distinction called for a deviation. Conformity was the rule, and very few states were permitted exceptions. For travelers who used several of the guides on extensive trips, this uniformity was convenient, but for state editors it could sometimes prove stifling. This cookie-cutter conformity did, however, prove beneficial in the editing process, wherein Washington editors used a comparative approach and soon knew what worked well and what did not. A Kentucky editor who had earlier complained about the administrative regimentation was later sent to Missouri to assist its staff in overcoming some problems with their guide that he had already overcome in his home state.[5]

The fact that a grand strategy had already been adopted for the guides did not necessarily mean that the Washington administrators had worked out all of the logistics regarding research, writing, editing, and publication. Those myriad details had to evolve over several months. Until they did, Indiana's FWP director devised his own scenario for the Hoosier guide and the role to be played by state fieldworkers, based on his own experience with writing popular history. Lockridge reported in January 1936 that fieldworkers with military experience would be researching and writing about the history of the army and navy in Indiana, and that those with scientific training would be digging up materials on the state's topography and flora and fauna.[6] No matter how logical this scenario might have seemed to Lockridge, it did not coincide with the evolving plans from Washington. As federal plans developed, the national office bombarded the state offices with memos and guidelines that added layer upon layer of instruction, technique, and deadlines. Successive guidelines often contradicted earlier ones and made life difficult for the understaffed and harried state directors. One of the federal administrators, George Cronyn, estimated that more than 650 pages of guidelines came from the national headquarters in the first year.[7] One FWP employee in California expressed understandable frustration to the *Saturday Review of Literature* about the plethora of federal instructions. This complaint probably spoke for employees in other states as well, but the editorial dominance of Washington prevailed.[8]

State fieldworkers ultimately received specific topics to research and varied techniques for digging up local history, folklore, and arcana to add color and flavor to the essays and tours within the emerging guide. Early in the process, Alsberg told the *Indianapolis Star* that the fieldworkers would be studying Indiana through a "figurative microscope" in order to uncover things that often had been overlooked and now would "quicken the interest" of both natives and tourists.[9] Regardless of their previous military or scientific backgrounds, they would visit their area museums, libraries, and cemeteries for information on Indians, historic buildings, major events, amusing incidents, and famous or infamous individuals who had distinguished the territory. They were to dig through old newspapers and history volumes and explore documents in city and county public offices for records dealing with trials, deaths, land, and natural phenomena. If necessary, they would interview elderly residents whose personal memories were the only apparent sources of information about local incidents.[10] Most often the fieldworkers submitted their research in a standard format that answered the journalistic who, what, where, when, and how questions concerning their assigned topic. Sometimes the fieldworkers would copy by hand, then later type, entire public records, newspaper articles, and pages from printed histories. These documents would accompany their raw data and be sent together to the state headquarters, where full-time staff would then turn the research into prose. On other occasions, the fieldworkers would write their own essays or articles as rough drafts to be edited in Indianapolis. Often these drafts would include a word count, to document the fulfillment of their weekly quota of "writing."

Examples of fieldworker research in the state FWP files reveal the sort of guidelines under which the FWP personnel operated and the varied ways in which they responded to them. Jerry Kirk from Terre Haute went out to survey the small communities in Vigo County and compile information on the origins of their names, famous people who had lived there, distinctive architectural features, existing public institutions, and the presence of ethnic populations. Kirk dutifully researched, observed, and reported his findings about the community of Bridge Junction in a literal and straightforward manner. "The name is due to the fact that it is located near a bridge. . . . No distinguished families or persons have ever lived here. . . . There is no architecture here. . . . There are no hospitals, colleges, libraries, or museums. . . . No foreign groups reside here." He concluded his report with a terse comment that explained everything with no editorializing: "Bridge Junction has no population."[11] Needless to say, Bridge Junction was not mentioned in the completed guide.

Going from the perfunctory to the poetic, Paul Yoder from St. Joseph County undertook an assignment that asked for a descriptive survey of antiques in South Bend. Yoder responded by visiting the Richard Elbel home and filing this inventory:

> They have in their reception room a love seat identical in design with that which stands in the first territorial governor's mansion at Vincennes. It is French, about one hundred fifty years old, has high crowns at the ends on the back, and three rose carvings there. It is claw footed. Mrs. Elbel has reupholstered it in satin damask, griffin design with floral figures. She secured the piece at the Walker tavern on Route 112, in Michigan."[12]

Federal and state FWP officials encouraged the fieldworkers to go beyond the usual secondary sources such as encyclopedias and local histories in order to get previously unused primary data. They suggested digging into local newspaper morgues and the files of local government offices. Two FWP researchers were so diligent in their pursuit of an assignment that their efforts got reported not only to the state headquarters but to the press as well. This unnamed pair had been digging up official documents in the office of the Wabash city clerk. The city clerk assisted at first, then grew weary of retrieving old records and replacing them when the FWP researchers were finished. She conferred with other city officials, and they mutually decided that "too much inspection was too much," Indiana guide book or not. Local officials consequently closed the files for several days until the city clerk acquiesced to WPA pressure and permitted the FWP researchers to continue their work, digging up raw data for the guide.[13]

Printed sources, whether standard secondary materials or primary documents in newspaper morgues and government offices, often needed verification for authenticity or supplements for depth and nuance. National guidelines instructed fieldworkers on the benefits of interviewing people to extract additional information not available in libraries or filing cabinets. The reasoning went that much local history had never been written down and existed only as memories, waiting to be transcribed by would-be historians. The Indiana guide editors wished to write about the Amish and Mennonites in northern Indiana, and naturally they consulted books and articles already written about these "Pennsylvania Dutch" settlers. For verification and supplementary material, FWP writer Allen Stranz from Indianapolis conducted a lengthy interview with a Mennonite native of Pennsylvania who now lived in Indiana. His report from the interview cited the usual descriptions of "prosperous farmers" and "clean housekeepers" and "thrifty, simple fashion." He concluded that the interview corroborated earlier research and that "our material in the files is substantially correct."[14]

To speed up research and to supplement fieldworkers, especially in rural areas where FWP personnel were scarce, national administrators suggested that the state directors farm out some assignments to associate volunteers. These unpaid associates could be teachers, newspaper reporters, librarians, students, and other people who wanted to assist in the compiling of local lore for the guide. Lockridge informed Washington officials that he had 2,690 associate volunteers lined up to help. Some, he said, were Republican and anti–New Deal, but all supported the guide. This extraordinary number included newspaper editors, librarians, school principals, and other individuals from almost every county in the state.[15] Lockridge probably compiled this list from previous lists of county contacts when he worked with the Governor's Commission on Unemployment Relief arranging educational programs and historical site recitals around the state. There is little indication that they assisted with

Ross Lockridge, historian, writer, and impresario,
was director of the Indiana FWP, 1935–37.
Photo courtesy Larry Lockridge.

THE INDIANAPOLIS NEWS

THURSDAY EVENING, FEBRUARY 27, 1941.

WPA Guide Offers History of State, Points of Interest, Folkways and Interesting Tours

Gordon Briggs, director of the Indiana FWP, 1937–42, featured in the *Indianapolis News*, 1941. Photo courtesy *Indianapolis Star.*

The "Liars' Bench" in Brown County, a source of many folktales for FWP fieldworkers. Photo courtesy Indiana FWP Collection, Cunningham Library, Indiana State University.

George Sargeant displaying pioneer tools in Martin County. Photographed by FWP fieldworker Emery C. Turner. Photo courtesy Indiana FWP Collection, Cunningham Library, Indiana State University.

Mint field photographed by FWP fieldworker Paul Yoder in
St. Joseph County. Photo courtesy Indiana FWP Collection,
Cunningham Library, Indiana State Library.

The Levi Coffin Home in Fountain City earned the title of "Grand Central Station of the Underground Railroad" and was featured three times in *Indiana: A Guide*. Photo courtesy Indiana FWP Collection, Cunningham Library, Indiana State University.

Indiana: A Guide, published in 1941, was the forty-seventh state guide published. This book was the major undertaking of the Indiana FWP. Courtesy of Indiana State Library.

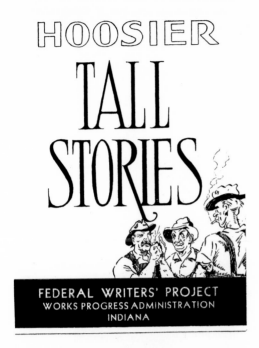

Hoosier Tall Stories, 2nd edition, 1939, was a popular collection of folklore and yarns gathered by Indiana FWP fieldworkers. Image courtesy of Indiana State Library.

Logo for FWP weekly newspaper column "It Happened in Indiana," which appeared in seventy Hoosier papers, 1940–42. Image courtesy Indiana FWP Collection, Cunningham Library, Indiana State University.

Rebecca Pitts, an editor in the state headquarters of the
Indiana Federal Writers' Project, wrote major portions
of *Indiana: A Guide*. Photo courtesy IUPUI University
Library, Special Collections and Archives.

much research or provided much data. This was an example of Lockridge's enthusiasm for public relations, which the national office soon began to question. One group of associates, however, was of some service in providing research materials to the FWP. The National Youth Administration found part-time jobs during the academic year for high school and college students. Some did research on guide topics when fieldworkers were not available. For example, in Spencer County, NYA student Inez Barnett copied old articles and documents from a scrapbook belonging to the Spencer County Historical Society. Her typing was littered with typos and strikeovers, but some of the information she submitted on the Rockport bluffs and Nancy Hanks Lincoln proved to be valuable enough to appear in the guide after considerable editing.[16]

All of this research by part-time fieldworkers fed into the state headquarters, where full-time editorial staff transformed the data and rough drafts into essays about the history and culture of the state. Prescribed topics determined the number and nature of the essays, but individual states were able to tweak the format if their reasons were compelling. For example, all of the guides included essays on the state's natural setting, history, early Indian contributions, and transportation. Most of the states wrote essays on the arts: painting, music, theater, literature, and architecture. Some of them grouped all of the arts together into one essay; others, with apparently a deeper heritage or more to boast of, wrote separate essays on each. The same grouping or dividing held true for commerce, industry, and labor. Some had lengthy essays on sports and recreation; others omitted the topic entirely. Likewise for agriculture, education, and religion. Indiana, specifically, included a major piece on agriculture, as could be expected, but chose, after several attempts, to forgo an essay on religion. Rebecca Pitts had written a preliminary piece on religion that the Washington editors deemed satisfactory, but state director Gordon F. Briggs later decided that it was "likely to be highly controversial and probably unsatisfactory to every denomination" in the Bible Belt.[17] The Indianapolis staff also chose, oddly enough, to do nothing with sports and recreation, but provided four separate essays on the arts. A few states convinced the national editors to permit a special essay on some indigenous sub-ject. For example, Kentucky wrote of its Thoroughbreds, Louisiana cooked up an essay on its cuisine, and Arizona provided the "Sun-burnt West of Yesterday," a romanticized elegy to the mythic cowboy. Indiana did not depart from the standard lineup.

The opening essay in the guides was generally an impressionist piece that set forth the character of the state and its inhabitants. This essay permitted considerably more creativity and individuality than the others. North Carolina, for example, explained the origins of its nickname in "Tar Heels All," and Oklahoma described "The Spirit of Oklahoma." New Hampshire claimed to be "The Merriest of the Puritans," while California boasted of "El Dorado Up to Date." Indiana chose to compromise with a simple "Indiana Today," wherein the editors concluded that "the average Hoosier is neither a highly polished urbanite nor wholly rustic. Rather, he is something in-between."[18] With very rare exception, the essays were anonymous, the product of several authors and editors. However, a small handful of noted writers did produce signed essays, generally on the state's character. For instance, Virginia historian Douglas Southhall Free-man and Kansas journalist William Allen White received credit for their work. Indiana had attempted to persuade state writers Booth Tarkington and Meredith Nicholson to write signed pieces, but this never came to fruition.[19]

Part 1 of the Hoosier guide, under the general headline "Indiana's Background," contained fourteen essays. The shortest was the anal-ysis of the contemporary Indiana character, which ran roughly five pages, and the longest, a chronological narrative of the state history, consumed thirty-six pages. These essays were written by a handful of the FWP editorial staff in Indianapolis, who, despite their anonymity, poured much effort and personality into their work and took pride in the results. Lockridge invested much time in several of the initial pieces before his departure, especially on Indians and the state his-tory through 1815. Gordon Briggs wrote several pieces on his own, such as folklore and transportation, and rewrote parts of others that had been started by Lockridge. Rebecca Pitts probably crafted more of the essays than anyone else and was not hesitant to defend her work. She wrote essays on natural setting, education, agriculture, and archaeology, among others. After two years on the job she said, "The Writers' Project has taught me a great deal about my own State, and not a little about good writing."[20] At one point she transferred to the regional office in Chicago to assist in revising copy there. Mildred Schmitt, from the Indiana WPA staff, shared office space with the FWP and, after the departure of Miss Pitts, rewrote some of the essays, including the one on architecture.[21] Some of the planned essays on religion and sports were jettisoned early on and never appeared in the book. Others were the product of so many contributors and revisions that clear individual authorship is impossible to attribute.

Typical of most state guides, individuals wrote the essays whether or not they possessed any expertise on the subject. To prevent egregious errors and omissions, and to guarantee a high level of accuracy, the national staff suggested that state editors have the essays critiqued by consultants who were authorities in the field. One of the Washington editors estimated that some ten thousand consultants around the country volunteered their services to read and comment on the essays before publication.[22] They were university professors, independent scholars, museum curators, artists, musicians, and other professionals who contributed skills and knowledge at no cost to the FWP. Indiana benefited greatly from this practice and found Hoosier consultants willing to assist on most of the essays. The essay on history required several consultants due to its length and the scope of the subject. Dr. Otho Winger from Manchester College, Dr. Andrew W. Crandall from DePauw University, Rev. James Mathew Gregoire from Vincennes, and Dr. Christopher B. Coleman, director of the Indiana State Library, all gave the essay critical readings during its development. The essay on architecture also needed the assistance of several readers. Lee Burns and Kurt Vonnegut from Indianapolis donated their expertise. Dr. Stith Thompson from Indiana University assisted with folklore, and state archaeologist Glenn A. Black aided with that subject. Several members of the Purdue University School of Agriculture critiqued this essay, and Wilbur Peat, director of the John Herron Art Institute, consulted on the arts and crafts piece. Drs. John and Erminie Voeglin and Dr. William A. Huggard from DePauw helped with the essays on Indians and literature.[23]

For the most part, the state headquarters found its relationship with these consultants to be convivial and invaluable. Briggs spent an entire day at the Purdue campus working with the School of Agriculture and commented that "personally, I think they did a swell job."[24] He also spent a day in Bloomington reviewing suggestions on folklore with Stith Thompson and found that time very profitable.[25] On occasion, however, the relationship was a bit strained. For example, Briggs disagreed frequently with architect Lee Burns on both style and deadlines. He recalled that he "wrested the manuscript away from [Burns] . . . by main force yesterday. He is a fine architect and a very pleasant gentleman; but as a writer he is not so hot."[26]

These fourteen essays emerged over months and years of researching by fieldworkers, writing by state editors, and critiquing by volunteer consultants. Then they were critiqued again, first in the regional FWP office in Chicago, and again in Washington. Depending on the length and quality of the originals, this editing and revising process could be repeated several times. Some of the editorial comments dealt with content, others with style, others with length, sometimes all of the above. In Chicago, John Frederick read the Hoosier copy with a critical eye. He was a professor of English at Northwestern University, director of the Illinois FWP, and regional FWP director for the Midwest.[27] In Washington, FWP director Henry Alsberg often read and critiqued copy in the early years, and a roving field editor, Stella B. Hanau, did much copyediting in the later period, frequently visiting state headquarters.[28] In addition, two of the editors in the Washington headquarters were native Hoosiers and gave the Indiana essays a close and personal commentary. One was George Cronyn from Anderson, who had pursued an academic and writing career before joining the FWP. Terre Haute resident Ruth Crawford assisted with regional FWP offices, then transferred to Washington.[29]

The essay on Indians is a good case study in the gradual evolution of a topic to a finished piece. Lockridge initially rejected the idea of treating Indians in a separate essay, preferring instead to integrate the material into the essay on history.[30] He ultimately relented on this point but still regarded this as his personal turf, considering his prior publications on Indiana pioneer days. He told the Washington staff, "I have given the subject of Indian lore and history in Indiana a great deal of attention for many years."[31] Lockridge's early draft of the piece included several lengthy speeches delivered by Indians, apparently a carryover from his historic site recitals in which he delivered orations by Little Turtle and Tecumseh. Washington editor Ruth Crawford determined that the speeches impeded the narrative and needed to be cut.[32] Following Lockridge's departure, Briggs admitted to national headquarters that the essay was not making progress and it might be helpful to see some successful models from other state guides. He shortly received essays on Indians from the Iowa and Nebraska projects.[33] Rebecca Pitts did not find these two models particularly helpful, and therefore she relied heavily on the *Handbook of American Indians* from the U.S. Bureau of Ethnology. She also consulted works by Hoosier historians Jacob P. Dunn and Logan Esarey for other details.[34] The final sixteen-page essay contained no Indian orations but considerable folklore from the Miami tribe, possibly gathered by fieldworker James Clarence Godfroy. His drafts on witchlore and superstitions show much similarity to portions of the finished manuscript.[35]

The essay on folklore and folkways is another good example of how raw data from fieldworkers evolved into an entertaining piece through a lengthy process of many consultations and editorial revisions. From Washington, folklore specialists John Lomax and Benjamin Botkin sent lists of items for states to research: superstitions, cemetery epitaphs, medical treatments, foods, games, and many other subjects. Indiana's original FWP folklore editor, Elsie Durre, prepared a supplement and index to these topics for fieldworkers, which, according to Lockridge, was adopted for use in other state FWP offices.[36] And Hoosier fieldworkers responded with a multitude of material gleaned from libraries, observation, and interviews. These bits of folklore arrived from almost every county, piling up in the state headquarters in quantities far exceeding the needs of the guide essay. One of the national folklore authorities was impressed at the resourcefulness of the Hoosier fieldworkers, especially Lauana Creel from Evansville. He praised her as "a natural collector, one of the few I have ever met."[37] Gordon Briggs filtered through this mass of material and drafted the manuscript. Folklore had long been one of his personal interests, and he belonged to several professional organizations in the field. He spent several hours with Indiana University folklorist Stith Thompson and produced the nine-page essay, which Alsberg declared was "excellent" and which was used as a model for other state editors.[38] The essay included the predictable discussions of the legendary John Chapman (Johnny Appleseed); fieldworkers from Allen County had sent more than twenty-five pages of material on Chapman's legacy.[39] Creole music from French settlers in Vincennes also received much attention; fieldworker Elizabeth Kargacos located many French folk tunes in Knox County and had them translated by a local teacher of French before sending them to Indianapolis. Briggs listed most of the songs in his essay.[40] The essay also included several gravestone epitaphs as examples of attitudes in earlier times. Fieldworker Cora Shand from Benton County found one cemetery inscription on a small white marble slab that testified to the hard times and short life span of pioneers.[41] Briggs quoted it in his manuscript. He also singled out various ethnic groups who had settled in the state and described some of their native customs and dubious medical practices. Briggs boasted that these compiled bits and pieces of mostly forgotten customs constituted "the best history of the State and its people."[42]

Tensions between state pride and federal directives surfaced in the production of the essay on arts and crafts. Its development from initial draft into final manuscript provoked several outbursts of Hoosier provincialism that had to be reconciled with national standards. Rebecca Pitts assumed primary responsibility for the piece, and her predispositions clashed with Washington editors' on several occasions. The result, as usual, was a compromise. There were no real controversies on major items, such as the Hoosier Group of painters, the influence of the Herron School of Art, and the Hoosier Salon. But an early draft of the essay did not include the Indiana sculptor

Janet Scudder, and editor Ruth Crawford called attention to this omission.[43] Pitts relented but explained in the final essay that most of Scudder's mature work was done outside the state of Indiana, presumably the reason for omitting her from the original manuscript. Also in an early draft she praised Terre Haute mural painter Gilbert Wilson, perhaps excessively, and the Washington critique insisted that her appraisal of his work be toned down from "magnificent" to merely "impressionistic."[44]

Another disagreement involved the German immigrant stone carver Rudolph Schwartz, who had designed statuary for the Soldiers and Sailors Monument in Indianapolis. Pitts declared that he was unworthy of mention since he had "perpetrated monstrosities all over the State." She lost this battle, and Schwartz appeared in the essay. A major controversy dealt with her refusal to discuss the Thomas Hart Benton murals on Indiana history, which the state had commissioned to appear at the 1933 World's Fair in Chicago. "Benton was not a Hoosier," Pitts insisted, and "a great number of Indiana people, including a majority of the best painters, felt very bitter at the time about the selection of Benton to paint those murals." These protestations notwithstanding, the final version of the essay included a brief discussion of Benton's work, but Pitts could have taken solace in that a scene from Wilson's mural appeared in the section of photo illustrations, but Benton's was absent. Miss Pitts complained about the constant revisions to the essay, and she questioned whether editors in Washington should have veto power over Indiana material written by Hoosiers.[45]

George Cronyn, as a Hoosier in Washington, got the task of explaining protocol to Indiana headquarters. "It must be remembered," he reminded them, "that the Washington office is the co-author of all the State guides," and it exercised "final authority over every word which is to be published."[46] He reiterated this position a few months later and explained that Indiana was no different from the other states in matters of critiques and revisions. The reputation of the American Guide series made it "absolutely imperative" for Hoosiers to live up to established standards.[47] And those standards originated in Washington, not in Indiana.

Adherence to federal standards for the American Guide series meant that Indiana had to modify several things in its written copy, in both style and substance. The ideal and average length of the guides was 500 pages, with rare exceptions such as Texas, which stretched beyond 700, and most states had to cut mercilessly to achieve that. When historian Ray A. Billington took over as the second director of the Massachusetts project, he found a swollen manuscript of roughly 650,000 words. He devoted much of his editorial work to condensing this to a manageable 250,000. He recalled years later that guide editors had to be ruthless so that "chapters became pages, pages became paragraphs, paragraphs became sentences."[48] The Indiana guide never had a chance to get this swollen because it was so late in development. Each essay and chapter was trimmed from the early stages. A few examples of cutting and condensing illustrate this point. An early version of the history essay came in at 15,000 words, and the critique suggested cutting it to 2,000.[49] The agriculture essay was regarded as "twice too long," and from its start in 1936 to its finish in 1940, it shrank from 5,500 words to 3,700.[50]

Other modifications in guide copy dealt with omissions, balance, point of view, and error. The original essay on music contained virtually no folk music, and the Washington editors suggested finding songs from Indian tribes, children's play songs, and ethnic music from immigrant groups.[51] Most of these suggestions were ultimately incorporated, probably at the expense of more obvious contemporary musicians such as Cole Porter and Hoagy Carmichael, who received only perfunctory coverage.

The early paucity of material regarding black Hoosiers also caught federal editors' attention because ample racial coverage was a stated goal of the guide. "What is the Negro's present social state?" they asked. "What do Negroes do industrially, agriculturally, professionally? Is there discrimination, segregation, residential restriction: Much remains to be said about these 112,000."[52] Indiana editors addressed these questions in several ways throughout the book, although blacks in the state did not receive a separate "racial elements" essay common to many of the other state guides. And matters of opinion and balance had to be reconciled.

In the essay on literature, editors questioned whether novelist Edward Eggleston merited three pages when Lew Wallace had received only seven lines. They also felt that Booth Tarkington was dismissed too lightly.[53] In the final version Eggleston dropped to one page, Wallace grew to ten lines, and Tarkington received more respect than previously. The essay flaunted his Pulitzer Prizes and argued that he had "few rivals in American Literature."[54] Factual mistakes were caught and corrected; for example, Quakers worshiped in meeting houses instead of churches.[55] When the Indiana staff had managed to jump through all the federal editorial hoops, they sometimes received enough praise to compensate for their months of conforming and adhering. Briggs's essay on the Hoosier character got this pat on the back: "The last version of 'Indiana Today' has rung the bell. . . . I congratulate you on having captured the rather elusive quality of the state and its people."[56]

Part 2 of the American Guide series allowed the states to highlight the history and special features of their "principal cities." By devoting roughly a third of the volume to this subject, the national editors revealed their bias toward the recent urbanization of the country. Even in part 1, which contained individual essays on natural setting and, in some of the states, pieces on agriculture, the balance drifted inexorably toward metropolitan concerns such as industry and the arts. In this second section, rural America was simply left behind while the states discussed their downtown scene and presumably their future. Only in rare exceptions was the section omitted, such as in Nevada, which in the 1930s did not admit to having any principal cities. The traditional Hoosier fondness for new-mown hay and sycamores in the moonlight gave way to a celebration of commercial architecture, ethnic immigrant festivals, and other sights and situations more commonly found in chamber of commerce literature than in nostalgic musings.

The selection of which Hoosier cities to celebrate in separate essays fell to the editorial staff in Indianapolis under the direction of Ross Lockridge. They initially picked twenty that ranged from the obvious, Indianapolis, which was the largest city in the state and its capital, to the surprising, French Lick, a small town that reveled in its mineral waters and resort hotels.[57] From these polar extremes it became apparent that Indiana's part 2 of the guide had as much to do with character and accomplishment as it did with urban population. Lockridge and his staff now had to convince the national editors that their choices were worthy. By 1940 this list of twenty had been whittled down to fourteen. The final list included Indianapolis and the other major metropolitan centers—Fort Wayne, South Bend, Evansville, and the northwest cluster called Cities of the Calumet: Gary, Hammond, East Chicago, and Whiting. Three others were included for reasons of current demographic and economic importance: Muncie, New Albany, and Terre Haute. And the final three— Corydon, New Harmony, and Vincennes—made the list due to their past distinctions, not their contemporary significance or urban character. Excluded after months of research, writing, and editing were French Lick, Anderson, Jeffersonville, Madison, Richmond, and Elkhart.

The six sites that national editors rejected for inclusion in part 2 failed to impress the Washington staff for a variety of reasons. Indiana editors had not made a compelling enough case for their size, uniqueness, or significant contribution to the state's development. Their exclusion from the essay section did not mean, however, that they were excluded from the guide; they would be recycled into the tours in part 3 in a slightly different format. French Lick, for instance, was unable to rise above its past reputation for resort hotels, one of which had recently closed during the Depression, and was recommended for the tour section.[58] Likewise, Madison failed to convince the editors that, beyond its distinctive nineteenth-century architecture, there was any other "particularly interesting material."[59] National critics were especially brutal toward Anderson. They found the discussion of its Indian Mound "of dubious authenticity," regarded the account of recent labor unrest "partisan and slightly incorrect," and dismissed Anderson College as "not an important college." Following another revision, which elicited the verdict that Anderson "does not warrant serious consideration," someone in the Indianapolis office penciled onto the final critique that the city should move to the tour section "and to Hell with it!"[60]

These fourteen essays on urban sites followed a procedure from research to completion that was similar to those in part 1. Fieldworkers observed, researched, and interviewed in the designated sites, then submitted their raw data or rough essays to the state headquarters. State editors transformed them into a standard format, and most were revised by Rebecca Pitts.[61] The essays adhered to a formula devised in the national office, then went through critical readings in Chicago and Washington and were revised accordingly. They each began with listings of transportation facilities, such as railroads and airports, followed by such accommodations as hotels and tourist camps, then theaters, parks, and recreational sites, and finally distinctive annual events. The major narrative was a combination of history and current description, known among editors as "the contemporary scene." Concluding the essay was another listing of "Points of Interest," such as major industries, museums, colleges, etc., and usually a map showing the locations of those points. Often material discarded from one of the essays in part 1 would resurface in one of the city pieces. For instance, when the essay on education did not have sufficient space for a detailed discussion of nineteenth-century experimental schools, editors shifted that discussion into the New Harmony essay in part 2. In the same manner, historical material concerning George Rogers Clark and William Henry Harrison that could not be accommodated in the essay on history could be shuffled into the essay on Vincennes. This frequent shifting of research and writing from one section to another necessitated equally frequent cross-referencing.

The rejection and recycling of Richmond from essay to tour site is a good example of the process of research, writing, revision, and editorial reassessment of priorities. Fieldworker Flora Mae Harris had lived in Richmond for many years, and she had researched printed histories, publications of the chamber of commerce, and the local newspapers. Her rough draft for the essay followed the required format, but it was disjointed and ran to twenty-five pages. Four items dominated the essay: the visit of presidential aspirant Henry Clay to the city in 1842, the campus of Earlham College, the Richmond Art Association, and the Hill Floral Products greenhouses.

She wrote this informative but wandering sentence about E. G. Hill, founder of the floral business:

> Oftimes he rejected as many as 16,000 rose plants in one long experiment, running over a period of three years, in search of a new shade or a better shaped bud and then finding results unsuccessful, would cheerfully begin anew.[62]

As state editor W. Clay Stearley revised Mrs. Harris's draft, it evolved in clarity if not in brevity:

> In the beginning, he often times rejected as many as 16,000 rose plants from all parts of the world in one long experiment. His work, started as a search for a new shade or a more shapely bud, sometimes continued for three years. And then if the results were unfavorable, he would cheerfully begin all over again.[63]

Ultimately the editors decided that Richmond "had nothing to recommend it except its moderate size" and that its distinctive attributes were better suited to the tour section than to the essay.[64] Mrs. Harris's four major items remained, but in a different format. They were now geared to accommodate visitors on a trip rather than readers of history. The status of Mr. Hill's experiment after the final revision by Rebecca Pitts was considerably reduced: "During his long experiments he rejected as many as 16,000 rose plants from all parts of the world, often working years to develop a new shade or a more shapely bud."[65]

To survive the editorial process meant that the Hoosier "principal cities" had to appear not only historically significant but interesting as well. The fourteen essays emerged in the prescribed format, well researched, tightly written, informative without being encyclopedic, and positive without sounding boosterish. The Indianapolis essay was the combined effort of at least four state editors who still had to satisfy national critics on a number of points. Washington editors wanted more architectural detail, less repetition, and specifics on when the Central Canal ceased being functional. Only then would they call the essay "a commendable piece of work."[66] One can detect the careful balance required by federal editors in this brief geo-graphical survey of the city: "Still further south are neighborhoods of trim houses, here and there a belt of slums, and Garfield Park with its sunken gardens."[67] They achieved this same balance between truth and beauty in the "Cities of the Calumet" essay. State editors could boast that it was "one of the world's greatest industrial centers" and still describe scenes more vivid than attractive. "Over the entire district," they claimed, "are the smoke of the steel mill, the smell of the oil refinery, and the glow of the blast furnace. Always there is the clang of forge, the roar of wheels, and the thunder of dumping slag."[68] The essay on Fort Wayne could not pass muster until the state editors included information on recent labor unrest and the medical accomplishments of native Alice Hamilton.[69] Similar re-quests for additions to the Terre Haute essay included the general strike of 1935 and the musical legacy of Paul Dresser.[70] New Har-mony was small but rich in history with its various utopian experi-ments. Ross Lockridge sent in a manuscript he had written that stretched over sixty-two pages, filled with colorful characters and amusing episodes. The Washington office sent back a nine-page cri-tique that listed the areas to be cut and condensed. Gordon Briggs did a rewrite and Rebecca Pitts did another revision before Wash-ington approved the final, which was not nearly as colorful or amus-ing, but which required only twelve pages.[71]

South Bend represents a revealing study in the evolution of a principal city from its first research phase to the final essay. Field-worker Paul Yoder's assignment was to gather observations for the "Contemporary Scene" section. He positioned himself at the corner of Michigan and Jefferson streets, observed, then filed this colorful report of bustling urban life.

> Apparently everybody in South Bend walks by this crowded cor-ner—or drives by. . . . [Streetcars] come thundering up and down the streets, plowing their ways through the almost unbroken lines of automobiles like yellow, hollow-eyed juggernauts seeking victims to crush. . . . The six-story Sherland Building, cat-a-corner across the intersection, . . . belches human beings in droves. The first Bank & Trust Bldg. straight across the street vomits its contribution

to the noonday rush. . . . We turn and see Kresge's 5 & 10 belching and swallowing both at the same time.

Yoder added an explanation that "I saw this all myself. . . . The Lord only knows whether this is what Indianapolis Office wants."[72] What the Indianapolis office wanted was something a bit more sedate and with fewer physiological verbs. Another fieldworker, Albert Strope, supplied an alternative and more acceptable version of downtown South Bend, which was edited by Clay Stearley, Gordon Briggs, and Rebecca Pitts. The final version is the same scene from a different street corner in tamer prose:

> Downtown South Bend is a bustling business center, locally called "Michiana" because it is the trade and financial heart of southern Michigan and northern Indiana. The center of activity lies at Michigan and Washington Streets. Most of the streets are usually crowded and noisy. . . . The skyline of the western and southern sections of the city is broken by the stacks of many factories, an impressive industrial scene.[73]

From the initial gathering of data in 1936 to its final editing in spring 1941, South Bend had changed, so the manuscript had to do the same. For example, streetcars had to be removed from the listing of transportation services because they had been discontinued. And due to the dislocations caused by World War II, it was uncertain whether the annual automobile show would be held at the Grenada Theater. That would be contingent on whether "new models are brought out."[74] Other changes in the manuscript involved expanding the material on the large Polish community, including more recent historical events, and eliminating some of the boosterish adjectives such as "greatest" and "most famous."[75] The finished piece included a section of almost three pages devoted to the campus of the University of Notre Dame, denoting its separate and significant status. No other city in part 2 devoted an appendix to one of its unique sites or institutions.

While parts 1 and 2 were narrative essays that described and analyzed the state and urban centers for their historical significance, the tours of part 3 were strictly utilitarian. They were to entice visitors and natives to travel and explore and possibly to spend time and money in the process. Even during the Depression, Americans traveled for both business and pleasure, and the automobile was part of the family, not a luxury to be disposed of during hard times. An estimated 35 million Americans took motoring trips during 1935, and they spent $7 billion annually on travel.[76] The American Guide series sought to provide these millions of tourists with a systematic scenario of things to see and do and to supply a generous helping of things that normally would not be found in a commercial travel guide. According to the FWP, part 3 would include "famous landmarks, historical figures, customs, folklore, scenery, climate, industrial and agricultural development, art collections, museums, monuments, sports, educational facilities, and other institutions which make up the life of the community."[77] The guides, although not planned as such, also served another utilitarian purpose—that of a repository for the excess materials that had not been used in parts 1 and 2.

Lacking a national park, a seacoast, mountains, or other major attractions with which to lure tourists, the Indiana guide would have to accentuate other sites and events of a less obvious nature. Not that Indiana was modest about its attributes, but in a field of forty-eight state guides, the competition was now fierce for visitors. In Vincennes there was little to see concerning the Revolutionary War, but George Rogers Clark and his military contribution to American freedom merited attention; the federal government had recently constructed a memorial there. And John Hunt Morgan's raid through southern Indiana might interest Civil War enthusiasts. The claims for Indiana as a mother of presidents were problematic, but three—William Henry Harrison, Abraham Lincoln, and Benjamin Harrison—had spent several years in the state. As far as sporting events were concerned, the oval track in Indianapolis was becoming America's premier auto racing site, and the stadium at Notre Dame was the scene of unmatched football weekends. Part 3 could feature all of these and more for the benefit of state pride as well as tourist attention. Hoosier fieldworkers, therefore, were responsible for nominating sites, events, and people for inclusion. This section encouraged boosterism just as the other two discouraged it. These tours were to be enticing and attractive, and fieldworkers were to suggest photo opportunities to accompany their site nominations. State editors and national critics, as usual, would winnow through the lists to select the winners in this race for visitors.

Fieldworkers from almost every county sent to Indianapolis a combination of the obvious and the obscure. From Porter County came several enthusiastic accounts of the Dunes State Park that described its scenic glories and vacation possibilities. Another item from Porter County was a leftover account from the folklore collection. It dealt with the strange hermit woman Diana of the Dunes, who had once lived in a driftwood hut and gained national notoriety. She no longer existed, but her legend exemplified the "lively items" that the national FWP staff encouraged the Indiana staff to find.[78] Iris Cook from Floyd County on the Ohio River sent in a list of thirty-nine sites of interest, far more than could be used.[79] Gordon Briggs worked with several fieldworkers, WPA staff, and other individuals in Spencer County to make the most of the Abraham Lincoln connection. In the completed tour, this small reconstructed pioneer village got considerable space to cover the Hoosier years of the sixteenth president.[80] Winona Lake in Kosciusko County received nominations from four fieldworkers in northern Indiana for its summertime Chautauqua programs and the massive Billy Sunday Tabernacle. Fieldworker Archie Koritz described Sunday's surprisingly modest home nearby as an "unpretentious frame bungalow," and his prose survived all the revisions and remained intact in the completed guide.[81]

State editors took these hundreds of nominated parks, towns, lakes, and museums and placed them on linear tours that crisscrossed the state. According to national regulations, all tours would run from north to south or from east to west.[82] Initially the Hoosier staff determined that twenty-seven tours would be sufficient to accommodate the sites, but by publication time the number had fallen to twenty.[83] Each route had to be driven to get exact mileage and correct descriptions. This became a time-consuming, expensive, and tedious process for both fieldworkers and the Indianapolis editorial staff. Briggs reported that the drivers and writers often felt "harried and hurried" to cover great distances in a short time, and as a result the written descriptions of the routes were often "sketchy and inadequate." Extra travel funds were then needed to travel the routes again for accuracy and more detail.[84] For example, fieldworker Allen Stranz traveled Highway 20 from the Ohio state line, passing through Angola, LaGrange, Elkhart, and Hammond to the Illinois line, a total of 154.5 miles. The draft of his tour was five pages long and ranged from fishing in Steuben County's Clear Lake to viewing Whiting's Standard Oil refinery.[85] Washington's Katherine Kellock responded to this draft with a dispiriting critique: "There is little in this copy that would induce a visitor to go out of his way to take this tour. Entirely devoid of human interest and local color."[86] This obviously called for another revision.

Each of Indiana's tours had to pass the critical eye of both the regional office in Chicago and the national office. Both had strong opinions about what needed to be included and how it should be written. Because the guides were federal publications, no hotels or restaurants on the tours were to be mentioned by name, in order to avoid any appearance of government favoritism or endorsement.[87] They also demanded more attention to "the dominant flora at various seasons" along the highways: trees, flowers, even goldenrod and Queen Anne's lace. And they requested that more precise architectural terminology be used; describing buildings as "interesting" and "colonial" was one of "the chief inadequacies of the tours."[88] Editors had rejected Elkhart for a separate essay in part 2, but they still wanted more colorful material for it, even in its abbreviated form. They asked why local author Ambrose Bierce had been so critical about the town and why the children's pet parade was not listed.[89] Even though the tours were by necessity perfunctory and formulaic, the editors demanded original prose. In Lockridge's final weeks as state director, he had apparently responded to encroaching deadlines by sending in some material that had been hastily or carelessly prepared. The national director chastised the Indianapolis staff severely. He pointed out that too much of the tour information on

George Rogers Clark and Abraham Lincoln had been "copied word-for-word from Lockridge's biographies of these two men. . . . We do not allow direct copying, even though it has been done with the author's permission."[90] New state director Briggs felt that he could address most of these criticisms with an addition to the Indiana editorial staff in 1938. Rebecca Pitts had departed after three years, and to fill her spot on tour revisions was Lavier Milstead, a journalist with newspaper experience in Missouri, Pennsylvania, and Kentucky. Briggs thought his work was "outstandingly good" with the redriving, researching, and rewriting.[91]

The completed twenty tours filled 208 pages and directed readers down Indiana's major highways into some nooks and crannies unknown to many experienced Hoosier travelers. One reviewer of earlier state guides had commented on the surprises that emerged from the jumbled treasures and trivia, and another critic later referred to the tours as "a storehouse of miscellaneous facts."[92] The Indiana guide did not fall short of uncovering the same kind of unexpected information. For instance, Tour 17 stopped on a farm in Stark County to visit the Old Libby Prison, once a barn in Virginia. It had become a Confederate prison during the Civil War, then was dismantled and moved to Chicago for the Columbian Exposition of 1893. From there it moved to Starke County to become a barn again. Names of several Union prisoners, carved on the beams, were still visible.[93] Tour 19, which started in Indianapolis and headed south on State Road 37 to Sulphur, was a 123.5 mile trip from the urban twentieth century back into the rural nineteenth century. At its terminus, one would find very few automobiles but many horses and small cabins, and conditions were not "affected greatly by modern civilization."[94] One of the recommended stops on Tour 5 was the jail at Crown Point. It had achieved a dubious notoriety in 1934 when Public Enemy Number One, John Dillinger, escaped by threatening the guard with a fake gun he had whittled in his cell.[95] In Tour 11 the Carnegie Library in Vevay displayed a piano brought from England in 1817 and played for forty years by a heartbroken woman who never left her house except "to wander alone in the moonlight."[96] This story from the banks of the Ohio River rivaled in poignancy the tale of Diana of the Dunes from the far northwest corner of the state. In Kokomo, the guide traveled once again to Hoosier extremes. Tour 16 described Elwood Haynes's "horseless carriage," which ushered the state into automobile history, and then reminded readers of Indiana's agricultural heritage. There in the city park stood a tribute to the "Largest Steer Raised in Indiana," a shorthorn Hereford that weighed 4,470 pounds.[97]

Just as the highway tours would lead travelers to parks, museums, and physical sites of the state, the connecting narrative would lead readers back into Indiana's past. Several major themes concerning Hoosier history emerge from these twenty tours. Numerous mentions of the Underground Railroad and the remaining structures along its routes recall this brief yet important chapter in race relations. Several abolitionists used their homes to assist southern slaves in their escape to freedom before the Civil War, and this once-illegal activity now got a favorable interpretation from fieldworkers and editors alike. The Levi Coffin House in Wayne County, once known as the Grand Central Station of the UGRR, is a good case in point. Equally frequent are the tributes paid to the influence of the canal boom of the 1830s and 1840s. Communities sprang up along the canal route, immigrants flooded in for construction work, and artificial lakes, such as Sylvan Lake in Noble County, were built to supply a steady source of water for the canal boats. This, too, was a brief but heady epoch in transportation history and financial speculation that led to the state's bankruptcy. Ross Lockridge's interest in the Civil War and his historical pilgrimage in 1935 along the route of Morgan's raid in southern Indiana produced a flurry of memoirs and research in old local records. One result of this was an almost inordinate amount of space in the guide devoted to the episode. Lengthy descriptions of the raid, from humorous to serious, fill the tours from Corydon east to the Ohio border. And failed experiments in education dot the landscape in these tours. In all sections of the state, small towns and aspiring cities briefly hosted a multitude of private and sectarian schools. Derelict brick buildings now stood as the only reminders of these aspirations for higher education and municipal growth that could not be sustained.

Following the three major sections of the guide was an appendix that contained a chronological timeline of Indiana history and a bibliography of suggested readings about the state. The chronology was a nine-page list of events, beginning in 1609, when the Northwest Territories were granted by royal charter, and ending in 1940, just months prior to the publication of the guide. Lockridge and his staff had prepared the chronology in 1936, and it required updating as more time elapsed. At closure, the final listing was the campaign for the presidency by Hoosier Wendell Willkie, who captured the state but not the office. The list contains both boosterish items and events that some Hoosiers might have preferred not be mentioned. Most of the material was distilled and condensed from the earlier essays, especially the one on history. This balance of the positive and negative typified previous guides and had led to some criticism about too much emphasis on the darker side of state histories. Indiana editors chose to brag about such things as the first free kindergarten in the United States at New Harmony in 1826 and Albert Beveridge's Pulitzer Prize for his biography of John Marshall in 1920. They also chose to remind readers about the cruel expulsion of the Potawatomi Indians in 1838 and the embarrassing murder trial of Ku Klux Klan leader D. C. Stephenson in 1925. Material about the KKK did not appear in the 1936 version of the chronology, but by 1938 it did, and the 1941 published guide boasted that the *Indianapolis Times* had won a Pulitzer Prize in 1928 for its work in exposing the KKK.[98]

Several inclusions in the chronology and bibliography could well have raised questions if critics had read the lists carefully. Many politicians got brief mention, but none so frequently as the perennial loser, Socialist Eugene V. Debs. Debs received nine listings; only William Henry Harrison, territorial governor and president, came close with six. Devoting this much space in the guide to a Socialist politician could have caused some conservatives to wonder if the state headquarters harbored radicals who were skewing the ideological tone of the book. The bibliography was an eclectic listing of books and pamphlets, which included scholarly monographs, popular biographies, and government publications, arranged in a format to roughly parallel the essays in part 1. Several of Ross Lockridge's books on state history joined the list, including the one on the old Fauntleroy home. Its inclusion was ironic because his work on this volume had caused tensions with the FWP Washington office during his state directorship. Lockridge was no longer on the payroll, but few other authors were as frequently mentioned for their literary legacy.

The Indianapolis staff had greater freedom in selecting visual illustrations than they had in making decisions about other aspects of the guide. Fieldworkers made suggestions and submitted snapshots of potential sites to state headquarters, then the Indiana editors supplemented them and sent them to Chicago and Washington for a critique. The national editors offered advice, but allowed the state considerable responsibility for choices and sources. This process depended on the initiative of fieldworkers and the ingenuity of the state staff, a process which, for the most part, worked well. For example, the ever resourceful Iris Cook sent a list of sites that she felt worthy of being photographed in southern Indiana and included some shots by an accomplished photographer with his permission to publish.[99] The state staff acquired permission to reprint photos from several Indiana newspapers, local chambers of commerce, and the State Department of Conservation. Purdue University was generous in supplying shots of agricultural scenes; various industries were equally forthcoming in sharing scenes of their manufacturing activities. The national editors assisted in getting illustrations from the United States Steel Corporation, the Farm Security Administration, the magazine *Life,* and the Library of Congress. Alsberg and his staff complimented Briggs and his staff on "a very good start on the collection," but made several suggestions for additional illustrations. "What about hogs?" they asked, and "the old swimming hole?" They felt a shot of the Culver Military Academy would be appropriate as well as the Lanier home in Madison. And they encouraged Briggs to "make a special effort to get a good street scene for Muncie—as 'Middletown.' "[100] Many of these suggestions bore fruit, but not all. The finished guide had 109 illustrations, grouped in eight portfolios or "signatures," suggested by the Washington staff, such as agriculture, education, industry, and historic buildings.[101] They ranged from bucolic vistas in Brown County to assembly-line production in the Studebaker plant in South Bend. They covered the obligatory basketball game, first state house in Corydon, and Bedford limestone carving. And they also included the less than obvious mint distillery in Elkhart and the old canal lock at Metamora. The state staff did honor Washington's suggestion to include a group portrait of hogs, but they declined to conjure up a view of the old swimming hole.

A recurring theme in most of the state guides, whether in the essays, tours, or photo portfolios, was that the New Deal had been a positive force for the United States. From Social Security assistance for the elderly, through Rural Electrification for farmers, to a newly built environment of Public Works Administration structures, the federal programs of the Roosevelt administration had created a better America. Nowhere was this so dramatically documented as in the Tennessee guide. It had devoted an entire essay to the impact of the TVA on flood control, cheap electricity, and improved recreation and agriculture. Few other states could match the intensity of this singular program, but most of them provided many smaller instances of New Deal solutions to their problems. Fieldworkers were encouraged to describe new Welfare State benefits such as parks, bridges, and activities funded by federal revenues.[102] Indiana was no exception to this inventory of good works. The CCC appears at least six times with its tree planting and trail building throughout Hoosier forestland. The PWA gets credit for constructing the new Shelby County courthouse and the Lockefield Garden apartments in Indianapolis. WPA is ubiquitous throughout the Indiana guide. WPA workers helped reconstruct the Lincoln Pioneer Village in Rockport, its NYA division helped keep students in school, and its music and theater programs helped sustain the arts. The FSA appears in two ways: Deshee Farms in southwest Indiana was an experiment in resettling farmers from unproductive land to a new community, and FSA documentary photographers supplied some of the portfolio illustrations of rural Indiana. All of these random bits of evidence supported a subtle yet constant case that the New Deal had built a better life and landscape for Indiana.

One responsibility that the federal government delegated to the state headquarters was to find an official sponsor to underwrite publication costs for the guide. The sponsor's potential subsidy to a commercial publisher in the event that the books did not sell as well as hoped would be approximately $2,500. As early as 1937, Alsberg pressured Lockridge to make the necessary arrangements, but Lockridge left the state directorship before completing any deal. Briggs continued the process, which was time-consuming and fraught with political entanglements. He acquired a tentative agreement in 1938 with Governor Clifford Townsend that would have the governor's office become the official sponsor, but the state attorney general ruled that the chief executive could not "sign a sponsorship contract involving the possibility of a subsidy to a private publishing house."[103] Briggs then worked with the Indiana General Assembly to permit a sponsorship and appropriation; Briggs helped draft the bill, and the governor encouraged its passage. The Senate passed the bill in early 1939 with little opposition, but it failed to get through the House in the last-minute flurry of competing bills.[104] Later that year, when federal mandates reconfigured the WPA and FWP and required each state's Writers' Program to have a state sponsor, Indiana resolved this problem. The department of public relations at Indiana State Teachers College became the official statewide sponsor for the state Writers' Program, which entailed providing 25 percent of its costs. This solved the problem because a separate sponsor for the guide was no longer necessary.[105]

When Indiana's leading publisher, Bobbs-Merrill, declined to publish the guide because of prior commitments, Oxford University Press assumed the job.[106] Bobbs-Merrill had been the obvious and sentimental choice because of its record with many Hoosier authors such as Riley and Nicholson. Oxford, however, had previously published several other state guides and possessed the experience to expedite the Indiana job, which was already many months behind schedule. FWP policy was to produce an affordable volume to promote sales, and Oxford, of course, wanted to make a profit. During this time, sales of 7,500 for a book of this type were considered very good, and a printing of 10,000 for guides had become the norm.[107]

Oxford therefore arranged for an initial printing of 10,000 copies of the Indiana guide that would arrive in stores in September 1941, priced at $2.75, typical of the series. Employees of the WPA and the faculty at Indiana State Teachers College could order advance copies at 40 percent less, or $1.71 each. Probably due to the success of the guides in other states and the long wait and attendant publicity, Indiana's initial printing was virtually sold out before the publication date.[108] The president of Indiana State Teachers College, Ralph N. Tirey, wrote a foreword and called the volume a "treasure trove" worthy of the "closest scrutiny."[109]

Reviewers of the Indiana guide were swift with their scrutiny and generally positive in their verdicts. Even the Japanese attack on Pearl Harbor and America's entry into the war did not deprive the book of widespread attention and critical appraisal. Outside of Indiana, reviewers focused on the volume as a whole and how it compared to earlier state guides. The *New York Herald Tribune* ranked it near the top of the series and appreciated the attention the book gave to Hoosier authors. Likewise, the *Christian Science Monitor* found it "interesting and readable" and an "excellent account" of the state's intangibles.[110] Back home in Indianapolis, reviewers focused on more provincial items, as might be expected. The *Indianapolis News* had given the guide a positive preview before its publication, including photos. The *Indianapolis Times* found the guide an "impressive piece of work," and the *Indianapolis Recorder,* the state's leading black paper, declared it encyclopedic and useful, but understandably lamented the "sparse" representation of the black experience. Editors of the *Indianapolis Star* had taken umbrage over a passage in the guide that referred to the *News* as the leading newspaper in the state and relayed their displeasure privately rather than in print.[111] Around the state, reviews tended to highlight how the guide treated local sites and events. The *Fort Wayne News-Sentinel* commented favorably on the illustrations by a hometown photographer and was pleased that a book written by so many "cooks" had not spoiled the broth. A few newspapers focused exclusively on the sections of the book that applied to their home turf. The *South Bend Tribune,* for example, felt that it was inexcusable for the guide not to mention that poet James Whitcomb Riley had briefly lived in South Bend. It also reported several incorrectly listed street names, a justifiable criticism. The *Elkhart Truth* had a similar complaint about mistaken dates and addresses. The *Vincennes Sun-Commercial* had nothing but praise, however. Its reviewer appreciated the good writing, the striking illustrations, and the amount of time the FWP personnel had spent compiling all the local details.[112]

The Indiana guide enjoyed an enduring legacy. More than six decades after its publication, copies are still available to resourceful book buyers. Oxford University Press kept the volume available and affordable for many years; their price had risen to $5 per copy by the 1950s, and they had gone into a fifth printing by the 1960s.[113] In 1973 Somerset Publishers reprinted the original, testifying to the continuing demand. In an abbreviated form the Indiana guide has appeared over the years in several anthologies and condensations of the national series. In 1978, the Indiana Historical Society decided to update and expand the 1941 guide, since so much of it had become unusable for current travelers. The new guide would contain many changes in both substance and style, but the intent replicated that of the FWP, to "awaken Hoosiers to the heritage and attractions of their home state."[114] By the time *Indiana: A New Historical Guide* appeared in 1989, almost fifty years had elapsed since the original, but its success paralleled that of its 1941 predecessor. Indiana had changed, and so had the people who put together the self-portraits. From anonymous writers on relief to professional historians and editors, the point of view was different. There apparently was a hunger in 1941 for Hoosier heritage that this volume fed by packaging research and analysis in a utilitarian format. The FWP had acknowledged the presence of a usable past and supplied a durable handbook for experiencing it. Five decades later, the IHS paid tribute to that persistent hunger by supplying a new means of accomplishing the same vicarious experience. The long legacy of the first guide made possible the production and success of the second.

FOUR

Other Publications

A small pamphlet, *Hoosier Tall Stories,* rolled from the FWP mimeo-graph machines in January 1937, the first of several provisional Indiana publications. In 1936 the national office encouraged many state headquarters to get a small project in print so the public would know that the FWP was doing "useful work."[1] Taxpayers and Congress could see immediate and tangible results from WPA work crews, but after a year of activity, what had the writers produced? In states such as Indiana, where progress on the guide was proceeding slowly, this national encouragement bordered on coercion. Henry Alsberg knew that Indiana fieldworkers had compiled vast amounts of folklore, far more than could ever be incorporated into the guide.[2] He worked with Ross Lockridge to recycle some of the yarns and folktales into a publication that Hoosiers would find both amusing and worthwhile until the guide finally arrived. *Hoosier Tall Stories* did this successfully. Another worthwhile diversion appeared in 1939, the *Calumet Region Historical Guide.* It was a smaller version of the state guide, devoted to the northwest corner of the state. And starting in 1940, the state staff began a free historical column for newspapers called "It Happened in Indiana." This became a popular feature around the state and generated good publicity for the Writers' Project. In the late summer of 1941, the Indiana Writers' Program published a small pamphlet in the American Recreation series. All of these publications depended on fieldworker labor, disseminated information that might never have appeared otherwise, and served as appetizers to keep Hoosiers in a favorable mood for the Indiana guide, the long-awaited main course that eventually appeared in late 1941. A final publication, a study guide for aliens preparing for naturalization exams, appeared the following year and indicated that wartime activities had swept up the Writers' Program.

Indiana fieldworkers had been especially enthusiastic about collecting folklore. The list of research topics prepared in Washington by John Lomax, the FWP's national advisor on folklore, had been supplemented and indexed by Indiana's folklore editor, Elsie Durre. A mass of stories, superstitions, folk medical remedies, gravestone inscriptions, and pioneer songs soon began to arrive in the Indianapolis headquarters. Upon Mrs. Durre's untimely death in 1936, she was succeeded by Bessie Roberts as folklore editor. Mrs. Roberts's background included newspaper work in Fort Wayne and Evansville, a syndicated column, and experience on the lecture circuit, and she had firm opinions about presenting the collection to its best advantage.[3] Lockridge also entertained a strong interest in folklore and theatrical presentations, and together they created the pamphlet. They culled through the many fieldworker submissions of amusing yarns and whoppers told by Hoosier raconteurs around the town square or "liars' bench." They selected approximately fifty of the stories for a small booklet, which had a working title of "Some Tall Tales and How They Grew," and shipped the manuscript off to Washington in September 1936. In addition to responding to Alsberg's pressure for a publication to mollify public opinion, the Indiana FWP envisioned this collection as an item that could be distributed to schools in the state.[4] Several other states such as Nebraska and Oregon had already issued or were preparing similar small collections of their folklore materials.[5]

The choice of topics by Roberts and Lockridge was either brilliant or very lucky or benefited from the fact that so much material was available to them. In the 1930s this booklet of rustic folktales would

likely strike both a nostalgic nerve and a funny bone in most Hoosiers. Several fieldworkers had submitted documented evidence that
a "liars' bench" actually existed in their county. The editors listed
these locations in Brown, Spencer, and Fountain counties and could
well have added more, including Wabash and Warren. The tales that
emanated from these benches were predominantly rural in tone and
masculine in voice, revealing the traditional Hoosier preference for
small towns and nineteenth-century deference to male leadership.
The topics leaned toward fishing, hunting, farming, carpentry, and
life on the rivers and in the woods. And most of the stories came
from interviews with elderly residents who had obviously spent time
at the bench, remembered the experience fondly, and were willing
to share the memories with fieldworkers.

Typical of most FWP publications, clear authorship of these stories
is difficult to determine, but some can be traced to the fieldworkers
who collected, transcribed, and sent them to state headquarters.
Roberts and Lockridge rewrote and edited the copy before submitting it for a critique in the national office. From Elkhart County,
roving fieldworker Albert Strope sent in a tale he called "Whopper"
about a Wakarusa carpenter who had shingled a house during a
heavy fog. According to the carpenter, after the fog lifted he discovered that he had finished shingling not only the roof, but two feet
of space beyond the eaves as well.[6] Strope, who had been an elementary school teacher before joining the FWP, knew how to structure a story and tell it entertainingly. His manuscript, therefore,
required very few changes except a new title, "He Roofed the Fog."
Fieldworker Arline Dickinson heard an outrageous tale in Grant
County about a boy who caught a young catfish. He tamed the fish,
raised it on dry land, and named it Tom. One day while following
the boy to school, it slipped off a foot log into a creek and drowned.
The editors took this brief tale, named it "Tom the Catfish," determined that the fish had been caught in the Mississinewa River, which
traversed Grant County, and expanded the tale with first-person dialogue.[7] Roberts and Lockridge gave just the opposite treatment to
a tale sent in from Warren County by Cecil Miller. His story was
about a mythical poisonous hoop snake that struck at a team of

horses pulling a wagon. It bit the wooden wagon tongue, which swelled up immensely and later, when sawed, yielded 350 feet of lumber. Miller's original tale had included dialogue and a secondary ending for a double punch line. The editors transformed the story into a straightforward narrative with no dialogue and with only one conclusion.[8] Apparently many fieldworkers from around the state sent in several variations on one story. The editors indicated that it was the "most frequently repeated tall story" of all. Titled "Drive On," it spun a yarn about Jeff, a man so lazy he chose to be buried alive rather than work for a living. On the way to the cemetery in his coffin, Jeff was offered a bushel of corn by a Good Samaritan to get a new start in life. "Jeff pondered this a moment and finally rose up to ask, 'Is the corn shelled?' 'Why no!' replied the Good Samaritan in astonishment. Jeff resignedly lay back again in the coffin. 'Drive on, boys,' said he. 'Drive on.' "[9]

The editorial process that transformed this little manuscript into a finished booklet probably came as a rude shock to the Indiana staff. This was, after all, their first publication, and they had not previously confronted the gauntlet of critiques and revisions that would later become standard procedure for them. Alsberg reported to Lockridge that John Lomax had read the manuscript and thought "very highly" of it.[10] When the complete Lomax critique arrived, Lockridge discovered that the folklorist expert also expected several major changes in the manuscript. While he found the tales "delightful in content," he disapproved of the "academic phrasing" that cluttered up the stories with terminology such as *corpulency* and *plebian* and *trysting*. He also felt that the introduction was not in harmony with the collection of tales. Whereas they were simple, fine narratives, the introductory comments were stilted and heavy.[11] The Indiana staff revised the newly named *Hoosier Tall Stories* "in accordance with suggestions by Mr. Lomax"[12] and proceeded to cut the manuscript into stencils for mimeographing. Somehow these stencils were intercepted by the national office, and the manuscript got a second significant overhaul. George Cronyn had some parts completely rewritten to achieve "the flavor of simple colloquial language." He also removed one story from the collection because it was a generic tale, having been previously published in a collection of Baron Munchausen stories and therefore not really indigenous to Indiana. Lockridge, somewhat chastened by this second round of editorial hoops, acquiesced to the changes and sent the manuscript on to James Dunton, the FWP Midwest field representative and Ohio director, who supervised the mimeographing.[13]

Hoosier Tall Stories was successful on several levels. Its creation taught the Indiana staff a great deal about writing, editing, and publishing. It also established the pecking order of priorities when state and national editorial decisions were in conflict. These would prove valuable as the guide moved closer to publication. *Hoosier Tall Stories* also turned into a popular item, proving Alsberg correct in that public opinion approved of the booklet and, by extension, the work of the FWP. Alsberg requested several copies for publicity purposes and sent them to a variety of venues, including the Scripps-Howard newspaper group.[14] Indiana printed slightly more than 1,200 copies and bound them in a greenish-gray construction paper cover. With some imagination, the title, in block print, could even be interpreted as having been chiseled into a small slab of Indiana limestone. Lockridge indicated that he was pleased with the monograph after all the trials leading to its completion. He said, "We shall rely upon it to establish our proud Hoosier claim that Indiana has 'bigger and better liars' than any state in the Union."[15] Requests for copies came in from every state, and it went into a second printing in 1939. The second printing was larger than the first, amounting to a combined total of 3,000 copies.[16] Although the content remained identical, the cover on the second run was more sophisticated, a pale blue card stock with dark blue lettering and a pen and ink drawing of three rustic Hoosiers in bibbed overalls, apparently getting ready for another round of yarn-spinning.

Small in size and modest in ambition, *Hoosier Tall Stories* nevertheless revealed the potential that existed in the growing folklore collection in Indiana. Lockridge spoke of the "richness" of the available material, which was "distinguished by the great amount and variety of its content." He hoped that more of it could be published later "so that the real measure of its merit can be exhibited."[17] A second booklet of similar tall tales about witches was in preparation, tentatively entitled "Pricking Thumbs," taken from a line in *Macbeth*. John Lomax had declared it even better than *Hoosier Tall Stories,* but it never reached publication. Folklore editor Bessie Roberts left the Indiana FWP late in 1936, Lockridge departed in 1937, and Lomax left the national office during this same time. In the midst of these departures the manuscript, now without a champion, remained in limbo.[18] In 1982, Professor Ronald L. Baker from Indiana State University successfully mined the FWP papers for his book *Hoosier Folk Legends.* Baker presented more than three hundred folktales from Indiana from early days up to modern times. Thirty-three of the tales in his book came from the FWP collection, including an account of Diana of the Dunes and another version of the dubious hoop snake.[19]

A much more ambitious publication than the folklore booklet was the *Calumet Region Historical Guide.* Several other states were putting together guides that focused on one city or distinctive region. They were generally smaller versions of the state guides, less expensive and quicker to produce. Alsberg strongly encouraged these efforts, especially in states where the major guide was slow in getting to the press. One enticement for producing a smaller, faster guide was that the national FWP office offered more freedom in editorial matters. Local and regional critiques would generally suffice, with less supervision from Washington.[20] The Kentucky FWP offered its readers *Lexington and the Bluegrass Country* in 1938, a year before its state guide, and Louisiana pushed *New Orleans City Guide* into print three years earlier than the state guide. Under the new Indiana leadership of Gordon Briggs, a special team of FWP workers in the northwestern corner of the state put together a guide for what had come to be known as "the Calumet region." Unemployment in this highly industrialized section was worse than in most other parts of the state, the fieldworkers there were numerous and productive, and the incentives for this publication were attractive in light of the glacial pace of the state guide.

The name of this book and region is derived from two rivers, the Grand Calumet and the Little Calumet, which run parallel to each other and the southern tip of Lake Michigan. From the dunes of Porter County through the industrial areas of Lake County, they run westward and cross into Illinois at Hammond. The diversity of their paths from rural to urban and the linkage they offer to the municipalities along their routes make the name an appropriate one for the area. The Calumet region, for the purpose of this guidebook, incorporates only the Indiana portions of the area from the Dunes State Park in the east to the state line in the west, from Lake Michigan in the north to roughly ten miles south of the shoreline. Gordon Briggs admitted that this geographical delineation was arbitrary and exclusive, so the guidebook stretched a bit, and several "towns, hamlets, and points of interest are treated as environs."[21] Always in the shadow of nearby Chicago, and late to develop as a population hub in Indiana, the region had long suffered a sort of identity crisis. Part of Indiana, yet separate from it historically, culturally, and environmentally, the Calumet area welcomed an opportunity to publish a guide of its own and not be just a small part of the state guide. This was an opportunity to tell a distinctive story about its own past and present, by its own writers and editors, without having to explain or apologize. Since the Region was the most industrialized section of Indiana, it was fitting that the editors should select the verb *manufacture* to describe the creation of the book. The editorial office was located in the Gary Commercial Club and Chamber of Commerce; the book was printed in East Chicago and bound in Hammond.[22]

Producing the Calumet guide was a local effort with generous assistance from the state FWP headquarters and the regional office in Chicago. FWP fieldworkers continued their normal assignments of researching and writing for the state guide through their district office in Gary. But starting in 1937 they also channeled their local materials to the Calumet office, sponsored by the Gary Board of Education and the editor of the *Gary Post-Tribune*.[23] Mrs. Naomi Harris Phillips had worked for the Gary FWP district office since 1936 and had edited and rewritten many manuscripts for fieldworkers in Lake and Porter counties. She had previously been a correspondent for the *Christian Science Monitor* and society editor for the *Gary Post-Tribune*. The state headquarters staff was well aware of her work, both its quality and quantity, since her initials, NHP, appeared at the bottom of hundreds of pages sent to Indianapolis. Gordon Briggs and John Frederick of the regional office in Chicago agreed that she would be an appropriate editor for this project, and she assumed the supervisory role from its inception to its completion, despite serious health problems toward the end.[24] Assisting Mrs. Phillips as the research editor was Frances L. Francoeur, a journalist of wide experience from Hammond. On occasion Briggs would send one of his full-time staffers from the state headquarters to Gary to assist Mrs. Phillips; for instance, he dispatched Howard Underwood, whom he regarded as a "very good" editor, from Indianapolis to spend a month helping out on the project.[25] The process of critiquing and editing the Calumet material in the Chicago regional office was swift and efficient, due in part to the physical proximity of the two offices, and also in part to the fact that Rebecca Pitts, who had written so much of the initial copy on the Indiana guide, had transferred to the Chicago office. There her assignments had less to do with writing Hoosier essays to be critiqued by outsiders and more to do with critiquing essays written by other Hoosiers.[26]

To assume that the Calumet guide was only a miniature version of the state guide would be a mistake. Exercising the freedom granted to these provisional publications, the editorial staff utilized the standard format for guides on some occasions but plowed new ground in other instances to produce a unique product, reflective of the subject under consideration. Briggs pointed out that the Calumet region was young, being largely a product of the twentieth century, and overwhelmingly industrial, therefore unlike most other urban centers of the state. With this situation as a given, the writers' job was to describe the contemporary scene of the area more so than to dig into its shallow past. To readers of the Calumet guide "who heretofore have found no romance in the whirring of wheels, the spinning of cylinders, the raising and lowering of giant cranes; to those who have found no beauty in spraying fountains of molten steel or in the red glow in the sky from a Bessemer furnace," this book would bring a better appreciation.[27] The first half of the book's 272 pages is a swift overview of the region's geography, character, history, religion, law, the arts, blacks, labor, and transportation. Then lengthy tours visit industrial sites, and briefer tours go to such "environs" as Valparaiso, Cedar Lake, and Munster. Concluding this first section is a sizable description and tour of Dune Country. The second half of the guide covers each of the four major cities. Parallel treatment of their statistical data, chronology, and points of interest accentuates their commonalities, while aptly named essays point out their distinctive qualities. Gary's character, for example, is presented in an essay entitled "Steel Engraving," while Hammond gets a "Lithograph" and East Chicago receives an "Industrial Mural." This gallery of urban portraits ends with Whiting, which is "Done in Oil." An appendix of maps offers guidance for the various tours, a bibliography suggests additional reading material, and portfolios of photographs illustrate the text and tours.

Although many FWP fieldworkers and guest authors wrote and revised the manuscript for the Calumet guide, some individuals emerge from the anonymous prose as major contributors to the volume. Mrs. Mae Patterson, a former president of the Gary school board, provided substantial material and commentary for the essay on the "work-study-play system" that William A. Wirt had inaugurated early in the city's educational history. This experimental program integrated academic and vocational training and influenced hundreds of other American schools. Mrs. Patterson had personal experience with the system and believed in its virtues, and the editors allotted her discussion almost five pages in the finished guide.[28] Another guest author was Mrs. Bess J. Sheehan, a high school teacher whose persistent efforts had helped in the establishment of the Indiana Dunes State Park in 1923. She lent her expertise to the lengthy essay and tour of Dune Country, which filled seventeen pages, including a botanically explicit listing of indigenous wildflowers.[29] Several fieldworkers conducted research and personally observed subjects in their home areas. The results of their activity appeared throughout the guide. Clive Beatty, for example, was especially prolific in submitting material related to Whiting, including a long essay on the city itself, an equally lengthy piece on the Standard Oil refinery there, and smaller submissions on literature and architecture.

Francis Francoeur submitted a detailed account of Hammond's Standard Steel Car Company, parts of which appeared in three locations in the finished guide. Audrey Laube and Archie Koritz were old enough to remember the steel strike of 1919 and the recent growth of powerful labor unions in Lake County. They both contributed heavily to the essay on working conditions.[30]

In his preface to the Calumet guide, Gordon Briggs maintained that the "true history of the twentieth century is the story of industrialism," and this theme permeates the book. The transformation of raw materials into finished goods and the impact of this process on the land and the people is the overpowering message in all aspects of the guide: essays, tours, and photographs. To accommodate industry, "swamps were drained, the channel of the Grand Calumet River was changed, and sand dunes 60 to 80 feet high were leveled."[31] This transformation of the natural landscape into a built environment for manufacturing products and profit set the stage for entrepreneurs and workers. Self-consciously dramatic prose describes the workplaces. U.S. Steel's Gary Works "stretches for miles along the flat gray Lake front . . . its narrow coke ovens (nearly one thousand of them) pressed together row on row like slices of toast in a gigantic toaster, with flames bursting out now and then between the slices."[32] The grounds of the Standard Oil plant in Whiting "are covered by an endless array of distilleries, their stacks jutting up like organ-pipes and huge oyster-grey cylindrical oil tanks."[33] On a tall water tower in East Chicago, a painting of the little Dutch girl looked down over the Cudahy Packing Company, where five hundred workers, mostly women, made Old Dutch Cleanser.[34] At the Queen Anne Candy Company in Hammond, "mountains of nuts, Brazils, pecans, cashews, walnuts, and almonds are picked by fingers so amazingly swift that no machine yet devised can replace them."[35] These industries represented more to the region than just places to work. In Gary "there is scarcely a church, hospital, fraternal or civic organization" that had not gotten contributions from U.S. Steel.[36] East Chicago's Inland Steel Corporation developed a residential subdivision called Sunnyside where garbage was collected, "lawns are watered and mowed, shrubbery and trees trimmed, and streets cleaned and kept in repair by the company."[37] In the early years of Whiting, the Standard Oil Company provided the town with water, lights, fire protection, a sewer system, and police protection,[38] and in 1923 Standard Oil constructed the Memorial Community House, the "most impressive building" in the city. It housed an auditorium, ballroom, banquet halls, and two gymnasia.[39] Of the forty-two photographs that illustrate the guide, one-third document some aspect of the industrial environment, testifying to the editors' belief in its predominance in Calumet life.

Contiguous to this industrial emphasis and integral to it is the attention given to labor, unions, and strikes. The essay on labor constitutes eleven pages, much longer than the discussions devoted to religion, the arts, and several other topics. The essay is chronological, moving from the days of no collective bargaining for the workers except in small craft unions, through years of struggle and failed strikes, to the New Deal with its championing of labor and the emergence of powerful industrial unions. The writers try valiantly to be fair in their treatment and show the arguments of both management and workers. They balance Judge Elbert Gary's policy of no unions in the steel industry with his local philanthropy and grievance policies. And they show how the company-provided pensions and hospitalization benefits mollify the employees' low wages, long hours, and dangerous working conditions.[40] But by 1919 the rising tensions resulted in a strike in the steel industry that was intertwined with the national Red Scare. It polarized the Calumet region and forced both state and federal governments to send in troops. The result was a standoff, with management holding firm and the workers retreating. Fieldworker Audrey Laube submitted a twenty-five-page account of this episode, filled with detail and passion. It survived editorial revision, but just barely. Most of the passion was tempered, and the printed version covered only two pages.[41] With the coming of the New Deal, labor unions received the blessing of the federal government and grew rapidly. Workers who had formerly had no collective bargaining options now saw a jurisdictional split between the American Federation of Labor and the Congress of Industrial Organizations. Fieldworker Archie Koritz wrote a lengthy piece covering this process. Like the account of the 1919 strike, it too was editorially tempered, although the final version refers to the "miracle" victory of the unions over the "vast industrial leviathan" of big steel.[42]

Ethnic heritage is one subject that sets the Calumet guide apart from the later and larger Indiana volume. Whereas the former revels in the diversity and multicultural nature of the region, the latter all but ignores the topic. The Indiana guide refers to Hoosiers as largely "homogeneous" descendants of northern European stock who had been little affected by recent foreign immigration into the Calumet.[43] State editors treat the Native Americans and French in a distant past tense; the Amish in Elkhart County and Belgians and Poles in St. Joseph County exist as isolated groups outside the Hoosier mainstream. To the contrary, the demographic mainstream described in the Calumet guide is an amalgam of nationalities, many from southern and eastern Europe. Maintaining their distinctiveness rather than rushing into assimilation, these groups augmented the labor force and added variety to the religious and cultural environment. Discussion of religion and the arts in the region is almost dominated by the contributions of these new Americans. Many of the Roman Catholic churches were congregations of Croatians, Slovaks, and Hungarians, and the Jewish temples and Greek Orthodox churches were more common than exceptional. These different ethnic groups were active in preserving and performing music from their native roots. Choral groups from Gary included the Choir Chopin, the Choir Karogeorge, and the Liederkranz Society. East Chicago hosted the Paderewski Choral Society, and Hammond had its Orpheus Choir. In addition there was a regional Jewish Symphony Orchestra and Father John Lach's Symphonic Boys Band of Whiting. Gary, being the largest of the Calumet cities, was also the most diverse, counting more foreign-born than native-born over the age of 35. The essay on Gary boasted of its retail stores featuring Italian ravioli, Polish hams, and Greek aptos, and listed among its points of interest settlement houses such as Neighborhood House and Friendship House, which offered classes in English language and Americanization.

Twenty-five percent of East Chicago's population in 1930 was foreign-born, and prior to the Depression the city had a sizable Hispanic community in the Little Mexico neighborhood. Whiting claimed an equal number of foreign-born; its essay estimated that almost 90 percent of the total population was of Slavic descent. Hammond claimed to be the least diverse in demography, with nearly 84 percent of its population being native-born whites. Of the 15 percent from other nations, Germans led the list.[44] In the guide's calendar of events, the monthly listings are replete with parades, picnics, and festivals that highlight the ethnic diversity of the region. One of the portfolios of photographs in the Calumet guide features a collage of ethnic businesses, ranging from a Greek café to a Hispanic cigar store. Apparently nonethnic businesses lacked sufficient visual distinctiveness to be included in the guide.

Another topic that distinguishes the Calumet guide from the Indiana guide is a separate essay on race. Many of the state guides contained discrete pieces on Indians and blacks. Indiana's guide did have an essay on Indians, but the editors chose to include material about blacks in other essays, especially history. Perhaps because the black population of the Calumet was approximately 10 percent of the total, more than double the percentage for Indiana at large,[45] the subject seemed worthy of an essay. The concentration of large numbers in a small geographical site intensified blacks' economic, social, and political clout. That concentration ranged from 20 percent of the Gary population down to Whiting, which, the editors noted without additional comment, "prohibits Negroes from living within its limits."[46] The essay is both historical and sociological, and the prose exhibits a genteel paternalism somewhat typical of many publications during the 1930s. It reflects prevailing attitudes of the time that included segregation, limited opportunities, and restricted freedoms for blacks, whether in the Calumet, Indiana, or the United States. Institutionally most schools were segregated, as were churches and hospitals. The editors mentioned almost condescendingly the many pool halls and "Harlemesque nightclubs" frequented by blacks but approved of the settlement houses and the Lake County Negro Children's Home, established for uplift and welfare. Professionally, several teachers, doctors, lawyers, and dentists were emerging in the black community, because "as a rule," according to the editors, "Negroes seek the services of their own race."[47] Politically, both political parties courted black voters, and several blacks had been elected to government posts. The essay on race in the Calumet closes with an inspirational story that sprang from the depths of the Great Depression. The story is based largely on a report submitted by fieldworker Micha R. Halsted.[48] A consumer cooperative movement, led by instructor Jacob L. Reddix of Gary's Roosevelt High School, established a grocery store, a gasoline service station, and a credit union. These were to "lift a race out of poverty and put it on the straight road to independence." The guide applauded its initial success as well as the "growing sense of racial solidarity" and the "spirit of self-sufficiency" that had developed.[49]

Bragging about local assets and attributes was something the national FWP office discouraged in the state guides, but it permitted, if not encouraged, this in the local guides. The Calumet guide indulged in this practice enough to be guilty of regional chauvinism. With editorial offices in the Gary Commercial Club and Chamber of Commerce, it was not surprising that the staff adopted an attitude of provincial pride and a prose style that bordered on boosterism. There was an unwritten assumption that the major audience for these city and regional guides was the local citizenry and potential visitors, so a generous dose of self-congratulations and puffery could not hurt anyone and might do some good. Gordon Briggs implied as much in the preface when he stated that the book could reveal local "treasures and resources" to strangers and could also give "a new pride of possession" to Calumet citizens.[50] The dunes, for example, represented not just a vacation spot by Lake Michigan; they were also "one of the most interesting natural phenomena in North America." Likewise, the manufacturing productivity of the region rose above mere national economics; it had become "one of the greatest industrial centers of the world."[51] Among the industries, size was a point to be mentioned with regard to the number of employees or items produced. Many of the individual plants claimed to be the "largest" of their type in the world, including the Gary Works of

U.S. Steel, the Standard Oil refinery in Whiting, and the sheet and tin mills of the Carnegie-Illinois Corporation. The heavily ethnic population strove to prove its Americanism during World War I, and according to the editors it did so with flying colors. Gary produced "the greatest patriotic demonstration in Indiana" during the war, and Hammond led the nation in the percentage of men who served in the military.[52] In the arts, quality did not depend on age. The young Gary Civic Theater had become in less than two decades "one of three outstanding civic theaters in the country," according to some observers.[53] This propensity for listing the oldest, largest, and finest reached a dubious height when the editors decided that some aspects of the region's racial segregation were worthy of attention. For instance, they noted that Gary's Roosevelt High School was one of the largest high schools for blacks in the Midwest, and that the black golf course, also in Gary, "was the first municipal Negro golf course in the United States."[54] In the annals of boosterism, if best is not attainable, first or most will suffice.

Perhaps because the Calumet guide had only minimal supervision from the national FWP staff, there was less emphasis on the positive impact of the New Deal than appeared in the state guides. There is brief mention of the Whiting Armory, which received construction funds from the WPA, and an equally fleeting discussion of the Federal Theatre Project children's program in Gary. The editors missed an opportunity to discuss the contributions of the Civilian Conservation Corps in the Dunes State Park or the considerable work done by the National Youth Administration in area schools. One major exception to this cursory treatment of the New Deal is the attention given to labor legislation. The passage of the National Industrial Recovery Act in 1933 opened the door temporarily for collective bargaining, and two years later, the National Labor Relations Act brought permanence and power to industrial unions in the Calumet. This shift in the relationship of management and labor was a major one made possible by the New Deal. By 1935 the federal government had openly chosen sides with workers instead of business. The editors labeled the change miraculous but withheld judgment on its long-term repercussions. Their verdict for this new balance of power was a diplomatic "only the future can tell."[55]

The legacy of the Calumet guide was more enduring than the modest goals set at the time of publication. Area individuals and institutions had reserved only 600 copies in advance, and a few extra copies went on sale for two dollars at local stores. Since this book was printed locally, not published by a commercial firm, it did not enjoy the normal publicity and marketing that would have accompanied a professional job. Newspapers in the region did take note of its arrival in January 1940, however, and their reactions were generally positive. The *Gary Post-Tribune* complimented the project, found the various essays fascinating, but wished for a more dramatic title for the book.[56] The *Calumet News* in East Chicago mentioned the guide twice. It lamented that the city of Gary had gotten the "lion's share" of the volume, but admitted that the book was well written with practical tours. In particular it found the essay on labor "fair-minded and well-balanced."[57] The *Chesterton Tribune* appreciated the illustrations that gave a "bird's-eye view" of the area, and was pleased that sites and events heretofore "unknown or overlooked" were now in print.[58] Local enthusiasm for the guide soon exhausted the supply, and not until 1975 was it reprinted by a firm in New York. More recent histories of the region continue to cite the guide, particularly as a contemporary source of opinions and attitudes from the 1930s.[59] It was in a very real sense a portrait of a region, warts and all.

The weekly newspaper series "It Happened in Indiana" was the first public activity of the newly renamed Writers' Program. When Congress restructured the WPA in late 1939, the former FWP became the WP, with 25 percent of its activities funded by its new state sponsor, the public relations department of Indiana State Teachers College. According to the prospectus, which the new sponsor completed in February 1940, they envisioned "furnishing free weekly columns to approximately one hundred Indiana newspapers." These columns would "be made up of material selected from the files of the Writers' Project" and would "contain little known sidelights on

Indiana history, humorous happenings in the past, bits of interesting folklore, and other miscellany of an interesting or unusual nature."[60]

This series appeared to benefit both the Indiana fieldworkers and the ISTC publicity office. The accumulated research materials submitted by the former would reach a wide audience prior to and beyond the publication of the guide, and the college would reap some tangential publicity in the process. Ross Lockridge had initially proposed a similar series back in 1937, when he was the state director, but the national director had quashed the idea, arguing that it would get in the way of a speedy completion of the state guide.[61] Now, with the national staff wielding less control and the state sponsor assuming more, Lockridge's original idea became a reality, although other individuals would be in charge.

"It Happened In Indiana" began appearing in the late spring of 1940 and solidified the relationship between the Indianapolis headquarters and the Terre Haute sponsoring institution. Gordon Briggs and his staff sifted through the piles of Hoosier history, folklore, and journalism, wrote the columns, and sent them to John Sembower and his public relations staff at the college. From Terre Haute, Sembower forwarded the columns to papers around the state, accompanied by a distinctive logo to appear at the head of the column.[62] The logo was a vertical rectangle featuring an outline of the state that contained in bold type the words "It Happened in Indiana." In smaller print, tucked into the lower right corner, or the southeast border of the state, was the message "Compiled by Indiana Writers' Program * Supplied by Indiana State Teachers College, Terre Haute." Although distinctive, the logo occupied considerable space, and some papers did not always print it, choosing sometimes to substitute a smaller headline stating simply "It Happened in Indiana." Omitting the logo saved space for the local paper, but it denied credit to the two entities responsible for the column. Readers with good memories would be able to associate the material with its originators; casual readers or those who failed to recall the logo would not. The original plan for this series had anticipated that one hundred papers would carry the column, but the actual number was closer to seventy, including both daily and weekly

96

papers, most of them "county seat weeklies," according to Sembower.[63] The series was scheduled to last as long as the Writers' Program partnership endured, and this was the case. The columns continued to appear until early 1942, when both the WPA and the Writers' Program were declining rapidly as the war made them redundant. A handful of fieldworkers and editors in Indianapolis kept the written Hoosier materials traveling west on the National Road to Terre Haute and then around the state almost until the Writers' Program died.

That Indiana history was so heavily featured in these columns was not surprising. Guidelines from Washington encouraged research into the past for the writing of the guide essays, and the fieldworkers were prolific in scouring through old newspapers and records for local events and colorful episodes. Many of these incidents that had happened in Indiana appeared in the columns in abbreviated form to educate as well as amuse readers. One episode early in the series typifies this dual goal. There was a village in Parke County so small during the 1870s that only one family owned a clock. This created a problem during the malaria season when taking quinine at regular times was required. Consequently, some resourceful citizens there fired guns and sounded horns "every two hours as a signal for the taking of the medicine."[64] Another column discussed canal days along the Wabash River in the 1850s. Readers learned of the mules, boats, crews, and cooks who plied the expensive artificial water route. The financially struggling canal companies did not get as much assistance from the General Assembly as they wanted, and an angry editorial in the *Wabash Gazette* castigated the state legislators as "pusillanimous nincompoops" and "thick-skulled asymptotes" for their lack of support.[65] Indians and military battles received much attention in these journalistic forays into the Hoosier past. During the Revolutionary War, the Lochry skirmish in Ohio County was a relatively minor event, but it got a memorable retelling in this column. While he was engaged in the Northwest Territory in 1781, American colonel Archibald Lochry encountered some Indian allies of the British forces. The story ends with a dramatic account of how Lochry "was tomahawked and scalped near the mouth of the creek which still bears his name."[66] In condensed but vivid prose, the historic episode wove together Native Americans, martyrdom, and Hoosier geographical place-names.

Gordon Briggs's fondness for folklore guaranteed that "It Happened in Indiana" would also feature many examples of Hoosier legends, tall tales, and sociological miscellany. Fieldworkers had been collecting this material since 1936, and vast amounts of it were available for use. For example, unusual epitaphs from Indiana cemeteries arrived from all corners of the state to document early attitudes about life and death. This one from 1849 appeared in Hamilton County:

> Here lies
> George Wise
> He was wise in life
> May he never be
> Otherwise[67]

The use of Native Americans as a source for geographical place-names became a common practice in the early days of the state. In Kosciusko County, for instance, developers of a resort at the largest lake considered naming it after Chief Flatbelly, who had once lived in the region. They overruled this, however, in favor of a more aesthetic Wawasee.[68] And indigenous wildlife influenced local traditions in small towns. In Knox County, the annual competitive search for wild morels produced heroes of a sort. The year that Clyde Stalcup claimed the championship, he found seventy-six, the largest of which weighed one pound. During the competition his basket ran out of space, so he stuffed the rest of the mushrooms into his shirt.[69]

As America drifted closer to war in 1941, the column featured items of a military nature. And following the Japanese attack at Pearl Harbor, subsequent stories discussed homefront activities, past and present. Some of these human interest features revealed much about continuity and change during wartime. Near Edinburg, the U.S. Army had located a site for a training camp and begun surveying the land and evacuating residents. These defense preparations forced Val Ulery, a blacksmith, to move from his home of more than eighty years.[70] In another episode, the editors of the Writers' Program drew parallels between President Roosevelt's current Lend-Lease aid to the Allies and a similar program during the Civil War. Fieldworkers in Floyd County had unearthed documents in the local courthouse that documented "muskets and other equipment Gov. Oliver P. Morton issued five men who enlisted in the Union Army in 1861."[71] And from all around the state, brief accounts of volunteerism, patriotism, and the inevitable xenophobia began to surface. The Indiana Gladiolus Society scheduled its annual show in La Porte and announced that there would be a prize for "the exhibit with the greatest patriotic appeal." The editors envisioned red, white, and blue gardens covering the state.[72] Recycling of tin cans and other metal products was reminiscent of the conservation efforts during the First World War. The Terre Haute Auto Club established collection sites for children to deposit old license plates that could be used in war matériel. One elderly resident of the Lafayette Soldiers' Home asked the local recruiting office to bend the eligibility rules for him. Pearl Harbor was still a fresh memory, and although he was 72, he wanted to enlist and "help whip the Japs."[73]

The history, folklore, and miscellany that appeared in "It Happened in Indiana" were never credited to their authors. Like most of the Writers' Program products, the prose was anonymous, and the fieldworkers who researched and compiled the information received no bylines, only WPA salaries. These fieldworkers probably could have felt some satisfaction or possessive pride in seeing their efforts appear in print if they read any of the seventy newspapers that carried the columns. Much of this material had been gathered between 1936 and 1938, the peak employment years for the FWP, and many of these writers no longer worked for the WPA in the early 1940s. Some of the stories, nevertheless, can be traced to the fieldworkers who discovered them in their far-flung locations and sent them to the Indianapolis headquarters. Their names are still attached to their manuscripts in the official records. They deserve recognition after many decades for their resourcefulness and creativity in excavating this load of Hoosier lore. Robert C. Irvin contributed the amusing epitaph for George Wise. Irvin was a fieldworker from Noblesville

who proved both versatile and resourceful. He submitted manuscripts on the Underground Railroad, historic buildings, and Indian
trails, and conducted interviews with former slaves. In his pursuit of
context for the cemetery epitaph, Irvin tracked down the only two
remaining descendents of George Wise, neither of whom knew anything about the small tombstone or its inscription.[74] Fieldworker
C. A. Anderson from Wabash wrote a lengthy manuscript on the
construction and operation of the canal system through his county.
From the thirty-four pages of carefully researched and documented
history, the Indianapolis FWP staff extracted a few punchy tidbits,
including the overwrought editorial from the *Wabash Gazette*.[75] The
story about the naming of Lake Wawasee came from a piece submitted by Pearl M. Roberts in Kosciusko County. She based her manuscript on a series of interviews with residents of the lake district
who traced the sequence of the lake's names. She indicated that the
community in 1894 had selected Wawasee as more "euphonious"
than Flatbelly; the FWP editors apparently decided that *aesthetic* was
a more aesthetic choice of words.[76]

The fourth publication, beyond the state guide, was a small pamphlet called *Indiana: Facts, Events, Places, Tours*. It appeared in July
1941, just two months before the release of the guide. *Indiana: Facts,
Events, Places, Tours* was part of a national recreation series in which
every state participated. These handbooks were short compilations
of information, largely aimed at tourists and visitors who sought a
quick source of answers about the state's natural resources, vacation
spots, and available facilities. They were approximately thirty pages
long and sold for around twenty cents.[77] This series, or one similar
to it, was planned in 1939 by the New York City FWP, and several
states had their manuscripts ready to print, but the project was
aborted. The Hoosier entry into this ill-fated group was illustrated
with photographs and entitled "Your Vacation in Indiana."[78] The reconfiguration of the WPA and FWP that year probably was responsible for stopping the series prior to the publication of the first titles.
The following year under the decentralized Writers' Program, the
series resumed life as the American Recreation series, sponsored by
the Virginia Conservation Commission. The pamphlets in this new

series were uniform in title, size, and content, and all were printed in 1940 and 1941 by the Bacon and Wieck firm in New York, which specialized in paperback publications.[79]

Most of the Indiana pamphlet is a distillation of those portions of the Indiana guide that Gordon Briggs and his staff deemed relevant for potential visitors to the state. At times the prose is verbatim, which, considering that the guide had tourism as one of its many goals, was a logical double use of the same materials. The pamphlet's "General Tourist Information" section repeats word for word some sections from the guide's unit on general information. For example, visitors are warned that "Rattlesnakes and copperheads, while not common, may be encountered in the hill regions of the southern part of the State."[80] And as a forewarning to imbibers, liquor is not sold "on Sundays, election days, and Christmas."[81] Details regarding the state's climate, highway system, hunting and fishing regulations, and tourist accommodations appear in almost identical format in both publications. The state park system is described enticingly in both the guide and the pamphlet, although the latter is easier to use. All the parks are grouped together in one section, whereas they are scattered throughout the various tours in the guide. The visitor, however, will glean the same material from both despite the difference in accessibility. For instance, at Clifty Falls State Park in the southern hills, the editors call attention twice to "deep ravines into which the sun shines only at noon."[82] And the scenic beauty at Turkey Run State Park is "unsurpassed" by any other park in the state, according to both accounts.[83] Also in both publications is a virtually identical monthly listing of events that visitors might wish to incorporate into their vacation plans. They range from the Creole King Balls at Vincennes in January to the tobacco auctions at Madison in December.

A decidedly rural emphasis distinguishes the pamphlet from the more urban-oriented guide. The unidentified photograph on the front cover sets the tone for what is to follow; a rippling brook flows past rugged cliffs and lush foliage. By omission and implication, the message is that people leave the city for recreation; they might live and work in cities, but they escape from them for vacations. While the Indiana guide devoted roughly a third of its space to essays on the major urban centers, the pamphlet mentions Indianapolis, Fort Wayne, Evansville, Gary, South Bend, and other urban sites only in passing. They are clearly not points of destination, and their art and historical museums, for instance, are merely listed statistically, not described by content or collection. This rural emphasis was typical of the American Recreation series; the decision had apparently been made that recreation was primarily an activity that took place outside of urban environments. But Indiana's pamphlet took this to an extreme. Connecticut, which was far more urban than Indiana, naturally included several of its historic urban museums and churches. Arizona, on the other hand, was overwhelmingly rural at the time, yet allotted considerable space to the attractions of Phoenix and Tucson.[84] To the contrary, the bulk of the Hoosier pamphlet is devoted to the bucolic corners of the state, which offer boating, swimming, fishing, hunting, and scenery. Lakes in northern Indiana and rivers and hills of southern Indiana get most of the attention, and the flat central section of the state is largely ignored. Those small urban centers that do rate discussion are the ones that offer attractions such as beaches and other recreational facilities. For example, the emphasis on Rome City is not the literary attraction of Gene Stratton-Porter's Limberlost Cabin but the nearby Sylvan Lake, "three and a half miles in length and offering good sport for canoe and motorboat enthusiasts."[85] Likewise, in French Lick, the descriptions deal less with the distinctive architectural and political heritage that characterized the guide's discussion and more with the golf courses, tennis courts, and "riding stables with miles of bridle paths through the surrounding hills."[86] Brown County gets more space in the pamphlet than any other subject or site. The attention given to this "mecca for nature lovers" typifies the rural bias of the booklet and highlights the kind of recreational activity that the Writers' Program accentuated. The rustic cartoon figure Abe Martin who frequented Brown County trails emerged more nearly as a Hoosier spokesman than did the unmentioned urban auto racers of Indianapolis or football players at Notre Dame.[87]

As an example of condensation, *Indiana: Facts, Events, Places, Tours* revealed Gordon Briggs's intense involvement with and intimate knowledge of the guide. As writer and editor, he had spent six years working through the drafts and revisions of the essays and tours. No one was better qualified to reduce the 500-page book to a 28-page pamphlet. Chapters became paragraphs; lists replaced analysis; non-recreational material ceased to exist. Hoosier history, folklore, art, industry, cities, and literature were reduced to a mere mention. Briggs had personally written the guide essay entitled "Indiana Today," which tried to capture the character and essence of the Hoosier state. For the pamphlet, those four pages were compressed into a comparable essay of two pages, entitled "Present Day Indiana," which also included enough history, geography, agriculture, industry, and the arts to create a coherent context. The result was a skillful job of miniaturization; Briggs and his staff succeeded in condensing a massive amount of material into a small space without destroying the meaning. What emerges from this midwestern mixture of agriculture and industry is a hybrid Hoosier, "famous for his easy-going manners, his love of politics, and his preeminence on the production of limestone, corn, and literature." And true to the guide's disingenuous denial of an urban mentality in the state, the pamphlet perpetrates the same attitude, maintaining that "the people of Indiana remain largely the friendly, democratic, small town folk made famous by Riley."[88] For visitors in search of a typical meal during their vacation, the pamphlet recommended a bountiful if stereotypical nineteenth-century menu of country-style fried chicken, pork chops, corn on the cob, and tomato juice.[89] Typical, maybe; tasty, no doubt; but decidedly not an uptown repast.

When *Indiana: Facts, Events, Places, Tours* arrived in July 1941, it quickly and quietly fell into a literary vacuum. The state Writers' Program staffers were gearing up for the publication of the guide in September, and their efforts to market and circulate the pamphlet were lackluster at best. The state WPA staff requested that district supervisors send lists of potential sales outlets for it to the New York publisher, but it is doubtful that review copies were forwarded to state newspapers. If so, they were largely ignored.[90] Today the pamphlet is regarded as a negligible piece of ephemera, located in only a few libraries. One of the Washington editors later assessed the American Recreation series as a symbol of the diminished ambitions of the FWP after it and the WPA were scaled down in 1939. He refers to the pamphlets as "hack work," lacking vision and originality.[91] His assessment is valid, although perhaps too severe. Granted, they did lack originality in their rigid format, condensed prose, and narrowly targeted audience. And they were more an exercise in recycling than in creativity. But they served several worthwhile purposes at the time. They offered employment to a few writers, many of whom had passed the age of reentering the job market. They distilled the essence of the larger guides and with their reduced size and cost were more accessible to a wider readership. And they offered handy advice to a large and expanding tourist market. More than 5 million people had visited Indiana's state parks and recreation areas in 1939 alone.[92] In the case of Indiana, a major reason for the pamphlet being so swiftly overlooked and soon forgotten was its denial of the state's demographics. The facts, events, places, and tours featured in its pages were the property of the rural minority. Hoosier urbanites had become a majority in 1920 and had increased that margin in the decades since. They and their urban attractions and amenities were omitted from the booklet because the editors gave recreation such a rural definition. The pamphlet *Indiana* had ignored these urban Hoosiers, and they, in turn, ignored it.

With the onset of World War II, both the WPA and the Writers' Program shifted part of their attention to defense projects to assist in wartime preparations. One of these projects in Indiana resulted in a small study guide for Americanization classes. Although this publication was not aimed at the general public, it did circulate widely among its intended audience. Following the attack on Pearl Harbor and the declaration of war in December 1941, there was a dramatic upsurge in the number of resident aliens seeking American citizenship. In cooperation with the Department of Justice and the Immigration and Naturalization Service, the WPA in Indiana assumed responsibility for helping these aliens prepare for their naturalization examinations. Unemployed teachers on relief taught citizenship or Americanization classes to familiarize these immigrants with the United States and Indiana constitutions, aspects of federal, state, and local government, and the duties that accompanied citizenship. These classes were conducted around the state in libraries, churches, schoolrooms, and community centers. In January 1942, more than nine hundred individuals were enrolled.[93] The Indiana WPA requested help from the Writers' Program in putting together a study guide for use in these classes.

John A. Linebarger, Indiana's WPA supervisor for the National Citizenship Education Program, was an experienced educator and administrator who knew how to plan for emergencies and delegate responsibilities. A graduate of DePauw University, he had taught and been principal or superintendent in Frankfort, Montezuma, and Rockville schools and had organized Chautauqua meetings around the state. In 1928 he had been the unsuccessful Democrat candidate for superintendent of public instruction.[94] Now with the responsibility for guiding resident aliens toward their citizenship exams, he confronted the competing pressures of wartime haste and intellectual integrity. Linebarger emphasized that the road to naturalization was not a "slipshod" process and that the citizenship examination was a "rigorous" one. But he also intended to provide classes that would facilitate the process and assist the immigrants toward their goal.[95] Materials on Indiana's constitution and government apparently were not as readily available for mass consumption as those for the federal government, so he worked with Gordon Briggs to get a brief and accessible Indiana booklet prepared for use in the WPA classes. Briggs logically delegated this study guide assignment to Ray Thurman, the WP regional supervisor with headquarters in Terre Haute. Thurman was a writer who specialized in advertising and trade journals and who enjoyed the respect of the teaching staff at Indiana State Teachers College and the editorial staff in Indianapolis.[96] He accepted this responsibility with its concomitant pressures of haste and integrity.

Ray Thurman took information about Indiana government that fieldworkers had previously compiled for the county guides and combined it with data from *Burns Statutes* and the 1940 Indiana *Yearbook*. He also used instructional materials from the social science consultants at ISTC, Dr. Olis Jamison and Charles Roll, both of whom had written books on Indiana history and government. The result, in March 1942, was a fifty-seven-page manuscript entitled "A Text for Americanization and Naturalization Classes."[97] This study guide did not pretend to be original or creative; it was a rapid synthesis of the state constitution, relevant legislation, textbook analysis, and standard civics lessons. Thurman rewrote the formal and scholarly materials into simple, readable prose, frequently using a question-and-answer format. The prevailing emphasis was democracy and patriotism during troubled times. He stressed the stability of the Constitution, "accepted by the people who are to live under it." And he pointed out that "liberty and justice are watchwords in America," protected by the judicial system. In a world currently threatened by fascist dictators, Hoosier citizens need not fear the military powers of the governor who does not declare martial law or dispatch troops unless local officials request them. Thurman also mixed humor with civic responsibility in his discussion of the Department of Conservation. "In an earlier day . . . the game warden, with his star shining brightly, pounced on a victim fishing, trapping or hunting out of season . . . their work today is more of an educational nature . . . the art of conserving these important gifts."[98] Briggs and his Indianapolis staff edited the manuscript for accuracy and style, made a few changes, and relinquished the booklet to Linebarger, who was anxious to use it in his statewide classes. Three months later, there were still more than eight hundred resident aliens enrolled in these naturalization sessions, making use of the study guide.[99] Because the war rapidly made the WPA unnecessary, this booklet was the final publication of the Writers' Program.

FIVE

Oral History

In the course of their research, most of the FWP fieldworkers indulged in a practice now known commonly as oral history, although this term was not in use in the 1930s. At its most basic, oral history is just another method of recapturing the past in order to preserve it for future generations. In the case of the Federal Writers' Project, the past being recaptured was human memory that had not been committed to the written page. Sometimes these oral memories were small fragments, such as menus for family meals or neighborhood folklore, and at other times the recollections were of broader significance, such as natural disasters or major events. These memories for the most part would never have been written down and thus would have been lost over time. As oral historians, the fieldworkers collected and preserved these pieces of the Hoosier past. A few of the oral histories appeared in books, pamphlets, and articles published by the WPA and have enriched our knowledge of Indiana's heritage; most of them, however, remain in storage with the other records of the Federal Writers' Project. Three Indiana projects in particular produced large collections of oral history that are worthy of study. Interviews with former slaves, Hoosiers who had witnessed the Confederate invasion of Indiana during the Civil War, and Native

Americans who remembered early tribal customs all unearthed fascinating details that deserved a wider audience. The fieldworkers who engaged in these activities provided a valuable link between the past and present as they captured these memories before they faded.

As a technique for pursuing and preserving the past, oral history has proven to be both invaluable and controversial. It has uncovered facts not available elsewhere and supplied personal vantage points that provide extra color and detail to the larger narrative. At the same time, it has offered accounts of dubious motive and questionable authenticity. The ancient Greek historian Herodotus tapped the recollections of participants for his accounts of the Persian Wars. His histories would have been much different without these memories. In the 1970s, Merle Miller wrote a biography of Harry Truman that used oral interviews to enhance the material from published documents. The results were more colorful and intimate than previous works about the former president. In the 1980s, Eleanor Arnold published several volumes of interviews called *Memories of Hoosier Homemakers,* which described farming, holidays, and activities from earlier days. Each of these examples used oral sources to help recapture and reconstruct the past. And each has been controversial in the sense that some historians have expressed concerns about the validity of the oral memoirs as fully trustworthy documentation of past events.

Historians question the validity of all sources in the normal process of research, analysis, and writing, and the FWP oral interviews are particularly vulnerable targets. The fallibility of human memory is an obvious area of concern, as is the time lapse between the event and the recollection of it. Even under the best conditions, people exaggerate and romanticize events and their role in them. Many memories are selective and exclusive, recalling only portions of episodes, and the details change with subsequent repetitions. And some interviews produce self-serving accounts that revise or refute other versions of the historical record. Historians have also raised questions about the interviewers themselves. The age, race, gender, and skill of the interviewer all can have an impact on the person being interviewed. Obviously, oral history as an avenue into the past is a productive yet precarious tool that must be used with great care.

The FWP fieldworkers in the 1930s were not trained historians or anthropologists; they were journalists, teachers, librarians, and housewives who had little or no experience in interviewing. And on most occasions, they worked without the benefit of mechanical recording devices. They took notes during their interviews and later transcribed these into typed manuscripts. Consequently, the results are flawed historical source material: incomplete, anecdotal, biased, and often dead wrong. But in many cases, these interviews are the only sources available. Historians have learned to make the most of imperfect circumstances and hope that the strength of a document outweighs its weakness. Such is the case with oral history and its role in painting a self-portrait of the Hoosier state. Unfortunately, Indiana was not involved in the Life Histories project conducted by the national office. These interviews in many states revealed much about the lives, vocations, and attitudes of working people during the 1930s and appeared in several published anthologies (see chapter 1).

The FWP oral history project in Indiana that received the most national supervision, generated the most systematic interviews, and got the most public exposure was the project to collect anecdotes from former slaves. Nationally this involved interviews with more than 2,300 elderly blacks who had lived in bondage in the South prior to emancipation in 1865. FWP fieldworkers in seventeen states participated in this activity, and fieldworkers in Indiana interviewed more than a hundred people who had moved north with their families after gaining their freedom.[1] This was a national program with formal guidelines from Washington officials, so there was a uniformity in purpose and technique that united the effort among participants. Never before had any institution attempted to compile systematic data from a large number of former slaves. For the first time since the Civil War ended, America would have a multitude of primary sources concerning one of the nation's darkest chapters. The potential findings would be an unprecedented body of information for historians, folklorists, and anthropologists. The result of this project was a collection called the "ex-slave narratives," and they were predictably rich in detail and controversial in value. Scholars have published and cited the memoirs in many articles and books, and they have debated the validity of the facts within the narratives and the techniques that produced the collection.

Before the FWP enterprise, a few scattered attempts to interview former slaves had established precedents for gathering memoirs. Faculty and students at Southern University in Louisiana and Fisk University in Tennessee had begun pioneer programs in the late 1920s and early 1930s. Professor Lawrence Reddick at Kentucky State College had participated in the program at Fisk, and in 1934 he suggested to Harry Hopkins that a similar program would be a good activity for the FERA. He argued that the history of slavery needed the slaves' point of view in order to make the story complete.[2] The FERA funded a small pilot interview project in the Midwest, and then the FWP began its national coordinated activity in 1936. John Lomax, the national advisor on folklore, devised questionnaires to guide fieldworkers in their interviews. The questionnaires listed topics and techniques to elicit memories. For instance, fieldworkers were to suggest subjects such as family history, working conditions, religion, food, educational opportunities, and attempted escapes.[3] Benjamin Botkin succeeded Lomax in 1938 and revised the questionnaire to gather additional information. Sterling Brown, a professor at Howard University, became the FWP's editor of Negro affairs and circulated additional guidelines regarding dialect.[4] The resulting interviews between 1936 and 1939 produced the narratives, most of which now reside in the Library of Congress. They became an aggregate autobiography of these former slaves and their lives during bondage, the Civil War, and the years of freedom that followed. As mentioned in chapter 1, Lomax published excerpts from some of the narratives in 1938; Botkin published many others in his 1945 book, *Lay My Burden Down;* and collections have appeared in numerous articles and books since then. George Rawick's massive compilation of the interview typescripts known as *The American Slave* finally made the narratives accessible to a wider audience in the 1970s.

Scholars have been predictably ambivalent about these interviews and narratives. Beyond their appreciation for the newly available raw data, they have lamented the missed opportunities that character-ized the enterprise.[5] Even though these narratives added many layers of primary information to that previously known about slave life, the information was suspect on several levels. The former slaves be-ing interviewed were, by necessity, elderly; two-thirds of them were over 80 in the mid-1930s. This meant that most of the interviewees were children during their bondage and knew of adult slave life only by secondhand reference to their relatives and acquaintances. It also meant that a time lapse of roughly seven decades separated them from their pre-emancipation days. Compounding the problems associated with memory was that of the interviewers. The FWP field-workers were amateurs in the new field of oral history, and the of-ficial guidelines left little freedom to pursue an interesting devel-opment beyond the scripted questions. The overwhelming number of fieldworkers were white, and the racial differences between them and their subjects might well have inhibited the open sharing of sensitive personal memories regarding master-slave relations. Dialect and speech patterns also created many problems for historians. Very few of the FWP fieldworkers were equipped with recording devices; they took notes by hand and later typed their interviews. Some tried to replicate the sound and rhythm of the interviews; others did not. Some transcribed the oral exchanges in first-person prose as if the interviewee were telling the story; others used third-person style with the interviewer telling the story secondhand. None of these prob-lems posed fatal barriers to accepting the FWP narrative as authentic voices from the past, but they did present serious caveats for scholars searching for reliability.

Indiana's participation in the gathering of memoirs from former slaves fit into the national pattern. Hoosier fieldworkers interviewed 134 elderly blacks, and their narratives ranged from one paragraph to several pages. This was typical in number and length. Arkansas produced the largest number of interviews, with 677, and Kansas the smallest, with only 3.[6] Also typical was the fact that not all of the narratives were deposited in the Library of Congress and later printed in Rawick's compilation in 1972. As other narratives surfaced in various repositories around the nation, Rawick added supplements to his subsequent editions of *The American Slave*. Several additional Hoosier interviews were similarly unearthed in the state records at Indiana State University and added to the national collection. The Indiana fieldworkers who conducted the interviews likewise typified the national norm. Of the eighteen FWP interviewers, all were white with the exception of Anna Pritchett from Marion County. And the diverse styles of the transcribed narratives also conformed to the overall collection. Some were perfunctory, with factual answers to specific questions; others were chatty and rambling discussions. A few of the fieldworkers wrote their narratives in first-person prose as though they had captured an extended autobiographical monologue; most, however, presented the information in third-person biographical style. In 1937, FWP director Henry Alsberg encouraged Gordon Briggs to try to get the fieldworkers to capture more of the former slaves' own words, but this apparently did not happen enough to satisfy the national staff. After the project was completed, the managing editor of the manuscripts declared that Indiana's were "less satisfactory than those from any of the other states," in part because fieldworkers had drafted so many in third-person prose.[7]

These 134 Indiana narratives went through several editorial revisions between their initial interviews in the 1930s and the twenty-first century. The transformations that occurred during these revisions proved, if nothing else, that history is a malleable commodity. The eighteen fieldworkers submitted their written versions of the interviews to the Indianapolis headquarters, where some, if not all of them, were edited by the state staff. Some of these narratives included brief remarks by the fieldworkers concerning family information or social context. They were then forwarded to Washington, where Benjamin Botkin also edited the narratives and arranged them into bound volumes for scholarly use. The Rawick publications in the 1970s duplicated those volumes for sale to libraries, which made the collection available to a general readership. In 2000, Ronald L. Baker published *Homeless, Friendless, and Penniless,* which made the entire collection of Indiana interviews available for the first time. Baker, a professor of English at Indiana State University, edited the narratives again "to improve readability, unity, and coherence,"[8] and supplemented the interviews with more biographical and contextual details. In addition to the narratives, the book includes Baker's analysis of what the former slaves revealed about their lives, religion, education, folklore, the Civil War, and what freedom meant to them. From the original fieldworkers' manuscripts through Baker's recent reworking of them, these narratives traveled many miles and survived several literary transformations, but they still shed valuable light on the past and the process of oral history.

Emery C. Turner interviewed two former slaves in Lawrence County, and the narratives that they produced survived the editorial process almost unscathed. Turner had taught school and worked as a journalist before the Depression, so he probably had more expertise at interviewing and writing than many of his colleagues in the FWP. His other manuscripts dealing with folklore and history were appropriately researched, and his interviews with workers in the limestone industry revealed a talent for asking probing questions and summarizing the results.[9] Turner had worked on the police beat for the *Louisville Herald-Post* until 1930, an assignment that undoubtedly developed his ability to ferret out facts and get to the point without redundant exposition. Many of his FWP pieces bore the traditional newspaperman's signal of "30" to signify a conclusion, something rarely used by nonjournalists. His narratives from Thomas Ash and Mary Crane, both from Mitchell and both in their 80s, indicate that they responded to his scripted questions and did not elaborate with much personal information. Ash and Crane had been children in Kentucky during slavery times and were understandably vague about dates and chronology. But they both had vivid memories and were comfortable enough with Turner to share some painful recollections. Crane recalled her father being auctioned for $25, and Ash remembered seeing other slaves "tied up to the whipping post and flogged for disobeying."[10] The narratives are brief and written as first-person reminiscences, with no attempt to replicate dialect or distinctive speech patterns. They are fluid and graceful to the point that the prose of the two former slaves emerges as almost identical. Turner's autobiographical style for his two interviews had, in fact, become his own voice. The finished interviews passed through Indianapolis to the Library of Congress with only minor corrections of typographical errors.[11] Turner's manuscripts also survived Baker's later reworking with only a few changes. Crane/Turner had used the word *nigger* several times, and Baker replaced some of them with a more politically correct *slave.*[12]

Lauana Creel from Evansville submitted twenty-two narratives, making her the second most prolific interviewer of the Indiana fieldworkers. Creel was a single, middle-aged music teacher who changed residences eight times during the Depression and sometimes lived with her brother or her widowed mother.[13] This migratory pattern probably indicated financial instability in the family and her need for joining the FWP. Gordon Briggs thought she was one of his best interviewers. He attributed this to the fact that she had grown up in the South and had been cared for by a "Negro mammy." This, according to Briggs, gave her "a rare ability for getting stories out of old Negroes."[14] The national folklore advisor also complimented her success in collecting folklore material,[15] and this interest shows up in the narratives. Frequently her interviews included information about rural superstitions, medical and religious practices, and songs from plantations. Her interviews, on the whole, were lengthy and interspersed with her personal observations about the interviewees' physical appearance, general demeanor, and surroundings. In addition to their recollections of life during slavery, Creel often included discussions of their life in Evansville since the Civil War and during the hard times of the current depression. Most of the writing is Creel's third-person summary account of the interviews, but she breaks the narrative on occasion with quotations that try to approximate the dialect of an elderly black person. For example, Katie Sutton explained why she sprinkled salt in the footprints of departing guests: "Dat's so dey kain leave no ill will behind em."[16] Creel's own prose in these narratives sometimes became effusive in an attempt to evoke sympathetic emotions. One example is the narrative of George T. Burns, who as a slave child was frozen to the bed one severe winter night, and his toes broke off. Not content to let these facts speak for themselves, Creel reconstructed the scene as the owner discovered the "motherless, hungry, desolate and unloved" child and "carried the small bundle of suffering humanity to the kitchen of her home and placed him near the big oven."[17] One of the Washington editors regarded Creel's writing as "melodramatic."[18] Ronald Baker, in his recent editing of the Creel narratives, not only got rid of much of the simulated dialect but also toned down the melodrama.

Two fieldworkers from Delaware County interviewed Joseph Allen separately, and the results present an excellent example of why historians have been cautious in their use of the ex-slave narratives.[19] The two interviews contradict each other on a few factual details, which presents a problem of credibility. They also vary in matters of content and emphasis, indicating that the two fieldworkers probably elicited different responses from Allen, remembered these selectively, and later wrote about the things they believed to be most important, based on their gender, experience, and personal viewpoint. Martha Freeman was a rural farm wife, and William W. Tuttle was a retired teacher and journalist from urban Muncie. In Freeman's interview there is a section in which Allen recalls being well fed as a slave, and then following emancipation he had to scratch like a "hen with one chick" in order to get enough to eat.[20] This barnyard analogy was apparently familiar and memorable to Freeman, but it does not appear in the Tuttle interview. Conversely, Tuttle's interview includes material about Allen's desire to learn to read and how his owner would punish him for his efforts at literacy. This episode on early education would naturally have greater appeal to a former teacher than to a farmer. Allen also shared with Tuttle memories of his youthful rebellion against female authority.[21] These did not appear in the Freeman interview, perhaps because Allen did not feel comfortable relating these gender-related stories to a woman. The basic chronology of Allen's life is similar in both interviews, but many aspects of his life diverge so dramatically, according to Freeman's and Tuttle's accounts, that Allen almost emerges as two different people. Hence, historians' caution is justifiable.

Anna Pritchett from Indianapolis held the distinction of being the only black interviewer from Indiana and of conducting the largest number of interviews, a total of twenty-four. Because several of her interviews were with children or grandchildren of former slaves, those were not included in the Library of Congress volumes. Pritchett's written narratives were mostly brief summaries of her interviews, and she rarely quoted directly, but when she did, there was no attempt to replicate dialect. She frequently described the appearance and living conditions of the person being interviewed, often in a judgmental way, with compliments for neatness and criticism for an untidy home or clothing. This apparently was a reflection of pride about her own middle-class status. Being in the FWP meant that Pritchett was officially, if temporarily, on relief; this situation seemed to affect her focus in the interviews. On several occasions she mentioned the inadequate pensions that elderly people received; Julia Bowman pointed out that during slavery there was never a time of "Want" as there was during the Depression.[22] Pritchett's background likewise colored her emphasis on education. Her extended family on Indianapolis's near northside included a dentist, a teacher, and a student at Indiana University.[23] And logically at least two of her interviews dealt with literacy: Belle Butler described the punishment given to slave children who tried to learn to read, and Joe Robinson, aged 84, was finally learning to read in a WPA class.[24] From Pritchett's twenty-four narratives, it is difficult to determine whether the subjects shared their reminiscences more freely with her, due to her race, than did other former slaves in their sessions with white interviewers. Her narratives are brief and perfunctory, with short sentences and paragraphs that seldom develop topics beyond factual answers to questions. Pritchett may have been industrious in locating a large number of former slaves in Marion County, but the narratives that resulted from her efforts lack detail and analysis. Because they constitute such a large portion of the Indiana collection, they could be partly responsible for Rawick's verdict on the state's contribution. He deemed many of them "not particularly significant for the general historian of slavery."[25] In his editing chores in 2000, Ronald

Baker did considerable rewriting, adding context and correcting details of the Pritchett narratives to enhance their value after the fact.

The collection of interviews dealing with the Confederate raid into Indiana during the Civil War is smaller than that of the former slaves and has never received public notice. But it reveals much about the Hoosier past and deserves the attention of historians. The collection corroborates old information about homefront activities and attitudes, and it adds layers of detail from a fresh vantage point. And like the interviews with former slaves, this collection contains both the strengths and the weakness that are inherent to oral history. Unlike the narratives from elderly blacks that sprang from a national project and adhered to rules from Washington, the Civil War memories came from an Indiana initiative and followed Hoosier guidelines. The FWP fieldworkers who participated in this project knew that they were capturing memories from the past that might never be preserved without their interviews and transcriptions. The record of this brief episode in 1863 is richer for their efforts in the 1930s, regardless of the inattention they received until the twenty-first century.

Briefly summarized, the Morgan raid occurred during July 1863, when the battles of Gettysburg and Vicksburg were heralding the doom of the South. Brigadier General John Hunt Morgan, a Confederate cavalryman from Kentucky, invaded Indiana with 2,500 troops and spent five days in the Hoosier state. Crossing the Ohio River downstream from Louisville at Mauckport on July 8, and leaving on July 13 north of Cincinnati at West Harrison, he was responsible for one major battle, a few skirmishes, considerable pillaging and destruction, approximately twenty deaths, and widespread fear.[26] The battle of Corydon early in the raid pitted the vastly outnumbered Home Guard against this Confederate cavalry, and they tried unsuccessfully to defend the town. The next four days saw the raiders head on a zigzag course north and east toward the state of Ohio, during which they burned bridges, ripped out railroad tracks, destroyed telegraph offices, looted stores, extorted payment in lieu of additional damage, "traded" their tired horses for fresh ones, and took money, food, and supplies along the way. The towns of Salem, Lexington, Vernon, and Versailles took the brunt of the invasion, and dozens of Hoosiers en route lost personal property and had to provide services for the raiders. Indiana governor Oliver P. Morton sent an urgent call for volunteers to defend the state, and 65,000 men rallied to the call.[27] Fortunately, this impromptu militia saw no real action, but General Edward Hobson and his Union troops pursued Morgan into Ohio, where he was ultimately captured and briefly imprisoned. As dramatic and daring as it was, this brief foray into the North gained nothing for the Confederacy other than a legendary reputation for the maverick cavalryman.

The oral memoirs of the John Hunt Morgan raid into southern Indiana were the end result of one of Ross Lockridge's historic site pilgrimages. He planned to restage the cavalry raid on its seventy-second anniversary in July 1935, when he was still a supervisor in the Emergency Education Division under Governor McNutt's Commission on Unemployment Relief. The publicity and pageantry associated with this reenactment would, Lockridge hoped, stimulate elderly Hoosiers to share their memories of the original event. Lockridge's associates in the commission would conduct interviews with people who had witnessed the raid. During the course of this pilgrimage and the subsequent interviews, Lockridge became the state director of the Federal Writers' Project. His change of status from state to federal administrator did not, however, interrupt his mission to gather the memories concerning the Civil War. He instructed the new FWP fieldworkers in those southern Indiana counties to continue the project as an adjunct enterprise to their normal activities of researching local history and folklore for the Indiana guide.

Lockridge's reenactment plans were larger than many of his previous "History-on-Wheels" activities, and his goals were more ambitious. In addition to organizing the usual music, parades, and speeches, he revealed an astute understanding of oral history. The pilgrimage would help to reconstruct this part of the past, and the interviews would help to preserve it. Just prior to the pilgrimage, he wrote that he hoped to attract "all the old people who were living" at the time of the Morgan raid and "who still remember that as children they actually saw" the events of 1863.[28] A flier distributed around Vernon issued a specific invitation to the elderly to attend and reminisce, and the Versailles newspaper reminded its readers that "it is the purpose of this series of programs to revive and recount the vivid memories."[29] This anniversary pilgrimage garnered good publicity and coverage in all the local newspapers along the route. At Corydon, Lew O'Bannon, editor of the *Corydon Democrat*, participated actively; his grandfather had been one of the Home Guard who had died in the original battle. Lieutenant Governor Townsend was the featured speaker on the Salem courthouse lawn. Near Vernon, CCC personnel set off explosions to simulate a military skirmish, and crowds attended ranging in size from 60 at St. Paul to 1,500 at Vernon.[30] Lockridge wrote an eight-page review of the reenactment, and his pleasure permeated the account. It was, he said, "an unqualified success in every particular." Of special significance was the "enumeration of interesting reminiscences by aged people who resided in the vicinity . . . [who] recounted vividly from memory significant incidents that they themselves observed on the occasion of the famous raid in Civil War days."[31]

The harvesting of old memories was successful, but it took much longer than the reenactment. In an addendum to his glowing review of the event, Lockridge instructed his county supervisors on the Governor's Commission to contact the elderly who had reminisced at the pilgrimage and to collect those memories on paper. He felt that collecting them would be a "substantial contribution . . . to the vital historic literature of these historic days." In addition to interviewing witnesses, his county supervisors were to gather press reports of the original raid and accounts from local and county histories. Lockridge instructed them to ignore obvious inaccuracies and inconsistencies in the recollections. They were simply to gather and send the material to his state office while the memories were still fresh and the enthusiasm was still high.[32] Only a few of his county supervisors completed their assignments before Lockridge's transition to the Federal Writers' Project. A small number of interviews and written memoirs trickled in, and a few copies of newspaper accounts and gleanings from county histories arrived at his office, but not the grand collection he had envisioned.[33] Subsequently, FWP fieldworkers in the southern Indiana counties took up the incomplete task and interviewed and collected materials through 1938. Together these two harvests provided a bountiful crop of Morgan memorabilia.

This cache of oral history about the Morgan raid is a disparate group of memoirs that received no publicity during the FWP period and have since been dispersed among several archives where they have been used only rarely. Of the approximately fifty recollections, some are secondary accounts based on tales passed down from ancestors or gleaned from older newspaper stories. They offer little that is new to historians. The remaining thirty-five are primary accounts by eyewitnesses. Most of them are interviews, but a few are firsthand reports written by the witnesses. Both share the common denominator of recalling the raid after seven decades of lapsed time. Similar to the slave narratives, these interviews were not tape-recorded, but were handwritten and later typed. Some of the fieldworkers were the same individuals who interviewed former slaves, and the results were similar: some first-person autobiographical recollections, some third-person summaries, some direct quotations with simulated dialect. The memoirs range in length from one paragraph to seven pages. Because they now reside in three separate archives, access to the entire group is complicated. The largest group is located in the Indiana FWP Collection at Indiana State University. The Library of Congress also holds fourteen memoirs, most of which are duplicates of the first group. A few extra, different from the others, are located in the New Albany Public Library. Of the thirty-five known memoirs in these repositories, so far only four have been cited in published works about the Morgan raid.[34]

The question of reliability is inevitable when dealing with children's memories after almost three-quarters of a century of lapsed time. Not all of the ages of the interviewees can be determined, but those that can average 83, making the average age of the witnesses in 1863 around 11; this raises the dual concern about clarity of youthful perception and sharpness of memory in advanced age. Another point of concern is how much these recollections have been influenced over the years by retelling, romanticizing, and mixing commonly shared stories from neighbors. Some of these interviewees could well have read books and articles about the event; other might have been swayed by Lockridge's 1935 reenactment. Although the gender balance among the interviewees is good, the racial mix is not; only one of the thirty-five interviewees was black. All of these are valid reasons to treat the recollections with caution. On the other hand, the memories were elicited, not volunteered; the Lockridge team sought out these recollections to illuminate and preserve past events, not to reshape them. This was not a case of the elderly waiting in line to become revisionist Civil War scholars. Because these interviews had no prescribed questions, unlike the slave narratives, they emerge as more spontaneous and personal, revealing greater amounts of individuality. Also because of the number of memories and the availability of corroboration with other contemporary accounts, they are less problematic than they might appear at first glance. As individual memoirs they probably offer historians little, but in the aggregate they offer much.

What were these children doing when John Hunt Morgan galloped through their lives in 1863? Youth is usually a self-centered period of life, and memory tends to personalize events as to their relationship with the participant or beholder. Not surprisingly, many of these memoirs, even after seven decades, recall the personal connections that the person or family members experienced at the time. Greenville Johnson from Scott County recalled that he was plowing corn when the raiders passed by. They asked him to fill their canteens with water, and there were so many to fill that he drained the shallow well in the process. Melvin Marling, of Jefferson County, was sent to warn his aunt of the approaching invasion. He had to run a mile across fields, a trip he still remembered because he had recently suffered a bad cut on his knee and the pain forced him to limp the entire way. In Harrison County, 5-year-old Charles Dome inadvertently became a traitor to the Union. When Morgan's troops questioned him as to the whereabouts of the community's men, the guileless boy volunteered that his father and the local militia were hiding in a nearby woods. Maston Harris, the only black interviewee in the collection, remembered that his mother in Hanover was so frightened by the Confederate raiders that she took her small children and loaded them in a wagon with flour and bacon. They escaped to a nearby village where she thought they would be safe and did not return for two weeks. Eliza Lawrence remembered that her grandmother came to stay with them for safety near Madison. "While with us she would not, at night, sleep in a bed but on the floor. She said by placing her head on the floor she would hear better when the rebels came."[35]

Horses form a common theme throughout the memoirs from 1863. This is logical because Morgan's men were cavalry, and rural southern Indiana was heavily dependent on horses for agriculture and transportation. Word spread quickly that the raiders were confiscating horses and "trading" their tired Kentucky mounts for fresh Hoosier ones. One resourceful farmer hid his prized black mare in a cellar under the kitchen. When the Confederates entered their home and were eating in that kitchen, the family feared the mare would make enough noise to betray her location. She remained silent, however, and the farmer kept her for years after that. Charles Burdsall, from Jefferson County, recalled that his father was a blacksmith in Dupont, and when Morgan's men stopped there, his father was forced to shoe some of the Confederate horses without compensation. The following day he performed the same task for some Union troops, for which he was paid. Elizabeth Swan in Dearborn County recalled that she was in such a rush to warn neighbors of the arriving raiders, she did not have time to put a saddle and bridle on the family horse. Instead, she rode bareback to deliver her warning. Harry McGrain from Corydon not only recalled the raiders trading their tired horses for fresh ones across the road from his home, but he also remembered seeing the cavalry horses bedecked with ribbons and lace streamers that the raiders had pillaged from stores.[36]

The pillaging, theft, and destruction of property that accompanied the Morgan raid has been well documented by contemporary adult accounts. But this collection of childhood memories reveals details not earlier recounted. E. A. Gladden of Scott County recalled that several local men were chopping down trees to block the way of the Confederates. Their attempt was in vain, and the raiders briefly captured them. "Pete Ringo had a new axe and one of the Confederates forced him to hit it three times, with all his strength, on a nearby rock, which of course completely ruined the axe." Pirene Vallile recounted a similar story of destruction and waste concerning the family orchard. "We had some large cherry trees in the yard as the men rode past they cut off the limbs and ate the cherries as they rode along." James Bland told about the night when the raiders set fire to a railroad bridge near Dupont. "The bridge was a good big covered bridge, weather boarded up the sides and shingled on top. . . . The light from the fire was very plain, so that Morgan's men could see us in our yard."[37]

The contradictions and exaggerations that characterized the contemporary accounts of Morgan's raid echo in these memories, even after decades of clarification. Lockridge reported after his 1935 reenactment that several of the elderly participants got into heated disagreements over their divergent memories on certain details.[38] Newspaper accounts in 1863 heralded Morgan's approximately 2,500 men as ranging from 3,000 to 11,000, thus creating understandable panic. As late as 1938, Middleton Robertson from Deputy, Indiana, still insisted that the raiders numbered 4,000 to 5,000.[39] Equally inconsistent were the beliefs that prevailed after seventy-two years concerning the motives for the raid. Several of the interviewees clung to the rumor that Morgan hoped to assist General Robert E. Lee at Gettysburg, even though that battle was finished prior to Morgan's raid. Others still believed that Morgan had intended to invade Indianapolis and release Confederate prisoners being held in Camp Morton. The passage of time seems not to have altered misconceptions developed in childhood.

The FWP fieldworkers who conducted these interviews influenced the outcome of the memoirs, just as they did in the slave narratives. Iris Cook conducted four of the interviews, and her background and personality are visible in the results. Born in Kentucky and raised in New Albany, not far from Morgan's route, she was single and free-spirited. As a teenager she was a professional musician in a local theater, and later she volunteered for military service with the Women's Army Corps.[40] Her interviews reveal the same flair for drama, humor, and the unusual that characterized her own life. Her interview with William Haughey, who lived only a block away from her, is a well-crafted piece of comedy. He told the story of three youngsters who headed out the pike to see the raiders. En route, they had to climb a high rail fence. One of his friends, according to Haughey, "was so fat that he got stuck in the rails and there he was, too scared to do anything but yell." His comrades managed to rescue him, and they escaped without encountering the enemy.[41] Another memoir displayed Cook's ability to spin a yarn and focus on the absurd elements. E. A. Gladden related to her an incident in Vienna in which one of the Confederates forced a local lawyer, William Marshall, "to dance on a plank at the point of his gun," and when his dancing failed to satisfy the Confederate, the latter "proceeded to show Marshall how it should be done. So the lawyer got free dancing lessons."[42] Grace Monroe from Jefferson County contributed several interviews, and her personal background also comes to the surface in the transcribed memoirs. After a period of single motherhood, she was now married to a carpenter in the small town of Hanover. The Depression had virtually halted new home construction, so they struggled to raise their four teenage children.[43] In her interview with Maston Harris, she included the information that his mother in 1863 "was a widow and lived with her five little boys in Hanover," a description that was almost autobiographical for Monroe.[44] Likewise in the interview about the farmer hiding his horse in a cellar, Monroe fleshes out the story with structural descriptions of the cellar, details with which the wife of a carpenter would be conversant.[45]

Why should we trust this new body of memoirs, and what do these examples of oral history offer that was not previously known? First, they are sufficient in number to create a critical mass that in its composite account is credible. Second, the memories corroborate earlier accounts; they reinforce known facts rather than contradict them with aberrant material. Third, the gender and geographical balance of the memories tend to strengthen the reliability of the stories; both boys and girls recalled the same episodes, and the behavior of the raiders remains constant from the beginning in Harrison County to Dearborn County at the end. Fourth, and probably most important, the focus is that of childhood. They recall the things that would attract a young person and be committed to memory: personal involvement, family activity, and familiar associations such as horses and food, particularly biscuits. A common thread in these memoirs is that, despite the passage of seventy-two years, the memories maintain the original innocence and guilelessness of youth. They are not embellished with adult face-saving subterfuges or sophisticated analysis. Seldom do you find here an attempt to discuss larger military strategy or the broader economic and political impact of the war. These memories recapture a youthful world, in which children are seldom independent agents but instead adjuncts to adult directives; they assisted their parents, ran errands for their elders, and agreed with their authority figures. That is what they experienced and felt in 1863, and that is what they remembered in the 1930s. Their memories ring true despite all the problematic circumstances surrounding their collection and storage. They deepen the pool of documentation for this Civil War episode in Indiana, and Ross Lockridge and his fieldworkers deserve credit for establishing this link with the past.

A third notable collection of interviews came from James Clarence Godfroy, a fieldworker from Wabash County who compiled an extraordinary amount of material through the process of oral history. This came naturally for him, since his Native American heritage included the storytelling tradition of passing tribal customs down through the generations by oral transmission. Godfroy was part Miami, a descendant of War Chief Francis Godfroy and Frances Slocum, the kidnapped white child raised by Indians. He had farmed, worked in factories, and performed in vaudeville, but his major interest seemed to be collecting and telling stories about the Miamis and other Native Americans from Indiana.[46] Some of his assignments for the FWP required him to do formal research in newspapers, local histories, and government documents. He proved more than competent at this, but his most prolific output of manuscripts came from interviews with various individuals he encountered in his FWP assignments. He listened to their stories, took notes, then transcribed them when he returned home. Most of these interviews dealt with history, folklore, Indian customs, and religious practices. Few if any of the other FWP fieldworkers mastered the art of capturing the "oral" quality in interviews as well as Godfroy. He seemed to craft the information to entertain as well as to instruct the listener.

The files of the Indiana FWP contain twenty manuscripts that were the result of interviews conducted by Godfroy, most of which were in 1936. He closed each manuscript with a precise attribution as to the source of the story and sometimes when and where the interview took place—for instance, by the banks of a river or in a lunchroom. Some of the stories were from family members who passed the information on to him when he was young, but he remained honest in documenting the source, despite the time and distance from the original interview. The "stories" that these interviews produced then became a part of his vast repertoire of anecdotes and tales, which he continued to tell for the rest of his life. Shortly before his death in 1962, a friend recorded and transcribed many of his stories for a book, *Miami Indian Stories,* which has since gone through several printings.[47] Most of his FWP material appears in the book, largely intact, with only minor editorial revisions, but unfortunately without citing the original sources. Over the years, these bits of oral history had become his through repetition as he passed them on to the next generation. The stories provide a rich collection of Miami lore, much of which might have been lost without his acting as its transmitter from the past to the present. But a skillful transmitter is what he was, not a creator. To trace the stories back to their origins, or authors, as it were, it is necessary to consult the FWP manuscripts and leapfrog over Godfroy back to his interviewees in the 1930s.

Several of the interviews deal with some aspect of the Miami history, and they reveal the gap between what the Indians and the white Americans thought was important in the past. In the 1930s, most written history was political and military and dealt with national and international forces. White history was macrocosmic. But to the Miami, history was microcosmic, dealing with personal and immediate matters. Everyday people dealing with natural forces dominated these oral versions of past events. Eva Bossley passed one such story on to Godfroy dealing with a famine of the 1830s, caused in part by an extensive drought. Many of the Miami people had to subsist on berries and nuts that grew in the forest. More fortunate than most was a chief who lived near Peru and grew a field of corn near a "wonderful spring." He shared this corn, which they harvested, dried, and often turned into corn soup. This process of careful cultivating and sharing managed "to pull them through until the following season."[48] Another interview with Perry Moore Jr. from Huntington, Indiana, produced a lengthy narrative concerning an American flag given by General Anthony Wayne to a Miami chief following the Treaty of Greenville in 1795. It had survived a tortuous path through many hands and was lost. When finally returned to its owners, the flag continued to symbolize friendship between two nations and "good luck to the tribe."[49] The priorities related in the interview dealt not with a known hero and his military and diplomatic accomplishments but with the impact that a gift had made on several generations of ordinary people.

The largest number of Godfroy interviews involve old beliefs and superstitions related to Miami religious practices. He collected and transmitted these folklore traditions without any comment concerning their validity. He wove facts and fantasy seamlessly into the same narrative cloth. Stories featuring witches came from interviews with Robert Lavouncher, Lewis and Frank Aveline, and John Mongosa. All the interviewees were of Miami blood, and all revealed the pervasiveness of the supernatural in everyday life.[50] Other interviews with John Quince and Comilius Bondy discussed special powers possessed by the animal world and the role of dreams in human behavior.[51] One interview with Godfroy's mother, Louise, linked the consumption of food to both the spiritual and animal worlds. According to her, "the old time INDIANS were and still are very peculiar about their eating. Should an old time INDIAN drop any food while eating, he would not pick it up and eat it, because he believed a dead spirit wanted this food." Leftover food was also never burned or buried.

Instead, it was placed outside for birds and animals. Louise also related that Miamis would not eat in the dark because that would make the spirits angry and they might cause fits or a twisted face.[52] These and many other quotidian details from the interviews link the Miami people to nature, spirituality, and the past.

Small victories by Indians over their enemies permeate these interviews, exposing a subtext of resentment in the Miami community about its relationship with the larger white world. Sometimes interviewees presented these victories humorously, indicating that the Miamis delighted in the superior Indian skills that made the victory possible while also acknowledging the fleeting nature of the victory itself. William Anthony told this episode to Godfroy about a long past battle.

> The Indians soon reached the fort. Among these was a sharp-shooter. He was very accurate in his shooting and a splendid marksman. This Indian climbed a large hickory tree which stood near the fort, situating himself so he could look down into it. Many of the officers in the fort were being picked off, could not tell where this shooting came from. When almost all of the officers were killed the Indian was located in the hickory tree by one of those in the fort. A canon was turned toward the tree, a canon-ball was shot into it. Out came Mr. Indian in a hurry. He ran so fast that he was never heard of again.[53]

On other occasions the description of victory contained no humor. One lengthy interview with James Witt described an American soldier in an undefined location who encountered an Indian squaw washing her clothes in a creek. He shot her in the back, killing her instantly but needlessly. The squaw's tribe later captured the guilty soldier. "The INDIANS placed him out stretched upon the ground tieing his hands and feet to stakes. With sharpened knives they began skinning the prisoner alive. . . . The hideless body was placed upon the fire and the Pale-face's hide was given to the squawless INDIAN. The INDIAN took the hide and later made a pair of Breeches."[54] This grisly story is related dispassionately, with neither apology nor boasting, just a bit of oral history about winning a minor battle in a larger lost cause.

These three collections of oral history, with all their questionable characteristics, provide unparalleled insight to different parts of the Hoosier past. They also reveal much about the interviewers who created the linkage that delivered the memories into the present. Many of the interviews with former slaves provided information about the lives of the former slaves after emancipation and how they had coped with freedom in their new homes in Indiana. Most of the memories of those who had witnessed the Morgan raid during the Civil War added a fresh perspective from a child's point of view. And the Godfroy interviews transmitted much unwritten information about the Miami heritage, philosophy, and lingering resentment about previous injustices. All of these collections suffer from the fallibility of human memory, time lapse, imperfect transmission of material, and amateur interviewers. And they also tended to present a "selective, defensive, and nostalgic" version of the past, which historian John Bodnar maintains is to be expected when the "public memory" is consulted.[55] But in their collective wisdom they offer historians a fuller and more colorful picture of the past, corroborating and enhancing available sources. The FWP fieldworkers, despite their limitations, provided a valuable service in two capacities. They helped to reconstruct the past by invoking old memories and to preserve it by transcribing and passing it on to future generations.

SIX

Almost Finished Projects

Among the hidden treasures in the Indiana FWP records are several projects that neared completion but were never published. A series of city and county histories, a second collection of folktales, a pictorial history of the state, a history of the Creole culture in Vincennes, and a study of the limestone industry were all on the brink of being added to the Hoosier bookshelf when the Second World War brought the federal public works experiment to an end. These projects occupied the fieldworkers and editors over a number of years, excavated many aspects of the Hoosier past, and produced some manuscripts that were original and entertaining contributions. Because the Indiana guide remained the first priority, these secondary projects remained on the back burner until the guide was finally published in late 1941. By then, the WPA/FWP was already in decline. Congress had slashed its budget, the major administrators had departed, and their successors had neither the funds nor the staff to undertake new projects or complete old ones. Kept in storage since the end of the FWP in 1942, these manuscripts offer an intriguing glimpse into several chapters of Indiana's past. They made use of sources, many of which are no longer available, and they reflected attitudes of a generation coping with unprecedented economic and international crises. Even as untrained historians, these Hoosier fieldworkers and editors tried to preserve some bits and pieces of the past. The facts they dug up and the interpretations they imposed offer a valuable resource that enriches the field of Indiana history. They also reveal much about the attitudes and priorities present in the state in the 1930s.

A proposed series of local histories started as a limited project for a few cities early in the Federal Writers' Project tenure. There was logic to the proposal, since fieldworkers were already researching local history to plug into the state guide in two sections: the essays on major cities and the tours that crossed most of the counties. Ross Lockridge especially favored the idea of local histories. They would be shorter and easier to publish than the bulky state guide, they could accommodate more local legends and folklore than the more formal state volume, and they would be good publicity for the Writers' Project until such time as the elusive guide was finally published. Several city histories were in progress in 1936, and some of them were nearing completion. An almost finished manuscript on South Bend was approximately fifty pages long, the product of at least three local fieldworkers: Albert Strope, Edgar Blackford, and Ruth Henspeter. Editors from both Indianapolis and Washington had made corrections and revisions to the manuscript. It included the swift surveys of history, industry, education, transportation, etc., that later characterized the state guide. The Indiana FWP district supervisor in South Bend predicted that it would be very useful for tourists and the chamber of commerce and suggested to Lockridge that either the local congressman or the president of Notre Dame should write the foreword.[1] A manuscript on Fort Wayne history was similar in length to the one for South Bend, but it had not yet been revised to the same level of readiness. In addition to the usual topics, it included a section on the "current scene" in 1936. Lockridge had once lived and taught in Fort Wayne, and much of the writing in this early draft is reminiscent of his colorful, dramatic prose, suggesting that he was largely responsible for its creation.[2] Other manuscripts were in progress for Indianapolis, Terre Haute, Evansville, Corydon, La Porte, and Michigan City. Another regional guide similar to the one for the Calumet was planned for the Falls Cities area, including Jeffersonville.[3]

None of these local history manuscripts ever reached publication, for a variety of reasons. Lockridge's forced departure from the FWP in 1937 removed one of the major champions for short local histories, national director Henry Alsberg believed that they were inhibiting progress on the state guide, and there was a problem finding local sponsors to underwrite the cost of publication. The Ohio River flood of January 1937 literally swept away the regional guide for the Falls Cities. The Jeffersonville Board of Trade had earlier agreed to sponsor the book, but was unable to do so after the deluge.[4] For some of these cities, the failure to publish was not a major loss. Fourteen cities eventually received their own sizable essays in the state guide, and although these were not individual and freestanding histories, they were current and reasonably accessible. But for the other communities that had manuscripts nearly ready for distribution, the failure to reach publication was a genuine loss. Fieldworkers such as Ruth Hagerty and Alvin Vanderwalker in Michigan City and La Porte saw their research and writing become victims of changing priorities and financial constraints. The information they had acquired from local authorities through personal interviews would never gain an audience, and some of the sites they described as important in the 1930s would disappear as the landscapes changed with future development. Their work as amateur historians exists today only in manuscript form in the FWP records. In particular, the editorial comments that decorate the pages in these drafts raise enlightening questions about what was considered important about the past then and now.

A series of county histories, similar to the ill-fated city volumes, became an even more ambitious project in 1938. Indiana State Teachers College volunteered to sponsor the publication of brief histories of all ninety-two counties for instructional use in schools. Gordon Briggs, the new state director, assured Henry Alsberg that the work on this series would not impede work on the state guide. He also indicated that they were "designed primarily for the use of teachers" and needed to be more flexible in their format than would be the case if they were just miniature versions of the state guide.[5] These ninety-two histories would be a combined enterprise of the Indiana FWP and the departments of social studies and public relations at the Terre Haute college. They would entail research and writing by FWP fieldworkers, editing by both FWP staff and social studies faculty, and publication and distribution to schools by the public relations department at the college. This consortium designed the scope and format that guided the project until the FWP ended. They envisioned for each county a history that would begin with early regional history, including "prehistoric inhabitants" and early explorations. Subsequent chapters would cover the founding of the counties and natural setting. "The topography, geology, physiography, and climate will be treated . . . in terms understandable by elementary students." Next would come discussions of commerce, industry, agriculture, transportation, cities and towns, and schools and churches. The next three sections would allow considerable flexibility: points of interest, noted personalities, and racial groups. Local sites of distinction and significant movers and shakers would be determined for their importance to the county; as for the racial groups topic, "in many counties it will be omitted" due presumably to the scarcity of racial minorities in some areas. The final two sections would be a chronology and a bibliography, both similar to that planned for the state guide. These would present a swift sequential chronicle of highlights and recommended readings for further study.[6]

Those county histories that came closest to being ready for publication followed this general format with a few modifications. Approximately twelve counties adhered to the plan and produced manuscripts of roughly a hundred pages each. From little Switzerland to large Vanderburgh, the fieldworkers submitted data and drafts to editors in Indianapolis, who polished, supplemented, and updated the materials. One of the Indianapolis editors assigned to the county history project, Margaret Schricker Robbins, recalled later that by 1939 parts of the early drafts were outdated, and she spent much time consulting various libraries in Indianapolis and offices in the state capitol to acquire recent information.[7] As time elapsed in the production of these volumes, an additional chapter joined the others; county government was an elementary civics lesson in taxation, government services, voting procedures, and law enforcement. Several of these chapters paid homage to such New Deal programs as Social Security, WPA, and CCC, which had infused new revenues and programs into the county. Fayette County fieldworker Alfred Smith concluded that the new Social Security system spared the recipients the "humility [*sic*] and sorrow" of a trip to the poor house.[8] The prescribed format for the histories guaranteed a basic consistency in the manuscripts but did not squelch local individuality. Fieldworkers managed to insert idiosyncratic materials and unique prose that survived the editing process. For example, the Howard County manuscript discussed the unusual class divisions in the community. Apparently, "there was a tendency among some of the good respectable citizens to grow old and cranky. . . . Consequently resentment against the long noses of Kokomo has always been an important part of its life."[9] And Warren County allotted considerable space to the undefeated high school football team of 1915 from Pine Village. Two decades later, the team still received the honor of being called the "wonder eleven."[10] Madison County decided that one of its notable persons deserved an entire chapter, not just a mention. Therefore, chapter 7 became "Young Jim Riley" and discussed at length the journalist who achieved dubious fame in the county by perpetrating a literary hoax, a poem he attempted to attribute to Edgar Allan Poe.

Several other counties produced manuscripts that revealed much work and ambition, but they would require considerable editorial revision if they were to see publication. They ranged from the 11-page draft on Adams County, which contained brief, undeveloped paragraphs in passive voice, to the 600-page opus on Delaware County, which included lists of seemingly every business enterprise in the county and a description of every building on the campus of Ball State Teachers College. The brevity of the former and the bloat of the latter needed major work prior to completion. Point of view was also a problem for some of the manuscripts. The Franklin County draft adhered to the basic outline of the series and paid tribute to the many immigrants who helped populate the county. Much of this history emerged from personal interviews and contained traditional ethnic stereotypes. For instance, it categorized the early German settlers as "stolid, home-loving, and industrious" people.[11] Crawford County's manuscript was incomplete but showed great potential with its ability to tell pioneer history with gusto and humor. One incident in particular covered the "hog wars" with neighboring Orange County farmers. Pigs from that county had customarily foraged for food in Crawford forests. Farmers finally stopped this invasion by shooting the foragers.[12] These and many other examples of compiled inventories, sociological insights, and whimsical recollections were doomed never to reach an audience. Readers in the future would have to wait for more disciplined, polished, politically correct versions of the past.

Despite the effort that fieldworkers and editors put into the production of these county histories, and despite the often unpolished gems that emerged, FWP administrators were indecisive about their publication. Official correspondence and occasional press releases concerning their status were unclear and contradictory. In July 1938, Briggs reported to Alsberg that work was progressing on the "abridged" guides for ninety-two counties, and a story in the *Indianapolis Star* reviewed the prospectus drawn up by the FWP and Indiana State Teachers College. The story emphasized that the publications would be in loose-leaf format for ease in updating and that the histories would feature "forgotten heroes" from each county.[13] The following year, the Midwest FWP director, John Frederick, endorsed this series and encouraged the early publication of those counties which were ready. This, he believed, would "satisfy the sponsor that reasonable progress is being made." Briggs soon reported to Alsberg that three of the series could be ready by June 1939, and Alsberg requested that his staff review them prior to their release.[14] These three were presumably the manuscripts of Allen, Lake, and St. Joseph counties. Margaret Robbins recalled that those three histories were nearly complete in the early summer of 1939, and she anticipated their imminent publication.[15] But nothing happened. Shortly before the publication of the Indiana guide in 1941, a story in the *Indianapolis News* reported that ten of the ninety-two county histories were finished but not yet published. Then shortly after the state guide appeared, an interview with Briggs in a Muncie paper indicated that only six of the series had been completed, and no decision had been made whether to publish the books individually as they were ready or to release the entire series together.[16]

By January 1942, the Indiana WPA office filed a status report on the Writers' Program: "Fieldwork has been completed on approximately 60 of the 92 counties. Manuscripts on 30 counties have been written, and are in pre-final form ready for final editing."[17] But the same week in which this encouraging report appeared, the director of public relations at Indiana State Teachers College, the official sponsor and presumed publisher of the series, admitted that he hoped a private publisher could be secured for the task.[18] In February 1942, a memo from Washington headquarters indicated that national defense activities would now take priority and that the program was to "curtail" county histories and local guides.[19] Regardless of the exact number and status of the manuscripts, it no longer mattered. The WPA and Writers' Program were phasing out, and the manuscripts went into storage in Terre Haute and Washington. To consult the histories, readers would have to research through archival collections for these accounts of their county's past. Nearly forty years after the FWP and the County History project died, the Indiana Historical Society came to the rescue. Recognizing that these unpolished gems could be valuable resources to state historians, the IHS photocopied and bound sixteen of the manuscripts for use in its library. Once an ambitious project, now a fragment of the original plan, the County History series finally occupies library shelves for public use. Tentative and incomplete, with editorial comments pointing out their flaws, the volumes provide a fascinating link to the past not available from other sources.

Another unpublished gem was a sequel to the successful *Hoosier Tall Stories*. This collection of folktales and whoppers, published in 1937 and reprinted in 1939, had achieved popularity nationally and had publicized the strength of the folklore collection gathered by Indiana fieldworkers. Even before its publication, Lockridge and his folklore editor, Bessie Roberts, were compiling a second booklet. This one was more specialized than the former; its focus was superstitions and witchcraft in Indiana. It had a tentative title, "Pricking Thumbs," based on a quotation from *Macbeth* in which the second witch chants, "By the pricking of my thumbs, something wicked this way comes." Roberts and Lockridge had compiled numerous stories, all of which dealt in some capacity with supernatural phenomena and their impact on Hoosiers. National FWP folklore advisor John Lomax had reviewed the manuscript and liked it even better than *Hoosier Tall Stories*.[20] Roberts and Lockridge revised the manuscript according to suggestions from the national headquarters and hoped to find a sponsor for its publication, with school distribution clearly in mind.[21]

The complete revised manuscript for "Pricking Thumbs" is unavailable, but a draft in the Indiana FWP Papers gives a good overview of its purpose and contents. The premise was that in olden times and rural places, supernatural forces caused unusual occurrences. For instance, if a churn failed to turn out butter, or eggs did not hatch, or a child had fits, then they were all bewitched. "As to the witch, she was usually an old woman, who, for some reasons of her own, had made a bargain with the Devil, who in turn agreed to share his evil power with her."[22] Not all of the power was negative; witches often could foretell future events, cure diseases, and suggest ways for preventing trouble and ensuring success. In modern times Hoosiers might not actually believe in witches, but they still maintained some of the old superstitions that accompanied the craft. For example, a buckeye carried in your pocket, "as every old-time Hoosier knows," will bring good luck. And the editors of the compiled stores insisted, "Herbert Hoover carried a Warrick County, Indiana, buckeye in his pocket during his 1928 presidential campaign." FWP fieldworkers had gathered tales from this long tradition, and the booklet now presented a collection "that folks in Indiana have believed in and told."[23]

As was the case with *Hoosier Tall Stories*, not all of the episodes can be traced to precise locations or to the fieldworkers who collected them. But some of them can be, and the collection tells much about the widespread prevalence of the witchcraft tradition in Indiana, the importance of oral history in uncovering the past, and the changes that occur during the editing process. The common themes that link the stories are obvious, as is the neutral stance of the narrator. Fieldworker Wallace Brown interviewed a Shelby County resident who recalled a story about a witch who shot a gun at invisible objects while lifting her foot and screaming. She claimed that the spirits of departed enemies annoyed her and that the bullets she made from melted coins were the only kind of ammunition that would destroy them.[24] Flora Mae Harris likewise gathered a story by interviewing Ephrain Hale Bowen in Jay County. It involved a young girl who had been bewitched and "would vomit pins in strings like fish hooks." Bowen had heard this story from his grandfather, "who saw that for himself."[25] Editors changed these two oral accounts only slightly, with a few stylistic modifications. Fieldworker Velsie Tyler in Floyd County read an amusing story in the *Louisville Courier-Journal* about an old witchwoman who lived in the Knobs region and constructed hex dolls from rags and potatoes. These hex or magic dolls represented real people and, when pricked with a pin or needle, would cause harm or death to the designated individuals. In the original newspaper account that Tyler copied and forwarded to Indianapolis, the columnist used a literary device, the Old Timer, to tell the story in dialect. But the editors changed the story by shortening it, altering the dialect, and omitting any reference to its source.[26] Entertainment value had apparently become more important than accuracy and attribution.

Despite the positive reviews "Pricking Thumbs" received in Washington, and despite the logic for publishing it as a sequel to the popular *Hoosier Tall Stories,* the manuscript died. There are several reasons for its demise. Both Ross Lockridge and Indiana folklore editor Bessie Roberts left the FWP during the revision process, and they had done most of the work on the collection. National folklore advisor John Lomax also departed from the Washington office. So "Pricking Thumbs" had lost its primary champions just at the time when they were needed to shepherd the manuscript through its final stages. But the stories did not die with the manuscript. In 1982,

Professor Ronald L. Baker from Indiana State University retrieved some of the tales from the manuscript and several others from the folklore collection for his book *Hoosier Folk Legends*. His analysis of witchcraft placed the FWP stories in a more international context than the original booklet had attempted, and his inclusion of later stories gave them additional comparative value.[27] By languishing in limbo for several decades, "Pricking Thumbs" missed its intended audience of students in the 1930s, but inadvertently became more important to a later generation of scholars. What had been intended as publicity and entertainment during the Depression years appeared later as intriguing insights into the migratory intellectual history of the Midwest.

The American Pictorial History Guide series was an ambitious plan from the national headquarters to publish visual profiles of the states. In late 1940, with most of the state guides either published or nearly so, and with national defense activities becoming a higher priority than unemployment relief, federal officials determined that the Writers' Program could assist in building American morale. "A nation-wide series of picture books displaying through words and photographs the distinctive features and beauties of each of the States" could promote patriotism based on knowledge of the past and pride in local traditions.[28] Since all of the state editors had compiled large collections of illustrations for their guides, and had sorted them into "portfolios" such as natural settings, industry, education, and recreation, they already possessed the raw material and schematic framework to begin this new project. It was common knowledge that the fieldworkers had gathered information on local history, folklore, and tour sites that far exceeded the capacity of the guides to absorb. These surplus materials could be recycled into the pictorial series, and the states would get additional exposure for their heritage and accomplishments. The Writers' Program secured Fleming Publishers in New York to undertake the series, and the agreed format was to be hardbound books of approximately sixty pages with a visual emphasis. By the end of 1941, a handful of these volumes had appeared, including Montana, Vermont, and Virginia.[29] The rest, including Indiana's, did not get finished soon enough to avoid the 1942 curtailment of projects deemed unnecessary to the war effort.

Gordon Briggs selected one of his assistant state supervisors, Dickson J. Preston, to oversee the production of "Indiana: The Hoosier State in Pictures." Preston was a native of Monticello, a graduate of DePauw University, and a former reporter and copy editor for the *Indianapolis Times*. Not yet 30, he had nevertheless worn many hats in the Indianapolis headquarters, including editorial work for the guide and some of the ill-fated county histories.[30] His approach to this visual profile of his native state paralleled that of the guide on which he had been laboring for two years. Indiana emerged in photographs and captions as a rural and agricultural state with a population that was predominantly of white, northern European ancestry. Heavy industry and ethnic migrants occupied small pockets of the state, but they were exceptions to Hoosier traditions. Ralph Tirey, president of Indiana State Teachers College, wrote a brief foreword to the book and argued that the rustic Indiana of James Whitcomb Riley's poems was now a thing of the past,[31] but Preston's selection of illustrations and his running narrative contradicted Tirey's assessment of contemporary Indiana. His bucolic predilections seem to have sprung from the small towns in which he had spent most of his life.

Preston depicted a Rileyesque Indiana divided into three sections that ascended chronologically and geographically from past to present and south to north. They were the older and southernmost settlements of the Ohio River valley and hill country, the central section or "heart" of Indiana, and the counties in the northern tier that developed more recently. Describing the communities of the first section as "sleepy" and "old-fashioned," ranging from the "gracious homes" of Madison to the "rusticity" of Brown County, Preston presented photographs of rail fences, tobacco farms, New Harmony, cider mills, hog butchering, county fairs, and the Lanier mansion.[32] For a brief excursion into the exceptional, Preston showed scenes from coal mining and limestone quarrying operations to indicate that "Southern Indiana is not altogether dreamy, picturesque and backward."[33] Indianapolis, of course, dominated the central section, and despite its urban scope, its landscape had "an air of spaciousness and dignity," and its people were still "distinctly rural" and enjoyed the State Fair exhibits and horse racing.[34] Outside the capital city, Preston saw "abundant spring rainfall, rich, level land, and hot July nights" that produced corn, wheat, soybeans, tomatoes, hogs, cattle, and sheep, all of which were pictured.[35] The third section could not omit mention and illustration of steel mills, automobile plants, and oil refineries, in which toiled "husky workers recruited from Eastern Europe." But, again, Preston modified this exceptional scene with illustrations of sand dunes, lakes, and fields of celery, mint, gladiolus, and onions that flourished in the dark Kankakee "muckland."[36]

Two brief sections followed the three geographical portfolios and departed somewhat, but not entirely, from the nostalgic theme. "Building the Future" focused on education, and "Recreation" devoted space to leisure-time activity. Preston's commentary admitted that Indiana had been slow and late to provide educational opportunities to Hoosiers, but that situation had changed. Photographs of private colleges such as Notre Dame, Earlham, DePauw, and Wabash, and public universities Purdue and Indiana displayed attractive campuses in sylvan settings. Secondary education received only the merest mention, with illustrations of Arsenal Tech in Indianapolis, the state's largest high school, and a view of a vocational welding class in Gary.[37] The "Recreation" section reaffirmed the promise that this book was to be "representative rather than inclusive,"[38] and reestablished the overall theme of a rural state and people. Fishing, hunting, and sailing were what average Hoosiers preferred to do in their spare time, and high school basketball and college football were favorite spectator events. Most of the visuals for this section were appropriate, although generic, scenes of rural outdoor pursuits.[39]

Based on the two manuscript drafts available, "Indiana: The Hoosier State in Pictures" was not quite ready for publication. Both drafts are dated September 1941, the same time the finished copy was shipped off to Washington.[40] They include several editorial comments that refer to additional illustrations and written copy that would be forthcoming. They also indicate that some of the photographs are the same ones that appeared in the state guide, a duplication that revealed a lapse in originality.[41] It is highly probable that national editors would have modified the simplistic ethnic stereotypes included in the manuscript, judging from their work with the state guide series. And it is likely that the Washington staff would have asked the Indiana staff to reconcile contradictions between the urban emphasis of Tirey's foreword and the rural focus of Preston's narrative. Another troubling feature of the manuscript was the rushed and artificial insertion of Indiana's wartime activity in 1941. Photographs and captions depicted state factories producing airplane engines and armored tanks for "national defense," explosives being made from soybeans, and WPA Americanization classes for alien workers in East Chicago.[42] As true as these activities were in 1941, they were transient phenomena, and their inclusion appeared to be a gratuitous attempt to make the book timely and relevant. These and other editorial concerns could have been addressed with additional time, a commodity which the Writers' Program no longer possessed. Consequently, the visual profile of Indiana remained forever a draft manuscript. Today it offers a rather limited and problematic view of the Hoosier past. It also offers an instructive view of a state in the midst of several transitions. Indiana in 1941 was caught between its rural past and its urban future, between peace and war, and between its memories and reality. The unfinished manuscript was an awkward, if ambitious, self-portrait, and the picture it produced was unfocused at best.

One area of research that the Indiana FWP pursued tenaciously was a study of the Creole culture of early Vincennes. Both state directors and several fieldworkers and editors expressed deep interest in French impact on the lower Wabash valley, and they produced several manuscripts dealing with this pocket of linguistic and ethnic heritage. Eighteenth-century French explorers had moved into the American Midwest from Louisiana and Canada and established profitable trading relations with the Native Americans. These French settlers introduced their language and Roman Catholicism to the area, and some of them married into tribal families. Vincennes was the center of this Creole culture in Indiana, and it possessed a character unlike any other community in the territory. The language, religion, architecture, music, food, and customs of the town set it apart from the rest of the territory. The era of the American Revolution brought swift political changes as the British took control of the area from the French, then shortly lost it to the Americans. But the Creoles of Vincennes, despite their shifting national citizenships, maintained aspects of their culture for several generations. Linguists, musicologists, and folklorists all had shown interest in the lingering traces of this special heritage. One folklorist, Joseph M. Carriere, visited there in 1934 and later wrote, "Although isolated from other people of their stock . . . the early inhabitants of Vincennes and their descendants kept the flame of French traditions burning bright even long after they had become entirely submerged among their neighbors of Anglo-Saxon and German extraction."[43] The Indiana FWP was determined to capture, preserve, and publicize this phenomenon before it disappeared completely. This was similar in concept to collecting life stories from former slaves or tall tales from rural storytellers, but geographically it covered only one small community in southwestern Indiana.

The FWP's first manuscript dealing with the Creole culture was a brief work compiled by Indiana's folklore editor, Bessie K. Roberts. Neither Roberts nor Lockridge could claim expertise in linguistics, music, or folklore, but both were writers, and both aimed their work at a broad audience. She was a journalist who specialized in human interest features, and he was a popularizer of history. They collaborated on the two booklets of stories from the large folklore collection, *Hoosier Tall Stories* and "Pricking Thumbs." In late 1936, just prior to her departure from the FWP, Mrs. Roberts had put together a seventy-one-page pamphlet on French folklore from old Vincennes. It was a collection of music, stories, and recipes that she had tentatively titled "The Trail of Song."[44] Before shipping the manuscript on to national headquarters, Lockridge sent it to Dr. Gino Ratti, chairman of the department of romance languages at Butler University and asked for his "suggestions and criticisms."[45] Ratti proved to be a model of the kind yet firm professor who returns a paper to a promising but underachieving student. He found the premise of the manuscript "well worthwhile," but its execution "careless and unscholarly." He recommended that in order for it to be publishable, the FWP should slow down, be more careful, and consult some experts on French music and folklore.[46] Lockridge, who was nothing if not resilient, followed the professor's advice about moving ahead with the original premise. He nevertheless forwarded "The Trail of Song" to Washington, where it languished, unedited and unpublished.

By 1940, with more time, scholarly advice, and editing, the Indiana FWP produced a larger and more ambitious manuscript called "The Creole (French) Pioneers at Old Post Vincennes."[47] At 277 pages divided into eight chapters, it attempted to be at least three things: a history of the Creoles at Vincennes until the dilution of their culture in the late nineteenth century, a collection of French songs with English translations, and a collection of folklore stories and legends. Its organization followed the advice of Dr. Morton Royse, a consultant on social-ethnic studies for the national FWP.[48] Most of the historical narrative came from published books and articles in local newspapers, and two elderly women compiled many of the songs. They were Josephine Theriac Caney, a descendant of a Creole family, and Anna O' Flynn, a retired teacher in the old French section of Vincennes.[49] Four fieldworkers, Loy Followell, Elizabeth Kargacos, Bernice Mutchmore, and Paul R. King, and their FWP district supervisor, Doyle Joyce, claimed authorship of the initial draft.[50] There were no professional scholars in this group, but they had, in fact, researched, interviewed, consulted experts, and written with more care and less haste than had been the case with "The Trail of Song."

This ambitious draft of 277 pages went through several revisions on its journey toward publication. Gordon Briggs received much mixed advice from various consultants. George Cronyn from the Washington headquarters believed that the dialect was confusing and needed major revision; Indiana University folklorist Stith Thompson disagreed and argued that the material should be kept in its current condition.[51] Benjamin A. Botkin, the FWP consultant on folklore, suggested that the historical material, favored by Royse, overpowered the folklore collection and should be condensed into a long introduction instead of appearing as separate chapters at the beginning and end.[52] Briggs and staff revised and condensed the historical materials and brought them into the twentieth century,[53] and Botkin felt this was an improvement. But his suggestions for further work were daunting, to say the least. He advised Briggs that some of the folk songs had been copied incorrectly and without attribution from other published collections. This "problem" needed to be addressed. Botkin also felt that the folktales were "wooden and stilted" and the overall presentation "disjointed and scrappy."[54] Briggs returned the much-revised manuscript to the Vincennes field-workers along with Botkin's critique. He attached a rather dispirited memo which indicated that although he thought the materials were "valuable and should be preserved," he would let them decide whether to attempt to bring the work "into acceptable form."[55] They apparently decided to abandon the project rather than undertake yet another major revision. Briggs was preoccupied with finishing the Indiana guide and could no longer devote time and effort to the Creoles. The abandoned draft manuscripts, now stored in several archives, show the series of changes that occurred as fieldworkers and editors responded to various criticisms over several years.[56]

Both Briggs and Botkin were correct about this ambitious project; yes, it was a valuable subject, and no, it was not ready for publication at that time. But its most valuable and original parts did not die with the mangled manuscript. They found an audience later, absorbed into other publications that presented their material in more successful formats. The historical narrative was the least valuable part of the manuscript. FWP fieldworkers had synthesized it from secondary sources, and it was neither original nor distinctive, so its loss was of little importance. Most of the folksongs appeared in 1946 in Cecelia Ray Berry's book *Folk Songs of Old Vincennes*. In her foreword, Berry credited the same two women, Anna O' Flynn and Josephine Theriac Caney, who had assisted the FWP fieldworkers with their manuscript; hence much of the same personal information carried over into this later publication. Ronald Baker rescued the bulk of the folklore and legends from the Creole manuscript and revised

145

them for his booklet *French Folklife in Old Vincennes* in 1989. Of particular interest were the Loup-Garou stories dealing with mythical bewitched animals that apparently permeated the oral literary tradition of early Indiana.[57] Although the Indiana FWP had failed in its attempt to publish this unique chapter from the Hoosier past, its excavation and preservation efforts ultimately assisted later scholars who completed the project.

Another Indiana project in the FWP's social-ethnic studies category was a study of the limestone industry. National consultant Morton Royse championed this work as part of a series on communities that centered around particular industries, such as iron in Mineville, New York, and rubber in Akron, Ohio.[58] The Indiana manuscript that emerged from this series started as a survey of Lawrence and Monroe counties, the site of many limestone quarries. As it progressed through several revisions over many months, the focus narrowed to an analysis of Bedford, the heart of the industry, and the title became "Limestone Town." By late 1939, with the manuscript in its final stages, the project collapsed along with the entire social ethnic series of industrial studies. Congress reconfigured the FWP that year, and Henry Alsberg and Morton Royse both left for other assignments. The Indiana editor most deeply involved in the "Limestone Town" revisions undertook another endeavor, and the book, now with its major advocates gone, quietly expired. Bedford suffered the same fate as Vincennes; outside forces conspired to keep its story untold. But unlike the Creoles, who were later rescued from literary oblivion, the stonecutters remained buried in archival storage boxes. Although never published, the research that went into the draft remains an impressive collection of historical data, industrial statistics, and personal interviews not available elsewhere.

Fieldworker Emery C. Turner was the primary excavator of historical data for this study, and he was well suited for the task. A native of Lawrence County and a professional journalist before the Depression, Turner returned to Bedford and briefly edited a trade magazine, *Bursts and Duds,* for the area limestone industry.[59] His personal knowledge of the local economy and his years of experience as a reporter combined to give him the relevant skills for collecting material and writing about limestone lore. He pored through decades of the Bedford newspaper for stories about the industry and compiled more than seventy typed pages of old articles.[60] With assistance from FWP fieldworkers Oman Nelson from Lawrence County and Estelle Dodson from neighboring Monroe County, Turner wrote a 123-page manuscript titled "The Limestone Industry of Lawrence and Monroe Counties." The foreword and introduction reveal the wide variety of documents and industry personnel that provided information for the study, and five chapters of text surveyed the geographic, economic, and technical aspects of extracting oolitic stone from the earth and turning it into a marketable product. Chapter 6, which consumes more than half of the manuscript, is an alphabetical listing of locations where contractors used Indiana limestone to construct the architectural landscape. Banks, libraries, and post offices were ubiquitous, but specific structures such as the Gothic National Cathedral in Washington, the Art Deco Rockefeller Center in New York, and the Neoclassic capitol in Indianapolis documented the versatility of Indiana's geological treasure. Turner weighted the content of his draft far more heavily toward historical development of the industry than Alsberg and Royse had envisioned for their social-ethnic series. There is little in the manuscript about workers, labor conditions, and the social impact of the industry on the community.[61]

Selected to transform this draft into a publishable book was Charles Bruce Millholland, whom Henry Alsberg considered "one of Indiana's best workers."[62] Millholland was a professional writer with a record for producing large quantities of prose in short periods. As a writer for the stage and screen, he could also marshal words into a more flamboyant form than Turner's workmanlike prose. He had written and produced a comic play while in high school in Indianapolis, and studied art and dance in Chicago. His major claim to literary distinction was the script for *Twentieth Century,* which became a Broadway hit and then a popular film. Shortly before joining the Indiana FWP, he had been in Hollywood adapting his brother's novel into a screenplay.[63] Morton Royse and Gordon Briggs had reviewed the initial limestone manuscript and agreed that it needed "overhauling" and "some additions." In particular, they wanted more on working conditions, the impact of the Depression, and "considerable personal history stuff."[64] To accomplish this task, Briggs sent Millholland to Bedford, under the tutelage of Emery Turner, to absorb local color, interview stonecutters and townspeople, and turn "Limestone Town" into a more dramatic manuscript.

From April to July 1939, the manuscript took on new dimensions that changed its style, purpose, and impact. Millholland spent several days in Bedford, interviewing more than a dozen people, some affiliated with the limestone industry and some not.[65] He then returned to Indianapolis and absorbed contemporary data concerning unemployment, federal public works projects, labor union activity, and social conditions. One of his other FWP assignments had been to edit county history manuscripts, including Lawrence County, so Millholland was familiar with the terrain. Using Turner's draft manuscript as a base, he expanded the straightforward historical tract into a social-ethnic study that followed most of Morton Royse's directives. From a brief objective study of an industry, the manuscript became an exposé of a community in turmoil. Millholland condemned working conditions as "unhealthy" and "dangerous," applauded the rise of labor unions, and praised New Deal programs such as WPA and NYA for alleviating some problems that local officials were "incapable" of handling.[66] He quoted frequently and at length from his interviews, using local voices to buttress his arguments. The result was, in fact, a dramatic exploration of an insular community hurt by the Depression and indecisive about its future. Briggs forwarded a copy of "Limestone Town" to John Frederick, the regional FWP director in Chicago, who made no attempt to disguise his displeasure. Technically, he found the manuscript poorly organized, with confused time references and awkward use of interview materials. But he found the premise of the author even more distressing. Frederick said that Millholland showed no objectiveness or finesse, displayed a "flagrantly" pro-labor bias, and indulged in "special pleading for government agencies."[67] In light of this less than encouraging critique, Briggs did not move forward with the book. Millholland's heart was not with the FWP anyway; a new play of his about Eugene V. Debs had run briefly in New York and needed his time for revisions.[68] The reorganized Writers' Program had left the Indianapolis office short-staffed, and the new state sponsor, Indiana State Teachers College, showed little interest in pursuing "Limestone Town" any further.

Beyond the backstage drama surrounding its demise, the manuscript of "Limestone Town" contains much material of great value to historians. Discounting Millholland's overheated prose and opinions, the study contains information about the industry and community in the 1930s that does not exist elsewhere. Although the chapters of the manuscript are scattered throughout the Lawrence County file of the FWP collection, they can be pieced together without much difficulty. Technical descriptions of quarrying and milling operations are written in layman's terms and are both informative and accessible. The material about working conditions in the late nineteenth century and early twentieth century reflects much about changing attitudes on safety and government regulations. Of particular interest are the interviews that Millholland conducted in 1939. They reveal fissures in the community regarding labor unions, government welfare, ethnic relations, and religion. Had "Limestone Town" been published, it probably would have created some controversy in Bedford. Muncie had endured the same kind of exposure with the publication of the *Middletown* books in the 1920s and 1930s, and the parallels with Bedford are apparent, although on a smaller scale. This manuscript was the product of a journalist and a playwright, not professional historians, and its facts and interpretations lacked scholarly balance and analysis. But it contains much raw material from the 1930s that could still prove useful to students of immigration, ethnology, and labor studies.

These five unpublished projects reveal an intriguing tension between the editorial staffs of the federal and state FWP. Whether the topics emanated from Washington, such as the pictorial history and the limestone ethnic study, or from Indianapolis, as with the Creoles, witch tales, and county histories, their failure to reach publication was the result of disagreements between the two. Each of the endeavors started with a valid premise, used valuable sources, and presented a fresh look at the materials. But each also possessed flaws that the national editors would not tolerate. Sometimes the presentations were not scholarly enough, sometimes they contained internal contradictions, and sometimes they were too personal and indulgent. Conflicting expectations of national and state editors invariably produced the same results; New Deal priorities vetoed Hoosier peculiarities. This was the new balance of power in both politics and publications.

SEVEN

Incomplete Projects

Scattered throughout several archives are the promising beginnings of numerous projects that the Indiana FWP never completed. Federal and state initiatives sent fieldworkers on various research missions that unearthed rich caches of raw material, but they failed to take shape as coherent manuscripts. Some of these were national undertakings that allotted Indiana a small portion; others were Hoosier enterprises to commemorate local sites, events, and individuals. Most of the projects were anchored in the distinctive New Deal emphasis on social history as opposed to political and military history. The 1930s saw a new wave of interest in the accomplishments of racial minorities, labor unions, migrant farmers, ethnic neighborhoods, and family heritage. Roosevelt's administration aided this new wave with documentary photographs and films from the Farm Security Administration. And editors within the FWP gave special attention to these areas of life by hiring consultants in sociology and folklore who championed the previously "forgotten man" of earlier historical writing. In Indiana, fieldworkers gathered but did not mold into finished form much information about the state's most famous poet, its worst flood, its favorite foods, and several other indigenous features of Hoosierdom. They compiled eyewitness accounts, oral interviews, and contemporary reflections that were as transient as they were valuable. This research into unique corners of the state's past produced a vast amount of largely undigested material that is still valid documentation, adds extra dimensions to the self-portrait of Indiana, and cannot be replicated elsewhere.

Ross Lockridge conceived and championed one of these unfinished projects, and it reflected his experience as an impresario and historian. He proposed a multifaceted enterprise to honor James Whitcomb Riley, the renowned poet of Indiana's rural past. In a prospectus for this project in 1936, Lockridge argued that Riley exemplified "our most distinctive expression of Hoosierism. . . . He used Hoosier language and voiced Hoosier sentiments more clearly than anyone else has ever done." Furthermore, Riley utilized the entire state as a stage for his talent. "He walked and talked and dreamed and wrote everywhere in Indiana. His poetic peregrinations traced every road and trail and stream in Hoosierdom." Lockridge envisioned a book that would document the many towns where Riley gave readings or performances and would then reprint the poems that resulted from his visits to specific sites around the state. The placement of markers at each of these locations where Riley had stood, written, and recited would supplement the monograph. This "universal-geographical" tribute would commemorate "the fact that his wandering feet pressed the soil of every part of Indiana, that the melodious tones of his voice vibrated in every county."[1] And to dramatize the book and markers, Lockridge and his FWP staff would organize pilgrimages to the sites and conduct programs complete with readings of his works and reminiscences by those who had known or heard him. The prospectus captured Lockridge, if not Riley, at his exuberant best. It involved researching, writing, erecting signs, and reenacting the past.

Pilgrimages were standard procedure for Lockridge, and in the autumn of 1936 they generated the same enthusiastic response that he had encountered in 1935 with his reenactment of the Morgan Civil War raid. Mooresville and Monrovia both hosted programs in which schools and local citizens participated. Then the erection of markers there, "signalizing Riley's early days in those places," began the process of pinpointing the poet's geographical omniscience. In Carroll County, the pilgrimage was more elaborate, due to Riley's many visits there, and the results were also more promising. Riley had written such poems as "From Delphi to Camden" and "On the Banks o' Deer Crick" about local sites. At the programs, students recited his poems and older residents reminisced about their relationship with him. One woman, Mrs. Elizabeth Fisher Murphy, shared information that whetted Lockridge's appetite for more details. She intimated that she and Riley had been youthful sweethearts and that he had written the poem "Curly Locks" about her.[2] At the time of their association in 1885 she had been Elizabeth Fisher, but she had since been married and widowed. In subsequent exchanges of letters with Lockridge and in an oral interview and a written memoir, she shared other recollections. She recalled that Riley was bow-legged, took notes in "a little black book," and vowed never to marry because that would spoil his poetic career. They discussed the water bugs at Deer Creek, which he spelled "worter bugs" in his poem, and he sent her a copy of "Curly Locks" shortly after he wrote it.[3] Lockridge thanked her effusively for her recollections and told her that many people had claimed to be the source for certain poems, but that she had given the "best and strongest showing that has been made by anyone on this important subject of Riley's poetical inspirations."[4]

From all over Indiana, other reminiscences by former Riley associates added to the collection of intimate and literary lore. Lockridge interviewed Marcus Dickey, Riley's former secretary, agent, and biographer. The result was eighteen pages of typed questions and answers that discussed Riley's travels, friends, and erratic spelling.[5] Another was a briefer interview with Ida Belle Sweenie, vocal instructor at the Jordan Conservatory of Music in Indianapolis. In 1887 she had accompanied Riley on a six-week tour. Her vocal solos preceded his recitals in opera houses and schools from Richmond to Vincennes. She told fieldworker Mildred Adams that at one stop in Evansville they had to improvise dressing rooms by stretching cords across a room and draping shawls for privacy. Sweenie recalled that Riley said it was like "dressing behind the clothesline with the wash up."[6] Martha Freeman interviewed an elderly woman in Winchester who remembered that Riley was contracted for a recital to raise funds for the library. On the evening of his performance, a heavy rain cut attendance drastically, and the library lost money on the affair.[7] Carl Wills interviewed five Riley associates and elicited a revealing morality story from one of them. Riley once returned to Greenfield to attend the funeral of a boyhood friend who had become a town ne'er-do-well. Despite warnings from Indianapolis advisors that this association with a local reprobate could hurt his reputation, Riley arrived at the funeral in a car filled with roses.[8]

To enhance these oral recollections from friends and associates, Lockridge solicited tributes from other Hoosier writers to add literary substance to the monograph. Several famous Indiana authors responded to the request, and their contributions were uniformly laudatory about the poet. John T. McCutcheon, a cartoonist and writer for the *Chicago Tribune,* had first met Riley on a train during one of the poet's lecture tours. He argued that "those journeyings about the state, on little jerk-water railroads, speaking in towns and villages close to humanity," gave Riley an inside knowledge of the state and helped turn the term *Hoosier* into a compliment.[9] Kate Milner Rabb, historian and columnist for the *Indianapolis Star,* appreciated Riley for his service as a social historian of a bygone era. In his poems, "we have preserved for us the dialect of the day, the folklore, the songs they sang in those days, the kind of jokes they made."[10] Meredith Nicholson, novelist, essayist, and diplomat, concurred with the assessment of Riley as a social historian and made the case that "his writings will become a valuable and trustworthy source to students" of Hoosier life. He added that Riley's patriotic verse was first-rate, and he did not know of another poem in America that better captured the emotions of the Civil War than "Good-by, Jim" ("The Old Man and Jim").[11] Booth Tarkington, the dean of Hoosier writers at the time and twice winner of the Pulitzer Prize, regretted that Riley had not lived long enough for motion pictures with sound to capture his genius. Tarkington said that Riley's artistry with words combined with stage presence and vocal skill to create genuine magic that "held spectators rapt and magnetized."[12] Such tributes from contemporary writers to one of their craft were both predictable and probably inflated, but they gave Lockridge professional validation to justify his efforts on this memorial monograph.

Fieldworkers around the state scoured local newspapers for accounts of Riley's appearances and drew connections between local sites and his poetry. Merton Knowles found a notice in the *Warren* (County) *Republican* about a Riley recital in the Nebeker Opera House in 1886; Cecil Miller sent in a clipping from the *Logansport Pharos* about Riley's appearance in 1903; Elizabeth Waiter found a notice in the *Peru Republican* about a Riley program in 1881.[13] This detective work in old newspapers produced a list nine pages long of sites and appearances, many of which had supposedly inspired poems. For example, following a visit to Fortville, Riley wrote "Squire Hawkins Story"; Union City was the setting for "The Adjustable Lunatic"; and Warsaw compelled him to write "The Argonaut," although "it was lost and has never been found."[14] No fieldworkers labored harder to make these links between location and poetry than six fieldworkers from the Calumet region. They submitted almost fifty pages of evidence, including press clippings, letters, and interviews, to make the case for northwest Indiana as a major catalyst for Riley's verse. It was relatively easy to document his recitals at Rensselaer and his hunting trips in the Kankakee marsh by citing several corroborating witnesses. Their efforts to prove that these visits had produced the poems "Little Cousin Jasper" and "The Little Town o' Tailholt" were equally resourceful, although less persuasive.[15]

This enthusiastic effort to compile information for the Riley Monograph lasted roughly a year—from mid-1936 to mid-1937—and it produced 800 pages of raw material. But it did not produce a publishable book for a number of reasons. Many of the interviews were repetitive. Most of the tributes were just that; they failed to go beyond praise and provide analysis. The collection of press clippings documented sites and dates of Riley's appearances, but the result was merely a list. Attempts to locate the source of inspiration for specific poems were mainly speculative and unprovable. Among this mass of research were several nuggets of fresh, original material, some of which have never appeared in biographies of Riley, but the bulk of the collection is, unfortunately, redundant. Lockridge probably sensed this as the collection grew, and consequently directed his efforts to the easier tasks of pilgrimages and markers rather than trying to shape the disparate mass into a coherent manuscript. In early January 1937, he postponed work on the monograph. He hoped to gain access in a few weeks to a new cache of documents. Later he indicated that he was waiting for Riley's biographer, Marcus Dickey, to return from Florida before continuing work on the project.[16] By the spring of 1937, Lockridge had, in a manner of speaking, been placed on probation by FWP officials in Washington for his failure to make sufficient progress on the Indiana guide, and in July he resigned under pressure. Any chance for completion of the Riley Monograph departed with him. Neither federal administrators nor the new state director displayed any interest in the project, and in 1940, some of the most interesting and potentially valuable materials were returned to their source, the alleged Curly Locks, Elizabeth Fisher Murphy of Delphi.[17]

A natural disaster of unprecedented magnitude prompted Lockridge to propose another monograph. The Ohio River flood in January and February 1937 broke all records for depth and devastation. Days of constant heavy rains pushed the river over its banks from Pittsburgh to the Mississippi River, causing panic and distress along its route. At some points in southern Indiana, the swollen river stretched twenty miles across, and it stood almost twenty-five feet deep in downtown Jeffersonville.[18] Thousands of Hoosier refugees fled from its path, and the area sustained millions of dollars in damages. This disaster, according to Lockridge, offered an opportunity for the FWP to become an eyewitness to history in the making. Unlike the Riley project, which was to unearth and preserve the past, this monograph would capture the present with firsthand accounts from fieldworkers in hip boots and rowboats. Despite the fact that transportation and communications were disrupted in the thirteen counties fronting the Ohio River, and that some of his fieldworkers were "marooned" and out of contact, Lockridge devised a plan for documenting the situation at the heart of the flood.[19] Individual

156

fieldworkers were to visit flooded sites, keep detailed records, conduct interviews, collect newspaper accounts, and compile the data into flood scrapbooks.[20] In the monthly narrative report of WPA activities for February 1937, while the flood was still raging, Lockridge discussed his plans for the monograph, the research for which was already under way.[21]

Only nine fieldworkers covered the thirteen flooded counties because some of the smaller, rural counties did not have any FWP personnel at the time. Grace Monroe, for example, covered her home area of Jefferson County, and she also trekked upstream to cover Ohio and Switzerland counties. Samuel Dixon, likewise, surveyed his home turf of Posey County and his eastern neighbors of Warrick and Vanderburgh. Iris Cook from Floyd County traveled more than any of the Indiana fieldworkers, perhaps because of her known resourcefulness and writing ability. Her territory stretched from distant Dearborn County in the east to neighboring Harrison County in the west. The conditions in which these fieldworkers worked were uncomfortable and precarious. A flooded road near Hanover forced Grace Monroe to abandon her car and "climb a very dangerous rocky trail to get back to civilization."[22] Samuel Dixon's harried supervisor stopped by Dixon's desk in the makeshift WPA headquarters in Evansville and admitted that he had just taken "his first bath in ten days."[23] Iris Cook told of slogging down New Albany's Main Street in high boots, hiking up Silver Hills with a pair of binoculars while the city lay before her "like a wounded animal," and watching an electrical substation short out with a flash that "could have been seen for miles."[24]

The subject under study was memorable to start with, and fieldworkers usually matched the material with their prose. As eyewitnesses to the disaster they brought an immediacy to the job, and as residents of the area they were frequently able to provide context that an outside observer might have missed. Iris Cook's interests as a writer were apparent in her reports. When she described the damage to her hometown New Albany public library, there was the sort of pain that only a lover of literature would feel. Her description of soggy books being hauled out in wheelbarrows and dumped into the

gutter was both sad and vivid.[25] Likewise, her account from Lawrenceburg was equally well crafted. Floodwaters had inundated the
Seagram's distillery there, "and when the waters receded they left a
battered line of empty whiskey barrels, strung all around the ruined
area like a necklace."[26] One of Samuel Dixon's normal assignments
as a fieldworker was to collect and transcribe folksongs, and the
flood allowed him to combine this pursuit with the disaster. The
Cypress Beach Dance Hall outside of Newburgh housed five hundred evacuees, and Dixon described the sense of dislocation,
crowded conditions, and winter weather. He also included an account of the refugees' evening amusements; they sang and danced
"to the music of a two string banjo and a blue noted harmonica."[27]
Accounts of lost pets and livestock sometimes overpowered these
human interest stories. Grace Monroe told of six rabbits rescued
from the flood in Rising Sun, one of which had a mouse hitchhiking
on its back.[28] Beulah Van Meter reported that rescue crews at Jeffersonville refused to allow dogs in their small boats. Some of the
pets drowned in sight of their owners, and others were shot.[29] From
Spencer County Nellie Kellams relayed a tale of resourceful team-
work. A Coast Guard boat rescued several chickens that were float-
ing down the river on a piece of driftwood. The crew transported
the fowls to Rockport, where a Red Cross unit served soup and coffee
around the clock. The Red Cross lost little time in turning the feath-
ered refugees into a hot meal for weary workers.[30] Lauana Creel was
the most productive writer among the fieldworkers; her reports exceeded 100 pages, and as the Ohio River rose, her prose escalated
dramatically to match the flood waters. She spoke of the "desolation
and ruin" in Crawford County, of how the river had Tell City in its
"paralyzing grip," and of "the staggering mass of relentless water"
that covered much of Evansville.[31] Her account of Leavenworth's
plight made no pretense of objectivity. The little town in Crawford
County suffered so much damage that officials immediately condemned it and announced plans for relocating it to higher ground.
Creel protested this move, calling it a "sacrilege" to abandon the
beautiful site and rich heritage.[32]

Regardless of the drama and color that these anecdotes contained, the bulk of the fieldworkers' manuscripts were repetitive accounts of standard material already covered in the local newspapers and official reports. And therein was the major reason that the 333 pages of FWP prose from the Indiana flood zone never materialized as a finished monograph. Area newspapers relocated their printing equipment and personnel in order to give massive coverage to the flood and its aftermath. Much of this contained interviews and photographs that were more graphic than the FWP reports. The Red Cross kept its own record of emergency work and list of donors; this made the FWP coverage of the same material redundant. Coast Guard and National Guard units compiled their own official reports, as did the CCC, which did rescue and rehabilitation work. The WPA in Indiana published a 32-page supplement to its monthly report that described its flood work in great detail. It itemized sandbagging crews, sewing units, cistern cleaning, privy installation, worker headcounts, and costs of materials.[33] Lockridge's plan for an eyewitness monograph to document this episode was a valid one at the beginning. He had the personnel on site, and they were willing to take extraordinary risks to gather appropriate materials while they were still fresh. But the natural disaster produced a surplus of written accounts of equal or superior quality from several private and government bodies. The Indiana FWP monograph simply became unnecessary in the midst of these publications, and the project never advanced beyond the status of individual research and compiled scrapbooks. Only a few bits and pieces were salvaged for inclusion in the Indiana guide, where this flood had, by 1941, receded to a few paragraphs of recent history.

Unlike the Ohio River, the Kankakee River did not flood. Instead, it meandered through thousands of acres of marshland in northwest Indiana. This swampy terrain was originally a home to fish, wild game, and migratory birds, all of which lured sportsmen to a hunters' paradise. By the late nineteenth century, farmers and developers had begun the slow process of dredging the river, straightening its course, and draining the swamps. The shallow Kankakee, which once twisted and turned for roughly 150 miles, had become, by the 1930s, a straight 40-mile channel rushing toward Illinois. Almost 600,000 acres of former marshland now raised corn and wheat, mint and onions, poultry and livestock. Lockridge believed that this transformation was the subject for a book. In 1936 he planned a monograph to chronicle the Kankakee from its geological beginnings, through its Indian trappers, French traders, and American hunters, to its current Hoosier farmers. It would be a dramatic trek from wilderness to agribusiness along the dual paths of capitalism and technology. This Kankakee monograph would not be a straight chronological story of man overcoming nature and pioneers evolving into entrepreneurs. To the contrary, Lockridge saw the book as a cautionary tale that documented the loss of innocence, the rape of nature, and the triumph of greedy "landsharks." But the monograph would conclude on a hopeful note. It was possible that Indiana could find redemption for its mistakes through a partial "restoration" of the Kankakee with government forests and protected game preserves.[34]

Alice Demmon became overseer of research and writing for the Kankakee monograph. She was the FWP district supervisor for northwest Indiana, with headquarters in Gary, but fieldworkers from as far east as South Bend and as far south as Rensselaer would report to her. She took Lockridge's one-page prospectus and fleshed it out to three pages which expanded its scope and detail but retained the cautionary message of the original. Eight counties fell within the Kankakee drainage area, and Demmon assigned fieldworkers to research the history of the area, to compile newspaper coverage of the drainage process, to interview elderly hunters and current farmers, and to pursue the possibilities of restoring some of the wilderness. Seven fieldworkers spent approximately a year—from mid-1936 to mid-1937—traveling, researching, and interviewing. Some worked only in their home counties, but others ventured further afield. Henrietta Graubman from Michigan City, Floyd L. Meharry from Rensselaer, and Archie Koritz from Valparaiso were especially resourceful and prolific in their reports. The results of the fieldworker research amounted to more than five hundred pages of material, all of which was to fit into the eight chapters of the Lockridge-Demmon monograph.[35]

The first three chapters of the proposed monograph covered the topography of the area, the early Indian residents, and the period "Under Four Flags," which incorporated French, Spanish, English, and finally United States occupancy. Fieldworker Clyde A'Neals submitted ten pages on the geography, botany, and Indians of the early days based on published local histories and state geological reports;[36] Archie Koritz and Henrietta Graubman both provided five pages each for "Under Four Flags" gleaned from standard histories by Logan Esarey, William Cockrum, and Julia Levering.[37] Alice Demmon took these rough reports and edited them into more polished versions. The monograph moved swiftly from the glacial era through the mound-building Indians to the later Miami and Potawatomies. She spent considerable time with LaSalle and his 1679 portage from the site of current South Bend to the head of the Kankakee River. And she devoted ample space to Americans gaining control of the territory from the British and to descriptions of the Hoosier pioneer era.[38] All of this was familiar history based on secondary sources that provided nothing exceptional or new to scholars of the period. But apparently Lockridge and Demmon felt the early chapters were necessary to set the stage for later developments.

"Hunters' Paradise" and "Reclamation" proved more original than the opening chapters but also one-sided in their point of view. Fieldworkers interviewed many elderly residents of the region and compiled reminiscences of life along the Kankakee before reclamation changed the landscape. Lockridge had suggested that Henry Dunker from St. Joseph County would be a good source,[39] and the result was a twenty-page interview with this outdoorsman who had been hunting and fishing in the swamps since 1876. He described muskrat houses, displayed his massive collection of Indian arrowheads gathered from the marshes, and lamented that the reclamation had ruined the flight patterns of migrating birds.[40] Another interviewee, Joe Johanni from La Porte County, compared the excitement of hunting mink in earlier days to the boredom of raising chickens in the 1930s.[41] There are many accounts of hunting lodges and gun clubs that sprang up to accommodate visiting sportsmen. From Starke County came tales of wealthy hunters who arrived carrying huge sums of cash for supplies and local guides.[42] Details on the reclamation process came largely from local newspapers. Fieldworkers collected debates between hunters and farmers, statistics on the miles of ditches and escalating property values, and accounts of the new large farms that had replaced bogs and former islands that were now landlocked hills. Most of the data collected and the interviews conducted favored hunters rather than farmers, and the composite verdict was a nostalgia for the past and a lost way of life. Henrietta Graubman reported that the old-timers "spend most of their time in dreaming of the river as it once was, when game was plentiful and when the river still had its many bends."[43] And Floyd Meharry concluded, "The abundance of game of all kinds paid better returns to the hunter than the Kankakee farmers realize today. . . . Drainage has destroyed the moisture of the earth adjacent to the Kankakee River so essential to plant and animal life."[44]

Likewise, "Original Tales" and "Persons and Places of Interest" provided laudatory and original viewpoints of a vanished landscape and lifestyle. Fieldworkers compiled stories of visits to the region by celebrities, especially writers, and the literary product that had resulted from these visits. One account described Lew Wallace and his houseboat, where he spent leisure time and, if legend could be believed, where he wrote part of his book *Ben Hur*.[45] James Whitcomb Riley apparently enjoyed hunting in the marshes, according to the elderly interviewee who had been his guide on several occasions, and several people claimed to have been guides for Benjamin Harrison, who would later become president. Novelist Maurice Thompson was an avid bow-hunter in the swamps, and he alluded to his archery exploits in both his poetry and prose.[46] In addition to these famous visitors, a native of the area, Will Pfrimmer, had published two books of poems that romanticized the untamed natural scenery. He was known as the Poet of the Kankakee, and both Clive Beatty and Floyd Meharry sent in assessments of his career and samples of his work.[47]

The projected final chapter of the monograph was to present a debate on the success and failure of reclamation and the potential for conserving the remaining pockets of wilderness and restoring others. In her prospectus, Alice Demmon presented the parameters for the debate. She explained that a movement was currently under way to return part of the Kankakee to its "original condition so far as possible" by flooding the low areas and "once more making the region a haven for waterfowl and fur-bearing animals." Opposed to that movement, she admitted, were "large land owners" who had invested time and money to reclaim the land for "great ranch lands" and "wonderful crops."[48] This chapter failed to materialize as planned. Extant fragments of the chapter in draft form argue the case for conserving and restoring the marshes and building private and state game preserves. The overwhelming majority of material gathered by FWP personnel supported this view. Fieldworkers simply had not gathered much data to counterbalance this position. They apparently did not seek out successful farmers for interviews to match their many talks with the garrulous and nostalgic trappers. Newspaper editorials that supported reclamation were from the early days of drainage activity; few statistics documented the new agricultural productivity; and fieldworkers granted only grudging support of the success stories in their manuscripts. The assessment by Henrietta Graubman was typical. Reclamation, she claimed, "broke these peoples' hearts and destroyed their hunters' paradise. Drainage benefitted a few but ruined many more."[49] Administrative lack of balance from the inception of the project and fieldworker sympathy for one side prevented any possibility of a genuine debate.

Several factors kept the Kankakee monograph from reaching publication. As was the case with Riley and the Ohio River flood, this proposal was one of Lockridge's personal enthusiasms. When he departed as state FWP director in late 1937, all research ceased on the project, and fieldworkers redirected their energies to the Indiana and Calumet guides. Alice Demmon edited a few of the reports into preliminary chapter drafts, which she forwarded to Gordon Briggs, the new director. She admitted having some personal doubts about the quality of the manuscript, and there is no record that Briggs encouraged any further work on it.[50] One of Lockridge's goals for the monograph had been for it to be a catalyst for creating game preserves in the region, and this activity was already under way. The state of Indiana had begun work on both the Kankakee and Jasper-Pulaski fish and wildlife areas in the 1930s, so Lockridge's crusade was really a moot point. Large portions of the manuscript were also not worthy of publication, and Demmon almost admitted this in her editorial reservations. The historical, literary, and scientific surveys were derivative and unoriginal, taken from secondary sources, and written by people who were not experts in the field. Those portions that were original, unfortunately, never moved beyond the research stage. Dozens of interviews with elderly hunters, fishermen, and guides present valuable personal insights into a way of life that all but vanished with the marshes. These oral histories, although collected, never found an audience and retreated silently into storage. They are joined there by dozens of compiled newspaper accounts of the reclamation debates from small local newspapers, most of which are not indexed. These interviews and press reports offer convenient and primary documentation of a turbulent chapter in the Hoosier past that, to date, remains unwritten.

"America Eats" was a proposal by national FWP administrators for an analysis of the national appetite. FWP director Henry Alsberg and one of his editors, Katherine Kellock, developed this project after reading an article on oyster suppers in the October 1937 issue of *Atlantic Monthly*. What this piece did, and what Alsberg and Kellock consequently envisioned, was a discussion of group gatherings that centered around food: traditions, preparations, and camaraderie. This was not to be a compilation of cookbook recipes; instead, they allotted each state one chapter to present "an account of a public or semi-public meal characteristic of those held in the state." Alsberg instructed state FWP directors to submit a list of three or four potential meals, and the Washington staff would select the appropriate one for each state to develop into an essay.[51] Typical of many other FWP enterprises, "America Eats" went through several changes of format before expiring, unfinished, in 1942. The failure to reach publication had more to do with the phasing out of the WPA/FWP during the war than to the lack of merit in the proposal or lack of cooperation from the states.

Indiana FWP director Gordon Briggs was eager to participate in the "America Eats" project, although its subsequent transformations caused several delays. He promptly responded to Alsberg's request for ideas and submitted nominations for three meals that he regarded as "typically Hoosier." After some negotiating, Briggs decided that he would focus the essay on either a "Company Dinner" or a "Harvest Supper."[52] Before Briggs could write the essay for the designated Indiana chapter, the project shifted into a new format. A second memorandum to state editors indicated that several regional essays would replace the compilation of individual state chapters. Not only was the format changing, but the national office also suggested that everyone affiliated with the FWP in the separate states was invited to submit materials for consideration. Fieldworkers, administrators, and clericals all could contribute information about group meals and traditions. From all points of the United States, essays and articles arrived for the national editor, Lyle Saxon, who then routed them to five regional editors. They ranged from the predictable Maine clambakes and Kentucky burgoo to the surprising Arizona son-of-a-bitch stew and Alabama possum party.[53]

Hoosier fieldworkers tapped their personal memories and interviewed many individuals about indigenous foods. The result was a vast collection of menus and recipes that documented a variety of food and folk traditions in Indiana. Pioneer days were represented by recipes for Indian pudding from Steuben County and johnnycake from Spencer County, allegedly the same kind that young Abraham Lincoln took with him on river trips to New Orleans.[54] Ethnic foods were heavily weighted toward German cuisine, with offerings of potato pancakes from Clark County, and from Ripley County grittsa, a loaf made of ground meat, barley, and herbs.[55] A Polish recipe from St. Joseph County gave instructions for making barczz from spare ribs and beets. And an exotic dessert of fried pumpkin blossoms from Shelby County came touted as "a delicacy not to be excelled."[56] Only a few of the fieldworkers followed Alsberg's instructions and worked these foods into communal activities. They dutifully described traditions and customs that accompanied specific meals. For example, Charles Willen from Vigo County described two gatherings: a rabbit supper for a church congregation and a high school banquet. Albert Strope from Mishawaka placed the process of making apple butter into an elaborate scenario of peeling apples, gossiping, and singing. Merton Knowles described a Warren County tradition of celebrating Thanksgiving not with turkey but with oysters. Whether stewed, fried, or raw, the "luscious bivalves" were followed by square dancing.[57]

Nelson Algren was the regional editor chosen to mix Indiana's cuisine with that of Illinois, Iowa, and other neighboring states. Algren was of German Jewish ancestry and had grown up in Chicago, so he was conversant with both ethnic and midwestern customs. An unemployed journalist during the Depression, he worked various jobs, from gas station attendant to fruit picker, and still managed to get his first novel published in 1935. He joined the Illinois FWP as a fieldworker in 1936 and became a supervisor the following year. The midwestern section of "America Eats" was largely Algren's personal project, and by his own recollection he finished the manuscript before entering military service in 1942.[58] It was a typical FWP project, in that research material arrived from dozens of anonymous fieldworkers, and Algren synthesized their disparate prose into his personal style. He took rural gatherings such as butchering hogs and making apple butter and presented them as generic midwestern activities not exclusive to just Indiana or Nebraska. Likewise he described ethnic traditions such as a Jewish Purim festival or a Polish Dyngus Day as standard urban customs whether in Chicago or South Bend. Algren mixed the past with the present, food menus with folk music, and short anecdotes with extended analysis. His finished manuscript of roughly eighty pages emerged as a midwestern gustatory encyclopedia, but it gave no attribution to sources or authors from the individual states.

It is possible to trace some of the material in the midwestern "America Eats" to its Hoosier origins, but most of the Indiana material is integrated so thoroughly into the text that it remains anonymous and thus Algren's own. The longest section of the manuscript devoted to a specifically Hoosier topic is about family reunions and stretches over three pages. Roughly three-quarters of the piece quotes verbatim from a five-page essay, copies of which are located in the Library of Congress and Indiana FWP files. It was probably written by Gordon Briggs, who had promised to personally write Indiana's chapter for the original book. The state office submitted the essay in December 1941, several months after the publication of the Indiana guide, so Briggs would have had time to draft the piece.[59] It also contains many of his stylistic and attitudinal trademarks: his tendency to group items in long lists; his sense of humor, much like that of George Ade, whom he was prone to quote; and his refusal to grant Indiana an urban personality. This essay has a rural slant and a funny tone. Algren obviously appreciated this and quoted the humorous portions at length. For instance, the family reunion has convened in the summertime at a park or churchyard. The women prepare the picnic meal of fried chicken, several kinds of potatoes, sliced tomatoes, deviled eggs, and assorted homemade relishes and preserves. Meanwhile, the men improvise games of baseball and horseshoes while taking occasional quaffs from a discreetly passed bottle of whiskey. The younger children huddle "a respectful distance from the main table, eyeing the food with wistful glances and trying to remember which of their fellows are the first cousins from Elwood. . . . When a slacking off in the first rush of eating is indicated by the gradual resumption of conversation, the servers start a second general attack, urging everyone to have another helping of everything. Then when only the most hardy are still chewing away on chicken legs or wishbones, the cakes are cut—angel food, devil's food, banana, marble, sponge, coconut, orange, burnt sugar, and lazy daisy. They are followed by pumpkin, cherry, apple, mince, peach, blackberry, and custard pies."[60] Algren unfortunately omitted the final paragraph of the Hoosier essay. Whether written by Briggs or not, it aptly described the real importance of reunions as having more to do with people than with food. Once the reunion is finished, according to the essay, "family ties have once again been reinforced with the lasting cement of fried chicken and apple pie."[61]

Although the FWP never published "America Eats," the midwestern section eventually found an audience. Algren left the FWP in 1942 and took his copy of the manuscript with him.[62] Later a Chicago restaurateur acquired Algren's copy, which the author described as the product of "a government writers' project. I did it because I needed the money."[63] In 1992, after his death, the University of Iowa Press published Algren's portion of "America Eats" and served up the communal cuisine of Indiana and the Midwest, a bit warmed over but still palatable. The Hoosier contribution to the book is limited and, like those of the other midwestern states, represents a tiny fraction of the compiled materials.[64] The Indiana FWP papers include a vast array of food information that fieldworkers gathered for "America Eats" and other projects. Almost every county file has folders labeled "Cuisine" and "Folklore," and almost all of those contain recipes and menus that link Indiana to its past by way of the dinner table. They range from persimmon pudding to onion pie, and from corn fritters to leather peaches. Both common and exotic, indigenous and otherwise, this collection from Hoosier cookbooks in the 1930s is a bounty as yet untapped and untasted.

National administrators had, from the beginning, instructed fieldworkers to gather materials for the state guides on ethnic neighborhoods, festivals, organizations, and customs. The resulting collection of music, folklore, and traditions linked to dozens of native homelands was far more than the state guides could publish. Consequently, FWP consultants on folklore and social-ethnic studies proposed several books to highlight America's diverse lifestyles and ethnic contributions to national life. Benjamin Botkin and Morton Royse, in particular, were champions at gathering and publishing material on ethnic heritage. Several books emerged from these efforts, including *The Armenians in Massachusetts* (1937) and *The Italians of New York* (1938).[65] Other than the ill-fated volume on Creoles in Vincennes, only one of the projected FWP books featuring ethnicity involved Indiana. "Pockets in America" was to be a collection of articles about ethnic communities that were relatively self-contained, still clinging to their national customs, and assimilating slowly into the American mainstream. Most of the early ethnic migrants to Indiana, such as the French, German, and Irish, had long since become Hoosiers, and they spoke of their ethnic heritage in the past tense. Many recent migrants to the industrial northwestern region still practiced some of their national traditions, but few of them constituted distinctive communities outside their churches and musical groups. A major exception to this rapid absorption into Hoosierdom and loss of ethnic identity was the Belgian colony in Mishawaka. This community, according to FWP administrators, retained many old-world characteristics and was worthy of inclusion as an ethnic "pocket" in the proposed book.

Indiana's contribution to "Pockets in America" had initially been more diverse than just the Belgian colony, but various developments narrowed the field to just one entry. One of the national FWP editors, George Cronyn, contacted Ross Lockridge in June 1937 for information about several possible Hoosier "pockets." He requested that Lockridge send information and photographs for New Harmony, Spring Mill village, and St. Meinrad.[66] Cronyn had grown up in Anderson, but had not lived in Indiana for many years. His suggestions had merit as unique sites, but not as ethnic communities in the 1930s. The German Rappites and utopians of New Harmony had long since departed, leaving a town in search of restoration and focus. Spring Mill village, the location of a limestone grist mill and distillery, had recently become a state park to highlight pioneer history. St. Meinrad, a German Catholic settlement in the nineteenth century, now hosted a monastery and seminary for students, many of whom were neither German nor Hoosier. These suggestions from Cronyn were not really appropriate for the "Pockets in America" volume, and Lockridge did not respond to his request, either because of their inappropriateness or because he was soon to depart as state FWP director. Cronyn later contacted Lockridge's successor, Gordon Briggs, with a more suitable nomination. He had noticed in the early drafts of the Indiana guide tour section a brief discussion of the Belgian community in Mishawaka and wondered if it could be expanded. He instructed Briggs that the essay should be lively, informal, and colorful, with an emphasis on human interest stories.[67]

In order to complete this assignment, Briggs depended on two fieldworkers from St. Joseph County who were noted for submitting colorful human interest material. Briggs would combine their information, add his lively humor, and submit a five-page article for the "Pockets in America" project. Albert Strope was an unemployed teacher who knew the Belgian community from personal observation, and Paul Yoder was an aspiring fiction writer who excelled at finding interesting people and extracting dramatic moments from their interviews. Together Strope and Yoder interviewed eight Belgian immigrants and worked the information into seventeen pages for Briggs to distill into his essay. Strope devoted considerable space to children and schools, and he emphasized old-world traditions that prevailed in Mishawaka's southside Belgian community. He described their orderly gardens, their love of pigeon racing, and their custom of wearing wooden shoes at home. One Mishawaka businessman also bred and sold Belgian horses from a nearby farm. As recently as 1936, he had imported twenty-two horses from Belgium to replenish his brood stock. Yoder supplied much detail on the Broederenkring, or neighborhood social club ("It is pronounced Brood her enk ring, with the accent on the first syllable, and with r's rolled"), and the women's dramatic society, which produced plays from the home country. "This," commented Yoder, "is a link binding them to their motherland." Yoder also stressed the community's proud and devout Catholicism. Briggs took these anecdotes from his fieldworkers and tied them together with his own distinctive voice. He enhanced Strope's description of tidy backyard gardens thusly: "In the rear of almost every house is a vegetable garden, meticulously kept, where cabbage, beets, corn, and all the common vegetables march in orderly rows." Briggs also amplified Yoder's discussion on religion. Yoder had commented that when the Mishawaka Belgians asserted their devotion to their church, you could hear it as far away as Gary; Briggs stretched the distance all the way to Omaha. Briggs concluded that this Hoosier pocket was uniquely ethnic but rapidly assimilating. He captured this transitional state by describing Belgian food in Mishawaka as though George Ade had sampled a "savory dish of red cabbage and apples cooked together, or an odd but toothsome mixture of spinach and potatoes."[68]

Despite an impressive collection of material from several states, "Pockets in America" remained only a collection, not a published book. Joining Indiana's Belgians were such diverse groups as the Yaqui Indians from Arizona, Greek sponge fishermen from Tarpon

Springs, Florida, and an isolated Mormon village in Boulder, Utah. The FWP submitted a book proposal for this project, but the publisher turned it down.[69] Benjamin Botkin and Morton Royse, the major champions of ethnic studies, both departed around the same time that Congress reorganized the FWP, and most of their projects remained unfinished. The state guides were to become the major priority. One of the national editors later lamented this failure of the ethnic collections to reach publication. He speculated that these books might have been a better reflection of the American character than the guidebooks.[70] These studies had described ethnic customs in a relatively pure state before they were lost through assimilation. In the 1920s, federal legislation drastically reduced the number of new immigrants who could enter the United States, so the period in which the FWP gathered its information was the last chance to observe undiluted ethnic traditions among sizable groups. This was certainly the case in Mishawaka. Briggs had noted in his essay the eagerness of the Indiana Belgians to Americanize and discontinue many of their old-world traditions. Today, in order to recapture the distinctive qualities of the Belgian colony in the 1930s, the fieldnote research by Albert Strope and Paul Yoder offers valuable primary documentation based on eyewitness accounts and personal interviews.

Three other national projects engaged the Indiana Writers' Program in research and compilation, and all three of these failed to reach publication, largely because of wartime priorities. "Hands That Built America" was a collaborative effort between the FWP and the Federal Art Project in which a book about American handicrafts would be illustrated with plates from the Index of American Design. The Indiana Writers' Program was compiling material for the proposed book when the national director, John Newsom, "suspended" the project in 1942.[71] Newsom likewise aborted plans for a book, tentatively titled "Indians of North America," for which the Hoosier state was planning a major contribution. This was to be an account of Native American heritage, and Indiana fieldworkers had compiled many pages of material, both historical and contemporary. In particular, the Miami Indian Clarence Godfroy had conducted many interviews regarding folklore and tribal customs.[72] Newsom had proposed in 1940 a series of factbooks in which each state would present reference material about schools, libraries, industries, hospitals, transportation, etc. These factbooks would be inexpensive, and they would be published in a format that permitted periodic updating with current data. The Indiana Writers' Program received a specific WPA appropriation in 1941 to finance the project and began work on what they referred to as "a compendium of information about the state, somewhat encyclopedic in type." But the war intervened; Newsom resigned as head of the Writers' Program to enter the military; and none of the states completed their factbooks.[73]

Several proposals from within Indiana met the same fate as their national counterparts; they were officially suspended or left unfinished in 1942. Following the 1939 reconfiguration of the FWP, Indiana State Teachers College became the official sponsor for the Hoosier Writers' Program. Briggs and two of his assistant state supervisors submitted an ambitious list of proposals for "a series of booklets, 50 to 100 pages each," which, they argued, would "bring great credit both to the Teachers College and the Writers' Project." This list included booklets on the Miami, Potawatomi, and Delaware Indians, Johnny Appleseed, the Rappite settlement in New Harmony, the Wabash and Erie Canal, and the Underground Railroad. On a more ambitious scale, they proposed full-length books on Indiana education and folklore. Briggs was in the midst of completing the Indiana guide and was fully aware of the surplus materials from the guide that could be recycled and expanded into these publications.[74] By the time the guide finally appeared in 1941, most of these proposals had been rejected or forgotten, and a few had been absorbed into national projects. But the state sponsor championed the book on education, and by early 1942 it had become "Education Moves Forward." This was to be an analysis of the social environment in Terre Haute and a proposal for schools "to do a better job of making good citizens." Newsom questioned the importance of the project for the Writers' Program and suggested that if it were to continue, the college might wish to assume responsibility for it. This did not happen, and the project died.[75] The sponsor also initiated a comparative study of two Hoosier cities, Lafayette and Terre Haute. Several members of the social studies faculty at the Teachers College devised a series of elaborate questionnaires to be used in Vigo and Tippecanoe counties. The intent was to gather current social and economic statistics about students, parents, and neighborhoods and to devise recommendations for remediation programs. They had administered only a few of the questionnaires by the time defense priorities replaced most other activities, including this project.[76]

As early as January 1942, John Sembower at Indiana State Teachers College sensed the problematic future of the Writers' Program. He spoke of wartime "storm warnings" that doomed the pending projects. And he lamented that the predominantly elderly and handicapped employees probably could not find work in defense-related jobs.[77] The WPA had already absorbed the diminished Writers' Program into its Community Service Division, and after Newsom's departure as national director in February 1942, it officially became the Writers' Unit of the WPA's War Services Subdivision.[78] Future Indiana plans entailed cooperating with other mobilization groups such as the new Indiana Defense Council to work on the *Defense Reporter* and a recreational guide for military personnel.[79] These activities were tentative, dependent upon outside agencies, and utilized little of the research or writing skills of the former Writers' Project. When word arrived in April 1942 that the Indiana project was officially terminated as "an economy measure curtailing non-military expenditures," it was no surprise to the twenty-five remaining personnel.[80] All that was left for Briggs and his small staff was to pack up the unfinished projects, fieldworker research, and administrative paperwork and place them in storage.

EIGHT

Research Inventories

Inventories of many fascinating Hoosier subjects occupy a large portion of the 60,000 pages of the Indiana FWP Papers. Fieldworkers gathered materials on such disparate topics as cemetery epitaphs, antiques, industrial jargon, and the Underground Railroad. They compiled much of this initially to use in the state guide, and it proved to be more than the book could handle. Some of it appeared in different formats, such as *Hoosier Tall Stories* and "It Happened in Indiana." But most of it was never used. The individual fieldworkers who trekked, pored, scoured, and interviewed to gather the information received no credit for compiling the materials, and the public never benefited from the accumulated mass. Archivists at Indiana State University Library have organized and indexed the entire collection of FWP activity, so the various inventories are easy to locate. The classification system replicates the one that the original FWP developed for fieldwork assignments, and divides the papers among the ninety-two counties that generated them. Thus, a scholar seeking information about pioneer food in Fort Wayne would consult the Allen County file labeled "Cuisine." Some counties produced more inventories than others, depending on the number and ingenuity of fieldworkers. It is often difficult to determine whether the fieldworkers reported these items as typical or aberrant, or simply what they could find at the time. Some of the fieldworkers researched the backgrounds of the inventory subjects, and others merely listed what they located. Almost all of the counties have files on cemeteries and Indians. Only twenty-nine have files on desperados, and four on orphanages. But the aggregate result is a gold mine of detail about the Hoosier past. Never before or since has there been such a comprehensive collection of quotidian material that documented daily life in the Hoosier state. Only a few researchers have consulted these inventory files. Indiana history is richer for their efforts, and other scholars should follow their lead in tapping these long-hidden treasures. They constitute a pointillistic self-portrait of Indiana with their thousands of details on hundreds of topics. The following eight topics are representative in their display of fieldworker research into obscure corners of the Hoosier past and character.

Antiques

Inventory files on antiques exist for thirty-seven counties, and they divulge much about what individuals preserved from their past and why. These physical remnants reflected family history, national heritage, and the settling of the Hoosier state. Whether typical or not, examples from four counties demonstrate what material culture can reveal about values, beliefs, and attitudes. In Knox County, fieldworker Loy Followell discovered several collections of antiques that spoke to the area's role in American independence and Indiana politics. Followell visited the Vincennes home of Mary Brouillette, a descendant of William Lindsay, who had fought in the Revolutionary War. She displayed on her dining room buffet a china water pitcher that had belonged to her military ancestor. The white vessel was adorned with a small blue painting of a colonial home and had been passed through several generations of the family.[1] Followell also described the family collection of Mrs. Paul Winter in Bicknell. She was a descendant of James "Blue Jeans" Williams, Indiana governor in the 1870s. His possessions, such as a walnut bedroom washstand and a walking cane with a gilt knob, sounded as rustic as the image

175

that the former governor cultivated.[2] From Muncie, William W. Tuttle reported that he had discovered in the Herman Myers home what was probably the oldest doll in Delaware County. It had traveled from Virginia in the 1820s in an ox-drawn wagon. Tuttle's journalism background was evident in his precise descriptions of the toy. Its head was made of glazed composition, and its eyes were "large and starey." Metal hinges linked the maple wood limbs, and the aged cloth body was "well onto a collapse."[3] Estella Dodson's inventories from Monroe County also revealed much about migration into and out of Indiana. She found in Elizabeth Beaty's Bloomington home a pewter oil lamp that had come west from Pennsylvania with Beaty's grandmother, and a carved redwood goblet that had returned east from California with a neighbor after the gold rush of 1849.[4] Clive Beatty's discovery of European antiques in Lake County was probably more typical than aberrant because of the large number of old-world immigrants who had settled in the Calumet region. Louis Wettengel had left Bohemia and settled in Hobart before the Civil War. His family home there contained many items that he had brought with him, and they still created a link between the two countries. Among the items were his 1827 baptismal certificate, written in German, and two trunks, one made from iron, the other of leather.[5] The antique accoutrements that Hoosiers treasured in the 1930s were physical manifestations of memories they chose to preserve. Several decades have elapsed since the inventories were compiled, and most of the antiques discussed have probably changed hands, some several times. Hence these inventories describe an Indiana that existed only at that point in time. These thirty-seven files, therefore, document a diverse and migratory people who built a cultural compost during the Depression with the things they carried into and cared for in Indiana.

Museums

Only twenty-eight county files exist for museums, but they document a zeal for institutional preservation of the Hoosier past. Museums, large and small, devoted energy and space to conserving and exhibiting pieces of their local heritage. The fieldworkers generally grouped art, natural, and history museums together, so the files are inclusive and not compartmentalized by subject. One exception to this was the exclusion of historic house museums that were shrines to a family or person. The homes of such dignitaries as James Whitcomb Riley and Benjamin Harrison, therefore, are listed separately in files labeled "Historic Buildings." Fieldworkers visited the museums, consulted with curators of those that had them, and quoted from brochures available at the museums or local chambers of commerce. They gathered this material for the tours section of the state guide, although they submitted far more material than was printed. Hence, much of the information in the inventories did not get public exposure. These inventories usually focused on the items that local museums most valued, so their choices reflected the institutions' priorities and what they felt was worthy of preserving. Many of the smaller museums were located in their county courthouses, indicating that their guardianship of local heritage had tacit government approval because of their physical location. Almost without exception, these museums contained collections of Indian relics, pioneer artifacts, and Civil War memorabilia. These formed a consistent core of the holdings around the state and revealed common threads about the Hoosier past, patterns of donations to the collections, and priorities for museum exhibits. Indian relics from arrowheads to pottery and blankets dominated the collections and for good reason. The earliest inhabitants of Indiana had left behind what fieldworker Sudie Knight from Evansville called a "bewildering array" of artifacts.[6] From the ancient mound builders to the modern Miami came physical evidence of their presence all over the state. Museums acquired many of these in a benign fashion, such as from farmers who plowed up spear points, but some were the result of systematic grave robbing, as was the case with Little Turtle's possessions in Allen County. Pioneer artifacts also were major components of these museums. These documented a rural and hardscrabble life for early Hoosiers. The artifacts from kitchens, springhouses, and barns are testimony to the ingenuity of their creators and the longevity of the materials. Quilts from the State Museum in Indianapolis, sausage grinders from the Union County Museum in Liberty, and candle molds from the private Roth Museum in Edinburg all were silent witnesses to resourceful pioneers. Legions of veterans from the Civil War donated their memorabilia to local museums, which often filled cases and entire rooms with them. Muskets, swords, flags, daguerreotypes, letters, and medical instruments documented the donors' service to the Union and propensity to bring things back from the battlefront. Fieldworker Wayne Price described one "rather gruesome" item from Versailles, a trophy of sorts brought home from the war to Ripley County. It was "a ring made out of the crushed bone of a confederate soldier's arm."[7]

Most of these museum inventories merited a brief mention in the state guide, but in a very abbreviated format. Editors omitted more than they printed, and some of the museums themselves were excluded when the book was published in 1941. Most of the fieldworkers submitted inventories that ranged from two to five pages in length; the guide usually granted a brief paragraph to each museum in the tour section, so the bulk of their material did not reach an audience. For example, the guide paragraph on the Northern Indiana Historical Museum in South Bend does not include fieldworker Paul Yoder's description of the cross-section of a tree said to have been gashed by a member of LaSalle's exploration party in 1679.[8] Neither does the guide mention Vivian Wilson's tribute to Ross Lockridge as one of the founders of the Fort Wayne Historical Museum.[9] Editors of the guide chose not to mention that WPA workers had created some of the display dioramas in the Indianapolis Children's Museum, an unusual omission, since they frequently mentioned New Deal accomplishments.[10] From Evansville, Sudie Knight submitted an inventory of the Temple of Fine Arts and History that ran to twenty-eight pages; the published account was only seven lines in the guide. Missing were her detailed descriptions of Filipino basketry, the oldest spinet in Vanderburgh County, and a wooden cabinet built by Abraham Lincoln.[11] Also missing in the guide were several of the institutions described by fieldworkers. For instance, public museums in Kokomo and Columbia City and private collections in Morgan and Clark counties receive no mention despite inventories of holdings with some distinction and rarity. The FWP files, therefore, contain some rich and unpublished information concerning what the museums and fieldworkers in the 1930s regarded as worthy remnants from the past.

Cemetery Epitaphs

Fieldworkers visited cemeteries in eighty-three Indiana counties and exhumed epitaphs from gravestones they found there. From the massive Crown Hill cemetery in Indianapolis to tiny family plots in rural communities, hundreds of epitaphs arrived in the FWP state headquarters. One Marion County fieldworker, Emile Walli, admitted that this project had more to do with copying than with creativity, but Walli and others sought and gathered words that bereaved families had inscribed for their departed.[12] Several patterns emerge from this large collection, some predictable, others surprising. One of the most prevalent patterns is the desire to honor the military service of deceased veterans. Regardless of their family or professional accomplishments, the participation of these men in American wars came first, and often to the exclusion of anything else. For example, the 1863 gravestone for Alexander Hewett in Knox said simply, "A veteran of two wars."[13] These inscriptions also expressed the overwhelming belief that the recently departed were now enjoying a better life beyond this one. A typical message of this sort appeared on Willie Mullings's stone in Jeffersonville: "A band of heavenly angels saw thee, loved thee and took thee home."[14] And in these preliberated times, women remained largely anonymous. Their roles as beloved and dutiful wives, mothers, and daughters overshadowed other pursuits that may have distinguished their lives. Finally, it is a bit jarring in the twenty-first century to read notations that fieldworkers made in a matter-of-fact way that some Hoosier cemeteries in the 1930s were "restricted for the burial of white persons only."[15]

The gravestones frequently indicated causes for death, and as the decades elapsed, the epitaphs reveal a transition from natural to technological killers. Fieldworker Grace Monroe discovered the Guhrt family stone in a Hanover cemetery, and it revealed much about the state of health in Indiana during pioneer times and the apparent lack of public education. Carved on the west side of the stone was the following:

Jamz W.
Eldest Sun of
W. B & M. K. Guhrt
Died
Jun 16, 1835
Sinhice K.
Eldest doter ov
W. B. & M. Guhrt
Died
Juli 1, 1835
Ajed 20 yearz.

An inscription on the reverse side documented their mother's death the previous year.[16] Deadly cholera epidemics often swept through the Midwest, and one had hit Jefferson County at this exact time, obviously taking much of the Guhrt family with it. Dorothy Woodworth recorded another cause of death that was probably too common in pioneer times. In the Sims Cemetery in Union County, a stone commemorated Susanna M. Haynes with no age or date but this brief inscription: "Killed by a rattlesnake bite."[17] The stone for William R. Johnson in Washington County tells nothing of his life except that he was "Killed by a cold blooded murderer" in 1866. Fieldworker Ina Mae Humphrey researched this incident and found that the accused murderer was in jail awaiting trial when he was "taken out and hanged under the bridge south of town."[18] When Elwood Haynes placed Indiana on the industrial map with his introduction of a horseless carriage in 1895, few people could have foretold its lethal consequences. But Helen Clark discovered a stone in Spencer County that told in macabre rhyme the story of John Paul Braun's death in 1915.

Oh, it's ashes to ashes and dust to dust
If the carriages don't get you,
Automobiles must.

180

So pause my friend as my tomb you view
And let this shred of advice soak into you.
Watch your step.[19]

From all points of the state and across the decades, gravestones offered up epitaphs that were identical, indicating that prefabricated messages were available for those who lacked the originality to compose their own. More frequently than not, these boilerplate inscriptions were poems, suggesting that rhyming and metered lines held more sentiment than straight prose. Raymond Butler found this verse for Ede Harding, who died in 1858 in Marion County.

Affliction sore for years I bore
Physicians were in vain.
At length God pleased to give me ease
And freed me from my pain.[20]

Variations of this quatrain appeared on a stone in South Bend in 1875 and in several other locations and decades.[21] The following poem was apparently a favorite in central Indiana. Fieldworkers copied it from stones in five cemeteries from as early as 1856 to as late as 1914.

Remember me as you pass by
As you are now so once was I
As I am now so must you be
Remember death and follow me.[22]

"Speak no ill of the dead" is a cliché that holds true for this collection of epitaphs. Inscriptions on stone rarely, if ever, depart from citing positive characteristics for those now beneath the ground. The exemplary attributes copied by fieldworkers create a composite Hoosier biography that is pleasant genealogy but untrustworthy history. Because infant mortality rates were high in the nineteenth century, gravestones for young children are numerous, and their messages understandably sweet. Botanical metaphors appeared frequently, such as "I was a flower too good for earth" and "Budded

181

on earth to bloom in Heaven," found in Floyd and Marion counties.[23] Emery Turner reported on one adult who had not lost his childhood goodness, according to his stone in Orange County.

> Upright and just
> He was in all his ways
> A bright example
> In degenerate days.[24]

In Lafayette, Albert S. White led a very distinguished life, and his burial plot gave witness to it. Fieldworker Fred C. Binz reviewed at length the career of the former politician and president of the Big Four Railroad, and described his gravestone, carved to resemble a tree trunk with a twelve-foot height and circumference. The epitaph did not diminish White's reputation.

> In all relations of life
> ADMIRABLE
> As a friend SINCERE
> As a citizen
> PUBLIC SPIRITED
> As a lawyer HONEST
> As a legislator WISE
> As a judge
> WITHOUT REPROACH[25]

Fieldworkers often labeled their submitted epitaphs as distinctive, unusual, and peculiar, indicating that they copied the atypical inscriptions and left the rest unrecorded. The inventory today speaks highly of the originality of its creators, perhaps because the majority of epitaphs were not memorable enough to be submitted. But the multitude of messages constitutes a valuable resource, both for their number and for their revelations about life and death in the Hoosier state. If taken at face value, they document the primacy of military service as a human endeavor, the second-class status of both women and blacks in early Indiana, a strong religious belief in a rewarding afterlife, high infant mortality rates, a sense of humor, and a predilection for rhymed poetry.

Underground Railroad

Documenting the freedom trail from southern slavery to Canadian freedom has been an elusive quest for historians. Fugitive slaves who received assistance along the route of the so-called Underground Railroad left few records because most of them were illiterate, and the abolitionist "conductors" were equally reluctant to publicize their actions, which violated federal law. But following the Civil War, the acts of courage and sites of refuge that characterized the Underground Railroad became mythic. Secret attics and hidden passageways proliferated as families enhanced or created romantic legends of how their ancestors helped thousands of runaways out of bondage. Several major escape routes did, in fact, cross through Indiana, and historians have sought to verify locations and stories that relate to this fascinating chapter in American history. FWP administrators in Washington encouraged the inclusion of black heritage in the state guides, and fieldworkers began sleuthing for material on the Underground Railroad. In Indiana they uncovered and submitted information from forty counties. Much of this was old material, based on hearsay and secondary sources. Some of it, however, was new and came from memoirs, letters, newspaper accounts, and interviews with elderly residents whose memories of the freedom trail were valuable primary sources.

Many fugitive slaves crossed the Ohio River from Kentucky, fled through Indiana, and exited into Michigan or northern Ohio. These crossing points around Cincinnati, Madison, New Albany, Leavenworth, and Evansville were places of concentrated activity before the slaves then took various routes northward. From these sites on the river's northern bank come several accounts that tell much about the Underground Railroad in Indiana. Fieldworker Iris Cook in New Albany interviewed the son of a Kentucky slave, whom Cook had known when she was a child. This interview revealed that slaves around Louisville would plan escapes in a Masonic lodge for blacks. They would cross the river in a skiff, hide in the hills back of New Albany, then head north through Salem.[26] In neighboring Clark County, fieldworker Beulah Van Meter was predisposed to research this subject. Her grandfather had been a slave owner in Kentucky, and her family memorabilia included printed songs about runaways.[27] She conducted interviews and cited memoirs to document Jeffersonville's role in this enterprise. One man recalled in his memoir seeing escaped slaves hiding outside his mother's tavern and slave hunters resting inside the tavern near the community of Borden.[28] In Evansville, Samuel Dixon and Lauana Creel compiled much material on routes and individuals from a variety of local sources, and Creel interviewed a former slave, George T. Burns, who praised the minister Calvin Fairbanks for helping many fugitives cross the Ohio River. Fairbanks was imprisoned for his illegal activities, but Burns believed that he was "one of the country's most self-sacrificing men. Ready to suffer the loss of liberty to emancipate others from bondage."[29] In Dearborn County, Edward Henson interviewed Mrs. Delight Kerr, who grew up on a farm adjoining a station on the UGRR. She had personally known many of the principals involved, and Henson visited the site to corroborate her stories. The homestead sat on a high ridge, visible across the Ohio River in Kentucky, and "it loomed up in the distance to the poor, weary, footsore, oppressed slave as a haven." Fugitives hid there in a secret cellar, whose entrance was concealed under the living room carpet. After they were fed and rested, they were entrusted to a trained pony who took them to their next stop in Napoleon, about thirty miles to the northwest.[30]

Farther north in the Hoosier state, abolitionist Quakers assumed a leadership role in the UGRR. Two sites in particular illustrate the part played by this religious group and the reputation they acquired. Quakers had founded Westfield in Hamilton County in 1834, and partly for that reason, several escape routes converged there on the way toward Canada. According to fieldworker Robert Irvin, the town was known as "North Central Station," because it was the receiving point for slaves from all points of the South. The town was known throughout the country as the "last hope" of the slave owners, for once slaves reached Westfield, there was little chance for owners to get them back.[31] In Wayne County, three lines of the UGRR merged from Cincinnati, Madison, and Jeffersonville. The home of Quaker

Samuel Charles in Richmond was a major stop on one route, and escaped slaves used the Charles washhouse, close to a spring, to launder their clothing.[32] Nearby in Fountain City (then called New-port), Quakers Levi and Katharine Coffin assisted more than two thousand runaways over a twenty-year period. Their brick home be-came known as "Grand Central Station," and Levi was known as the president of the UGRR.[33] After the Coffins moved to Cincinnati, their home became a hotel, then a private residence, but its secret hiding places remained intact. Fieldworker Flora Mae Harris be-came deeply involved with this Wayne County assignment, citing his-torical memoirs and local newspapers, visiting and describing sites, and writing a poem about one of the fugitives.

Predictably, many of the fieldworker reports on the UGRR are characterized by the same problems that have plagued scholars. Much of the material is vague, hard to verify, and more legendary than historical. Too frequently such phrases as "it is strongly believed that" and "according to local legend"[34] accompany the stories about individuals and sites. Another weakness, one that compromises the credibility of some interviews, is the verbatim quoting of dialogue that purportedly took place decades ago between conductors and escapees. Descendants or neighbors of the principals involved ac-cepted these dialogues as authentic and passed them on to field-workers. Several of the counties through which the UGRR ran be-came boosterish and competitive about the merits of their abolition heritage. Delaware, Jay, Steuben, and Wayne all made claims that Eliza Harris, a slave featured in the novel *Uncle Tom's Cabin*, had stopped at their stations during her escape. Fieldworkers sometimes got caught up in this aggrandizement rather than attempting to ver-ify evidence. Flora Mae Harris, for example, asserted that it was a "fact" that "Simeon and Rachel Holliday, mentioned in Chapter XII of the novel, were Levi and Katharine Coffin, and that Eliza and her little boy spent two weeks with them at Newport."[35]

Imperfect as they are as historical documents, the forty county files of UGRR material in the Indiana collection still provide a help-ful repository of information. This subject remains popular and pro-vocative for students and scholars. The state of Indiana now operates the Levi Coffin House as a historic site, and Cincinnati, Ohio, hosts a museum dedicated to the Freedom Trail. Materials gathered by fieldworkers, no matter how flawed, can lead researchers to other obscure sources. They listed articles from local newspapers that are not indexed, and they cited diaries and memoirs, some of which were privately printed and are now difficult to locate. Many of the interviews with participants have not been published, and those individuals are no longer around. One of the few researchers who has consulted these files is former state representative Hurley Goodall. He compiled more than three hundred pages of material, which the Indiana Department of Natural Resources published in 2000, entitled *Underground Railroad*. This compilation suggests that other scholars could find the FWP collection equally rewarding as they pursue this elusive subject.

Historic Architecture

Preservation of the built environment was a minor concern in the United States until the 1930s. Then both private and public groups began to take seriously architectural landmarks, many of which were threatened by neglect or destruction. The Rockefeller family generated widespread public interest when they began to restore and reconstruct Colonial Williamsburg in the late 1920s. One small but notable New Deal project was the Historic American Building Survey (HABS), which began under the Civil Works Administration in 1933 and continued under various federal agencies. This project employed architects to document historic structures with line drawings and photographs. In Indiana, dozens of such buildings became the subjects of government attention before HABS discontinued its work during World War II. Another federal action was the Historic Sites Act of 1935, which permitted the Department of the Interior to designate significant sites as National Historic Landmarks. FWP editors consciously echoed this new interest. Many of the state guides, including Indiana's, included a separate chapter on architecture, mostly about historic sites, and a portfolio of photographs devoted to the same topic. Editors instructed fieldworkers to locate and describe historic structures as points of interest for the tour section of the state guides. Many of these descriptions were featured in the Indiana guide, but many more were not used and now occupy files labeled "Buildings," "Public Buildings," "Bridges," "Monuments and Landmarks," and "Historic Houses." These inventory files from almost all of the counties contain information about structures that the fieldworkers considered distinctive in the 1930s. Whether they were covered bridges, log cabins, courthouses, stately mansions, or rustic barns, FWP employees regarded them as significant legacies from the past, not just old buildings.

The fieldworkers were neither historians nor architects, and they generally selected buildings in their communities for their age and associational value rather than their artistic merit. This was a predictable response by laymen, but despite their narrow vision, they produced the largest collection of materials concerning Indiana's built environment that had ever been assembled. These documents, no matter how unsophisticated, now constitute valuable raw data for future scholars. Pearl Roberts, for example, described an 1835 home in Elkhart County as the first brick house to be built in Goshen,[36] and Cornet Burnworth from Knox County insisted that a home in Vincennes was the only pioneer log house left in the city.[37] Elizabeth Kargacos gave only a perfunctory description of an 1808 house in Bruceville, but thought it deserved attention because Abraham Lincoln had slept there in 1844.[38] Robert Irvin's nomination of James Whitcomb Riley's childhood home in Greenfield logically had far more to do with the poet's tenure there than its structural details.[39] The only substantial submission from Fayette County was the 1831 Elmhurst estate, which fieldworker Dorothy Woodworth described merely as a "stately building of unusual architecture." According to Woodworth, what gave Elmhurst significance was that this Connersville site had been owned variously by a congressman, a secretary of the interior, and a United States treasurer, and it had been visited frequently by President Benjamin Harrison.[40] Grace Monroe, in Jefferson County, probably had the richest source material of any of the fieldworkers, and she approached her task enthusiastically. She was aware that the HABS team had completed surveys of four buildings in Madison and that the Lanier Mansion was already a state property, but she lacked the technical vocabulary to adequately capture the distinguished landscape. Her descriptions of the sites ranged from "picturesque" to "imposing" to "striking." But she dutifully recorded dates, locations, architects, owners, and other basic information.[41]

The files from Orange County are representative of the FWP collection in that some of the submissions later appeared in the Indiana guide, and others were filed away unused, but most provided insights into what the fieldworkers regarded as important about Hoosier architectural heritage. Two of the structures that appeared in the guide were obvious choices. The French Lick Springs Resort had a long legacy associated with mineral water, gambling, and the Democratic Party. The nearby West Baden Springs Hotel had recently become a Jesuit school, but its massive dome alone qualified as an architectural wonder. The Indiana guide also gave considerable coverage to the 1850 Greek Revival county courthouse and the 1825 William Bowles home, both located in Paoli. The former possessed architectural merit, and the latter had associational value because its owner had been a leader of the infamous Knights of the Golden Circle during the Civil War. Emery Turner also nominated another Paoli structure that ended up unused in the "Historic Houses" file. Carpenters had constructed the William Lindley farmhouse and barn with "massive hand-hewn timbers" in 1846; it was still in use in the 1930s and, according to Turner's research, had once held sessions of the Orange County circuit court. For a journalist with no training in this field, Turner had an innate appreciation for vernacular design. He indicated that recent renovations to the Lindley site did not hide "the original timbers, still in good state of preservation."[42]

The fieldworkers were resourceful at uncovering and documenting historic buildings; they were less effective at describing their styles and analyzing their significance. That dichotomy was to be expected and does not diminish their contribution to historic preservation. Editors and consultants could and did enhance the fieldworker compilations with their professional expertise and nomenclature. The Indiana guide included a vast amount of material about the state's architectural heritage and reflected the newly developed appreciation for the built environment. A few of the structures listed later gained designations as National Historic Landmarks, such as the West Baden Springs Hotel. After the creation of the National Register of Historic Places in 1966, many more of these sites entered its lists, such as the Shrewsbury House in Madison and Elmhurst in Connersville. The hundreds of nominations that fieldworkers submitted but which the guide did not use remain today an untapped resource for researching Indiana's architectural past. Part of their documentation came from descendants of the original owners who are now deceased, and some of the descriptions came from personal observation in the 1930s. Decades of remodeling has altered many of these structures, and others have been lost to decay and destruction. One unused submission from Knox County raises intriguing questions about the status of the nominee and other buildings not deemed significant enough to be included in the guide. Elizabeth Kargacos described the wooden country home of Francis Vigo, built around 1800. Workers disassembled this house in 1934 and, according to Kargacos, carefully labeled and stored its parts for future reassembly. And there the story ended. Whatever happened to the dismantled home that belonged to one of Indiana's founding fathers? According to a state official, the Indiana Department of Natural Resources recycled these stored logs in 1954 to build a replica of Elihu Stout's print shop.[43] These files from the 1930s can probably answer similar questions for historians and preservationists about Indiana's built environment.

Trade Jargon

One of the many FWP research categories was specialized vocabulary. Fieldworkers were to collect slang phrases, indigenous dialect, and other distinctive speech patterns. In Indiana, for example, Emery Turner submitted several words that rural Lawrence County natives used instead of standard English, such as "juberous" for dubious and "low" for think.[44] James Clarence Godfroy submitted a short list of Indian vocabulary from Wabash County that contained *at-che-pong* for snapping turtle and *mek-kah* for forest.[45] Most of the linguistic submissions, however, are examples of occupational or trade jargon. National FWP administrators envisioned a book devoted to this subject, and they suggested that such industries as rubber in Ohio and automobiles in Michigan would possess rich vernacular vocabularies. New York City's writers had already begun compiling trade jargon to enhance the collection of neighborhood and ethnic vocabularies. When Congress reduced WPA/FWP activities in 1939, this project ended, and no publications resulted from the amassed lexicons.[46] Hoosier fieldworkers in thirty-six counties had collected examples of trade jargon that represented industries distinctive to the state. These files are labeled "Linguistic Materials" and contain specific vocabularies that are often akin to words from an ancient or foreign country. Many of the words and phrases are from occupations that have changed greatly or departed the Hoosier state and have thus become a lost language.

Limestone, coal, glass, and automobiles all represented industries of great importance to Indiana. Others, such as steel and oil refining, are not included in the files because Lake County fieldworkers did not collect linguistic materials. Fieldworkers visited sites of these occupations, interviewed employees, and compiled lexicons from them. Some of the inventories simply provided words with translations; others explored origins of the terminology. Estella Dodson gathered jargon from the Shawnee Stone Company in Monroe Country and compiled words that would be unintelligible to people outside the limestone industry. Who else would know that "dog holes" were locations for stonehooks, a "banker" was a bench on which a stonecutter worked, "gangs" were machines for sawing stone, and "Dutchmen" were mortised patches in a piece of finished stone?[47] The coal industry had produced equally exotic terminology, and Walter Harris submitted several examples from Clay County. A "sounder" was a worker who tested mine roofs to prevent cave-ins, "bug dust" was extremely fine cuttings of coal, and a "gob picker" extracted stone and debris from coal.[48] William Tuttle and Martha Freeman interviewed employees of the Ball Brothers glass plant in

Muncie: "dog ears" were retention rings on fruit jars, "shoestrings" were thin ribbons of zinc, and "goose eggs" were used to shape clay pots for melting glass.[49] Albert Strope and Paul Yoder visited South Bend's Studebaker complex and provided translations for some of the language there. A "tack spitter" was a trimmer on the automobile assembly line, a "horse" was a rack on which fenders were clamped, and "orange peeling" meant a puckered and defective paint job.[50]

The circus represented an important but exotic trade in Indiana because of the winter quartering grounds for several circuses in Peru. Agriculture, likewise, was distinctive because it had once dominated the state's economy but was now experiencing a gradual decline. Martha Freeman and Ed Clinton discovered that many words associated with the circus were actually euphemisms to mask unattractive or surreptitious concepts. "Bats," for instance, were old, worn-out horses to be butchered and fed to other circus animals; a "capper" was an employee who feigned winning at gambling to lure other patrons into a game; and a "glamm show" was a circus that permitted pickpockets to travel as part of the crew. The fieldworkers also discovered that some of the jargon had a humorous linguistic logic. A "merry-go-round" was not a carnival ride; instead, it was four or more workmen in a circle driving tent stakes. And "windjammers" were musicians in the circus band who played "empty marches" after performances to accompany the emptying of the seats.[51] Many fieldworkers submitted jargon from agricultural activities, and they revealed a trade in rapid transition. Many of the terms involved orders that farmers would shout as directions to horses or mules. "Gee" and "haw" and similar commands were fast disappearing as machines replaced draft animals in the fields.[52] One fascinating feature of agricultural jargon was the pervasiveness of porcine terms. Swine had been a dominant part of the rural Indiana economy since the early nineteenth century, so it was not surprising that they had wandered into the vocabulary. "Hogging down" meant allowing pigs to feed in a cornfield; "root, hog, or die" was an expression of immediate necessity; and "to hog" was to plant in a lazy, halfhearted way, such as sowing oats in corn stubble rather than plowing the field again.[53]

These thirty-six files of linguistic materials constitute a small dictionary of what fieldworkers regarded as unique vocabulary in Indiana in the 1930s. Some of the words and phrases are from an earlier pioneer period and have since passed out of usage. Other are slang and dialect that came into the state with national, ethnic, and regional migrations. A few of the submissions document variant pronunciations that sounded strange to the fieldworkers. Indiana was, in fact, a linguistic crossroads where many forms of speech joined the Hoosier mixture. The most distinctive and valuable compilations in these files are the lists of trade jargon. They represented a specialized vocabulary, used and understood by exclusive practitioners in discrete occupations. As these trades have changed through time and technology, some of this jargon has become archaic and no longer understandable. A few of these industries have exited the Hoosier state, and the jargon is no longer needed here. What the fieldworkers captured in the 1930s was a transient language that, for the most part, now exists only on paper as a record of historic workplace communication.

Ethnicity

Many of the state guides contained separate chapters devoted to Indians and blacks. A few of the states with large immigrant populations also devoted chapters to those ethnic groups as major contributors to the development of the state. With the exception of a brief chapter on Indians, the Hoosier guide did neither of these, although fieldworkers gathered hundreds of pages that documented the role of various ethnic groups in building the state and its character. State FWP director Gordon Briggs argued in the guide that Indiana was demographically "homogeneous" except for the Calumet region.[54] While German and Irish immigrants had been numerous before the Civil War, they had largely assimilated into the mainstream. The recent migrants to the industrial Northwest were atypical and had not really affected the character of the state in a substantial way. Correct or not in his assessment of ethnic contributions, Briggs kept the guide almost as homogeneous as his attitude. The fieldworker accounts of ethnic groups went largely uncited and ended up in the FWP files. They contain a wealth of information about racial, national, and ethnic traditions that were still alive in Indiana in the 1930s. These files document an Indiana far more diverse and multicultural than the guide revealed.

Fieldworkers compiled files in almost all of the counties for Indians and in nearly half for blacks (filed as Negroes). This large number is testimony to the widespread location of the two groups throughout Indiana and to their significant impact on the history of the state. Whereas the chapter on Indians in the guide focused on tribes, battles, and treaties, the material gathered by fieldworkers is more anecdotal and social. They range from oral histories in DuBois County that recall stereotypical red savages who drank, scalped, and stole[55] to thoroughly researched biographies of Frances Slocum, the white girl who became an honorary Miami Indian. James Clarence Godfroy submitted numerous essays that explained burial rituals, hunting routines, and medical practices from his Miami ancestors.[56] White fieldworkers compiled the files on blacks, and they devote more space to current conditions than to historical activity. Marion County's file surveyed the churches, schools, businesses, and clubs that catered to blacks in Indianapolis, and the Lake County file gave considerable attention to the new cooperative stores in Gary.[57] Most of the files report, without comment, the pervasive racial segregation that characterized the state in the 1930s, such as separate schools, YMCAs, and playgrounds. Hallie Winger's report from Grant County is typical in its discretion and omissions. She indicated that some black families in Marion were politically active and prosperous in 1936, but she made no mention of the lynchings that had polarized the community in 1930.[58]

Other ethnic files generally reflected demographic ratios across the state during the 1930s. There are seventeen county files for Germans, fourteen for Irish, then down the geographical list to three for Lithuania and one for Albania. Not surprisingly, the urban Marion, Lake, and St. Joseph counties were the most ethnically diverse of the ninety-two. Most of the files for Germans concentrate on cultural contributions that these immigrants made to Indiana and do not focus on the repressions they suffered during the war. For example, the Fort Wayne Turnverein (gymnastics society) was instrumental in getting physical education classes introduced into Allen County schools, and the Maennerchor (men's choral group) in Evansville and Indianapolis enriched the music offerings of those cities.[59] Fieldworker Alfred Smith learned from an interview that early German immigrants to Oldenburg in Franklin County continued to wear their traditional wooden shoes. During the winter the clatter they made on frozen ground was almost "deafening."[60] Many of the files for the Irish commented on customs that continued to distinguish them from their American neighbors. For instance, "wakes" for the deceased served as both religious and social occasions. An early Irish settlement in New Albany, near the Ohio River, came to be known as Bog Hollow because it was reminiscent of the swampy terrain in the old country.[61] Several immigrants to Jefferson County had prospered to such an extent as pork packers and factory hands that they sent loads of corn from Madison back home to Ireland during the great potato famine.[62]

These ethnic files contain multitudes of stories, many based on unpublished interviews, and serve as a needed antidote to the demographically homogeneous Indiana guide. The ones featuring Indians, blacks, Germans, Irish, Italians, Greeks, and Poles are numerous enough to provide a critical mass of information that reveals cultural patterns across the state. Others, such as Albanians, Bulgarians, and Czechs, are so limited in number as to offer only anecdotal information, no matter how fascinating. One of the few scholars to consult the FWP ethnic files is Professor William Giffin of Indiana State University. His article on the Irish in *Peopling Indiana: The Ethnic Experience,* published in 1996 by the Indiana Historical Society, makes frequent and valuable use of the materials. Giffin's work is evidence that other scholars of ethnicity in the Hoosier state could find their efforts there just as productive.

Folklore

National FWP administrators and consultants had a predilection for folklore, and they encouraged the gathering of information ranging from folksongs to witch tales. Consequently, fieldworkers gathered massive amounts of material from around the nation. More than half of the state guides contained essays about folklore, and several of the states published smaller booklets featuring other aspects of their collections. Shortly after the FWP ended, one of the national consultants, Benjamin A. Botkin, published *A Treasury of American Folklore* in 1944. This anthology of yarns, legends, songs, and tales drew heavily from the FWP collection, including Indiana's, and soon became a classic in the field. Both of Indiana's state directors were also interested in the subject, and the compilation of Hoosier folklore grew large and diverse. Ross Lockridge oversaw the publication of the pamphlet *Hoosier Tall Stories* and was preparing one on witch tales when he left the project. Gordon Briggs wrote an essay on folklore for the state guide, which used several of the fieldworkers' submissions, and he recycled many others in the weekly newspaper column "It Happened in Indiana." As was frequently the case, fieldworkers gathered far more material than the FWP could publish. The storage files, as a result, are filled with folklore that Hoosiers shared with fieldworkers in the 1930s but that has gone largely unused since then.

These Hoosier files are numerous and eclectic. Alphabetically they cover the following aspects of folklore: "Cures and Remedies," "Devil Tales," "Folk Customs—Dances, Games, etc.," "Folklore and Legends," "Folk Personalities, Folk Poems, Folk Sayings, Folk Songs and Rhymes," "Folkways," "Folk Wit and Humor," "Ghost Stories, Music and Folk Music," "Superstitions," "Tales and Sayings," "Tall Tales," and "Witch Tales." A sampling from two of these categories will indicate the nature of their contents. In their search for cures and remedies, fieldworkers compiled a pioneer pharmacopoeia gathered from interviews and old newspapers. From Starke County, Hazel Giles sent in this treatment for erysipelas: Fill a fire shovel with hot coals and pass it three times over the head of the afflicted.[63] Iris Cook found a sure cure for the flux in Floyd County: Concoct a syrup from one pound of white sugar and a pint of vinegar.[64] Sharlotte Miller discovered the ultimate ointment for burns, bites, and cuts in Noble County: Prepare a salve by mixing a pound of leaves from the live-forever plant with a pound of unsalted butter or lard and frying until soft in an iron skillet.[65] Elderly Hoosiers around the state also recalled folk songs from their youths, mainly ballads from England and slave songs from the South. In Vanderburgh County, an enterprising team of fieldworkers uncovered a variety of musical treasures: folk songs from Germany, England, and Scotland as well as southern slave songs. What also distinguishes this group of fieldworkers was their success in unearthing local songs. Helen Clark interviewed 86-year-old Philip Voelker, who recalled learning to sing "The Canal Will Be Frozen Tonight" while skating as a young man on the Wabash and Erie Canal, "the social sport of the winter in Evansville." Clark included the verses along with her transcription of the melody.[66] Odie Salm went upstream to Cannelton and interviewed 75-year-old Frederick Heck, who, as a young man in 1876, had helped write the song "Cannelton Jail." Inmates inside the jail and friends outside with a guitar combined their talents to compose this ten-verse lamentation: the bedbugs were plentiful, the cornbread was "heavy as lead," and their verdict was, "It ain't a picnic, it's a jail."[67]

Professor Ronald L. Baker has spent several years poring through the Indiana FWP folklore files. His research there is featured prominently in two books, *Hoosier Folk Legends* (1982) and *Jokelore: Humorous Folktales from Indiana* (1986). Both of these highlight many of the fieldworker submissions on Hoosier wit, ghosts, witches, and legendary characters. Baker's success in finding fascinating and valuable material in these folklore files suggests what could be found in the dozens of inventories as yet unutilized. These eight inventory topics—antiques, museums, cemetery epitaphs, Underground Railroad, historic architecture, trade jargon, ethnicity, and folklore—typify the materials that fieldworkers compiled for other categories from around the state. They reveal, in their fragmented accounts, a self-portrait of Indiana that is far more complex and textured than the official one published by the FWP in 1941.

NINE

Conclusions and Legacy

The WPA passed away quietly in 1943, with a war replacing the Depression and defense contracts providing jobs for the unemployed. This public works phenomenon had been mammoth in scope and impact. It spent more than $12 billion and employed roughly 9 million Americans to build roads, paint murals, and can beans among the myriad part-time jobs it created. In Indiana, the WPA spent slightly over $300 million on projects ranging from the Naval Ammunition Depot in Lawrence County to the Children's Theater project in Gary. Its peak month was October 1938, when 105,000 Hoosiers worked for the WPA.[1] Some of the projects created a physical legacy, such as bridges, parks, and public buildings, many of which are still in use. Other projects were ephemeral in nature, such as sewing rooms and orchestra concerts, whose products were designed to be worn or heard and then disappear. Despite its size, and perhaps because of it, the WPA was generally not loved. Frequently accused of being socialism, often attacked for make-work boondoggling, and sometimes involved in partisan New Deal politics, the WPA was a large and easy target for conservative critics. When the state office closed in 1943, the *Indianapolis News* noted that the passing went "unwept, unsung, and all but unhonored." According to the editors, the WPA had produced a few good public works, but "half the money was wasted." Hopefully, for most of the workers "the scars of that humiliating experiment have healed."[2] This was a harsh verdict for the recently deceased giant.

Would the Federal Writers' Project receive the same kind of verdict? After all, it was a part of the WPA and shared both the strengths and weaknesses of its parent organization. Its two best-known activities generally got positive reactions. The publication of its guide series had met with favorable reviews and good sales, and historians gave guarded praise to its collection of interviews with former slaves. Several political critics, on the other hand, declared that the FWP harbored too many radicals and that its publications were too negative in their treatment of American democracy and capitalism. Congress in effect punished the FWP in 1939 by forcing it to find private sponsorship for part of its activity. Most of the periodicals that noted its death bade it a fond farewell, and scholars from the 1960s to the early twenty-first century have been kind to the FWP and its legacy. They approved of government support for unemployed artists, appreciated the sustaining benefits that the program offered to struggling writers during the Depression, and applauded the quality of the work they produced. The demise of the FWP in Indiana, almost a year prior to that of the WPA, was so quiet that few newspapers noted the passing or made editorial comment. Since then only a handful of scholars have mentioned its work or used its records. The virtual silence that surrounds the Indiana FWP should not, however, be interpreted as a negative verdict. To ignore something is not necessarily to condemn it.

Because of its small size, it is easy to dismiss the Writers' Project as a welfare program. At its peak, it hired only 6,500 white-collar Americans, and in Indiana it rarely had more than 150 people on its payroll. Due to frequent turnover of personnel within the WPA, it is possible that as many as 10,000 so-called writers worked for the project between 1935 and 1943.[3] The same kind of estimate would place no more than 300 Hoosiers within its ranks. These are insignificant numbers considering the multitudes who worked on other public works projects. And the amount of money the FWP placed in the hands of consumers barely made a dent in the Depression. Nationally the project spent roughly $27 million, a not inconsiderable sum, but it amounted to less than 1 percent of the WPA total.[4] In Indiana that would have totaled less than $1.5 million spread over nearly seven years. The average Hoosier fieldworker of the FWP earned slightly under $100 per month.[5] In light of the billions of dollars paid to millions of American relief workers, the FWP financial picture is a miniature portrait in the New Deal gallery.

That portrait takes on more positive dimensions when the statistics are fleshed out with human stories. Harry Hopkins's famous remark that artists needed to eat just as other people did served as a justification for creating white-collar relief jobs. Whenever possible, the WPA tried to tailor jobs to the skills of the unemployed rather than putting a musician to work at road construction or asking a stenographer to dig ditches. Hence the FWP permitted writers, or reasonably literate individuals, to work at a professional trade. Helping these workers to maintain their dignity was as much a part of this experiment as was the salary for these temporarily displaced occupants of the middle class. As fieldworker Emery C. Turner argued in a guest editorial for the *Indianapolis Star*, he felt his work was valuable and he took pride in it.[6] An examination of several Hoosier FWP employees reveals that their skills were appropriately utilized in many of their assignments, and they performed as professionals, not just workers doing whatever was available. Their experiences with the FWP allowed them to continue the type of work they were trained to do, such as researching, interviewing, analyzing, writing, and editing. If they were young, these assignments permitted them to keep their skills polished and ready to use again in the private sector when the economy improved. If they were older, the experience allowed them to maintain a familiar routine without having to master strange new techniques at the end of their careers. In either case, the maintenance of a professional lifestyle during the national emergency helped alleviate family disruptions that would have occurred if different or distant work opportunities had become necessary. This unprecedented federal subsidy for writers actually appears to have been more of a humane experience than the humiliation described by the *Indianapolis News.* The presence of the FWP, in Indiana at least, seems to have prevented more scars than it inflicted.

Five full-time employees at the state headquarters in Indianapolis are examples of how the FWP either perpetuated or enhanced their careers as writers.

- When Ross Lockridge resigned as Indiana FWP director in 1937, he was denied credit for his visions, which shaped the future of the program. But he returned to his previous dual career as impresario and writer. He directed the Hoosier Historical Institute, an agency of the Indiana University Foundation, which allowed him to continue his pilgrimages, making speeches and placing historical markers around the state. Lockridge also published four more books before his death in 1952. He and his son, Ross Jr., completed *The Old Fauntleroy Home,* which they had started during the FWP period, and his *Story of Indiana* became a standard junior high school text for several years.[7]

- Whereas FWP administrative chores had temporarily slowed Lockridge's productivity, they accelerated and climaxed the writing career of his successor, Gordon Briggs. Previously Briggs had been a journalist and public relations officer whose work was more frequently anonymous than not. With the appearance of *Indiana: A Guide* in 1941, he was officially and publicly the chief editor and partial author. When the Indiana FWP ended in 1942, so did Briggs's writing career. He died in 1954, at age 62, while employed as a purchasing agent for the Indianapolis Board of Park Commissioners.[8]

- Before Dickson J. Preston became assistant state director of the Indiana FWP at age 25, he had only limited experience as a journalist with the *Indianapolis Times.* At the FWP he rapidly added new skills to his résumé, including editing county histories and writing the unpublished "Pictorial History of Indiana." He later used those skills, from 1943 through 1966, when he worked for the *Cleveland Press* and the Scripps-Howard syndicate in Washington, D.C. Then he devoted his energies to writing history, something he had begun with the FWP. Among his many books were a biography, *Young Frederick Douglass,* and *Newspapers of Maryland's Eastern Shore.*[9]

- Bessie Roberts had journalism experience in Fort Wayne and Evansville before becoming an editor for the Indiana FWP. While there she collaborated with Lockridge on two collections of folklore. After leaving the FWP, she returned to Fort Wayne, where she continued to pursue her interests in folklore and history. She became the author of several books, one of which, *Fort Wayne's Family Album,* received an award from the American Association for State and Local History in 1960.[10]

- Rebecca Pitts had earlier envisioned a career as a writer in New York, a goal she pursued following her work as an FWP editor. In the late 1940s she returned to Indiana and taught English at several colleges. The cold war tensions at that time briefly threatened her teaching career, and she attributed her dismissal from Butler University in 1948 to her early ties with communism. As the Red Scare receded, she flourished as both teacher and writer, primarily at the Indianapolis campus of Indiana University. She channeled her radicalism into the environmental and feminist movements, and at the time of her death in 1983, she was working on a book of poetry, *Brief Authority,* which appeared posthumously.[11]

A few of the Indiana fieldworkers had been professional writers before joining the FWP. They had pursued careers as playwrights and journalists, primarily, and the Depression temporarily halted their livelihoods. Their stints as fieldworkers offered them an opportunity to continue their work as writers until returning to the private sector or retiring.

- Charles Bruce Millholland from Indianapolis was one of the few Hoosier fieldworkers who had been successful as a creative writer, both on Broadway and in Hollywood, before joining the FWP. Typical of many fieldworkers, he performed numerous tasks, but his largest endeavor was the ill-fated monograph on Bedford's limestone industry. He left the FWP and continued to pursue a career in show business as a playwright and actor. When younger producers transformed his play *Twentieth Century* into a musical in 1978, he received new levels of celebrity and royalties.[12]

- Emery Turner's journalism career stopped when his employer, the *Louisville Herald Post,* went out of business during the Depression. Turner was one of the more versatile and prolific fieldworkers, filing reports on historic buildings, slave interviews, trade jargon, and many other assignments. Turner was 52 when the FWP met its demise, and he did not resume his journalism career. He held a variety of jobs in his hometown of Bedford before his death in 1956.[13]

- William W. Tuttle was already 65 when he joined the FWP in Muncie. He had been a teacher and a grocer in addition to writing newspaper columns for twenty-five years. Like Turner, he was versatile and prolific on a variety of assignments, and likewise, largely due to his advanced age, did not resume a writing career. He died two years after the FWP expired while employed by Western Union.[14]

The majority of fieldworkers, both nationally and in Indiana, were not writers by trade. They were unemployed professionals such as teachers, librarians, and musicians for whom writing was not an alien concept, so they could easily transfer from relief rolls to the WPA and the FWP. Their experience as fieldworkers often enhanced their writing credentials and their attitude about the craft.

- Iris Cook was a professional violinist in New Albany who proved adventurous and resourceful as a fieldworker. Her many interviews and passionate reports about the Ohio River flood were typical of her work. During the Second World War, she volunteered for the Women's Army Corps, and following the war she continued her education, worked for the Kentucky Commission for Handicapped Children, and played violin with the Louisville Orchestra.[15]

• Lauana Creel had been a music teacher in Evansville, and her record as a fieldworker rivaled that of Iris Cook. Her interviews and reports were lengthy and often emotional, and national consultants praised her success in gathering folklore materials. She was 57 when the FWP died, and she subsequently held a variety of clerical positions, but she listed her occupation in the city directory as "writer," a tribute to the impact the FWP had on her self-identity.[16]

• Albert Strope had taught for many years in Mishawaka. As a fieldworker he collected tall tales, interviewed former slaves, and charted routes and sites for the tour section of the Indiana guide. Strope did not return to teaching after the Depression; instead, he worked at the Oliver farm equipment plant until his retirement in 1963.[17]

• James Clarence Godfroy had been a farmer, factory worker, and vaudeville performer. But the job he took most seriously was that of storyteller, an imparter of Miami oral history from one generation to the next. The FWP made good use of this skill by allowing him to conduct interviews and put in written form many of the tribal traditions and folklore. Godfroy continued his eclectic trades until his death in 1962. Shortly before his death, he dictated many of his stories to a neighbor, Martha McClurg, who had them transcribed and published in 1961 as *Miami Indian Stories*. A large number of these stories are almost verbatim renditions of his FWP reports. His decades of repetitive storytelling froze the material so that the oral and written versions were identical. At the time of his death, he was one of the few fieldworkers who had become an author of a published book.

Although the economic impact of the FWP was minimal and the effect on employees temporary and transitional, the published results of the program were permanent and assessable. Just as WPA workers graced the Indiana landscape with new roads, sidewalks, and public buildings, FWP employees contributed to Hoosier bookshelves and libraries the printed words that were the end product of their labors. These books and articles were tangible products that had both an immediate impact on literary consumers during the Depression and an indefinite shelf life for future readers. Today they represent the result of an unprecedented government relief project and provide a window for experiencing the attitudes of a now-distant generation of Hoosiers.

Since most of these publications received popular acceptance when they appeared, it would seem that their opinions were in synch with those of the state's population. Through inclusion and omission, the fieldworkers and editors revealed their personal attitudes and priorities about natural resources, history, race, ethnicity, gender, urbanization, and the arts. Hoosier critics and audiences at the time appeared to concur with the interpretations and conclusions. After the Second World War, as new viewpoints replaced old traditions, some of the interpretations in the FWP publications met with critical scrutiny and challenge. These publications, therefore, are a kind of literary time capsule for a generation. They reflect the period in which they were written, their intellectual positions exposed on the printed page for later generations to accept or contest.

Indiana: A Guide was the major undertaking of the Hoosier FWP, the best-known of its publications, and the most accessible to future readers. The book took six years to complete, making it the forty-seventh of the state guides to appear, and one national critic regarded it as one of the best of the series.[18] The national FWP editors dictated the format of the American Guide series, but there was allowance for state individuality. Indiana took advantage of this allowance and produced a book that reflected much of its own character, for better or for worse. Unlike many of the other states, Indiana did not include separate essays on blacks, immigration, or sports, choosing instead to integrate the material into other essays.

The first two topics probably indicated the low priority that Indiana FWP editors placed on the contributions of these small populations, and the latter an admission that basketball and auto racing were so woven into the fabric of Hoosier life that they were inseparable from everyday activities. Although women formed roughly half of the Indiana FWP staff, women make scant appearance in the guide. This absence reflects the silent roles women played in the early days of the state and their deferential attitude about editorial decisions. National administrators had to remind the state editors to include information about more Hoosier women, such as physician Alice Hamilton and sculptor Janet Scudder.[19] And despite the mandated essays on principal cities, Indiana's guide maintained a firm pattern of urban denial. Some of the cities included in this section were not urban at all but were distinctive historical communities, such as Corydon and New Harmony. The state's personality, said the editors, was still rural regardless of the fact that the federal census had proven otherwise. Essays on natural setting and agriculture emphasized the prevailing rural qualities of Indiana, and the state editors praised the work of county agricultural and home demonstration agents. These ambassadors from Purdue University, according to the editors, had made a campus of the "entire state."[20]

Although a period piece of the Great Depression, *Indiana: A Guide* has enjoyed both popularity and longevity. Most of the reviews of the book in state newspapers were positive, discounting some quibbles over factual mistakes, and the book sold well. This vote of confidence by the Hoosier public convinced Oxford University Press to keep the book available with five printings through the 1960s. In 1973 Somerset reissued the book to meet the continuing demand. Other institutions have paid tribute to its impact. The staff of the public library in Fort Wayne found the essay on their city so helpful as a reference tool that they reprinted it as a booklet in 1957.[21] The Indiana Historical Society regarded the tours section as a valuable service to people who wanted to visit both the Hoosier past and contemporary sites. Consequently they published *Indiana: A New Historical Guide* in 1989. It was a tribute to the FWP guides in that the concept of annotated tours was worthy of repeating.

205

Several scholars have also paid tribute to the enduring appeal of the series by revisiting parts of them in anthologies. The Indiana guide has been well represented in these collections. Historian Bernard Weisberger reprinted eight excerpts and one photograph in his *WPA Guide to America*. These excerpts featured items that he found unique or especially well written, such as the community of Gnaw Bone, the story of Diana of the Dunes, and the analysis of the Hoosier character. In *Remembering America,* Archie Hobson reprinted twelve items and displayed particular interest in the Conn cornet factory in Elkhart, the town of Santa Claus, and the dramatic prose that described the industrial landscape of the Calumet region.

Other publications of the Indiana FWP were distinctive but more limited in their circulation and impact than the guide. The *Calumet Region Historical Guide* was the only truly urban publication that the Hoosier project produced. It surveyed the most industrialized and ethnically diverse region of the state and dealt candidly with racial, religious, ethnic, and national differences that barely affected other sections of the state. Produced and circulated primarily within the region in 1940, the book made little impact on the rest of Indiana. Calumet area newspapers reviewed it positively; it sold well locally and was reprinted in 1975, testifying to its continuing appeal. Outside of the region, however, copies of the book are difficult to locate. *Hoosier Tall Stories* had a brief and popular life in 1937. This mimeographed collection was a showcase for folktales and whoppers that were passed around at rural meeting sites such as the liars' bench. It circulated to schools and libraries and served as a model for other state writers' projects. Despite its brief flurry of fame, the inexpensive format doomed it to a short life span, and today it can be found mostly in library collections. *Indiana: Facts, Events, Places, Tours,* although a slick and handy compendium of travel information, made barely a splash in Indiana. It was printed out of state, was aimed at tourists, and received hardly any in-state publicity. Small in format and containing mainly recycled materials from the guide, it is mostly forgotten and difficult to locate today. The newspaper column "It Happened in Indiana" appeared weekly in approximately seventy state newspapers. Because it was supplied free of cost, many of the papers gladly printed it, so it had wide exposure. Filled with history, folklore, and Hoosier ephemera, it may have elevated the name recognition of the FWP among leisure readers. Because its goals were merely to amuse or gently enlighten, its impact was minimal. Today "It Happened in Indiana" is known only to individuals who stumble across it while researching in Indiana newspapers from 1940 to 1942. The study guide written by the Indiana FWP for American naturalization classes circulated only among resident aliens who were preparing for citizenship examinations. Designed exclusively for this purpose, it had no publicity or impact outside this specific audience.

The public impact of the FWP slave narratives was slow and controversial, but ultimately significant. These interviews with elderly black Hoosiers were part of a national program that gathered biographical information from more than two thousand individuals in seventeen states. Approximately a hundred of the interviews took place in Indiana and produced a rich cache of material about life during slavery. They also produced valuable information about life after slavery for these new citizens who had migrated to Indiana, where they struggled to get education, jobs, and decent housing in a largely segregated society. Most had been hit hard by the Depression, and they welcomed the New Deal relief programs. At the time of the interviews in 1937 and 1938, very little publicity accompanied the project, and they received virtually no public attention. And like the national collection, they were rarely used by scholars where they were stored in the Library of Congress. Not until they were published in the 1970s did most Americans become aware of their existence and potential value. Despite debates and caveats about their trustworthiness as historical documents, the interviews have been used increasingly as a source of information about life in bondage and the trials of freedom after the Civil War. In recent years the collection has received widespread coverage. The Smithsonian Institution sponsored an audio documentary, broadcast by public radio stations, in which actors read portions of the interviews. This program, *Remembering Slavery,* included a book of the same title, in which historian Ira Berlin and others placed the FWP and the slave narratives in context. HBO television recognized this growing interest and produced a popular documentary called *Unchained Memories,* which accomplished visually what *Remembering Slavery* had done aurally. It, too, came with a companion book that provided additional details about the FWP and the richness of the interview collection.[22] This production featured John W. Fields, a former slave who had moved to Lafayette, Indiana, where he enjoyed a successful and literate life. Ronald Baker's book *Homeless, Friendless, and Penniless* made the Indiana interviews fully and easily accessible in 2000. His book probably informed more Hoosiers about the narratives than anything in their long, quiet history. After many decades of being ignored, then questioned, this unique chapter of the past finally found an audience. What had begun as an exercise to capture and preserve historical memory has become a resource for mass entertainment.

Beyond the immediate impact of the publications and the delayed reception of the slave narratives, the work of the Indiana FWP has received scant attention. This is unfortunate because the overwhelming majority of the fieldworkers' reports involved interviews and research that are now difficult or impossible to locate. A few of the unfinished or unpublished projects have eventually become available to the public. For example, the Indiana Historical Society copied and bound some of the county histories for use in its library; Nelson Algren's *America Eats* belatedly reached publication; Ronald Baker adapted parts of the manuscript on Creole heritage in Vincennes into his book on the same subject; and the Indiana Department of Natural Resources printed Hurley Goodall's collection of FWP material concerning the Underground Railroad. Many other projects, representing months of research, writing, and editing, still rest unread in storage in Terre Haute. Some are more nearly finished than others, such as Gordon Briggs's article on the Belgian colony of Mishawaka, Dickson J. Preston's pictorial history of Indiana, and Bessie Roberts's collection of witch stories, "Pricking Thumbs." Others were still unformed masses of raw but valuable research, such as the Kankakee monograph, the James Whitcomb Riley memorial project, the sociological study of Bedford, and first-hand accounts of the Ohio River flood in 1937. And the inventories of information about dozens of topics ranging from antiques to Yugoslavian immigrants contain data and anecdotes about the Hoosier state found nowhere else.

Roosevelt's New Deal established the WPA/FWP in 1935, the same year it created Social Security, the National Labor Relations Act, and the Public Utility Holding Company Act. The collective creation of these new programs appeared to many conservatives as an attempt to increase the power of the federal government, compete with private enterprise, punish big business, become partners with organized labor unions, and establish a welfare state that would subvert individual initiative. In short, the New Deal seemed to these critics a radical attack on traditional capitalism and earned it the status of being, at the least, socialistic. The investigations of the Dies Committee in 1938 showed just how strongly many conservatives believed that communist influence had infiltrated the government, especially the Federal Theater and Writers' projects. Indiana's FWP escaped the wrath of this conservative backlash, despite the youthful left-wing writings of some of its personnel, but the charge of New Deal radicalism was a difficult one to shake off. Washington administrators set standards and demanded adherence to federal guidelines. State directors and editors who could not or would not comply were fired, as was the case with Ross Lockridge, or forced to rewrite, as did Rebecca Pitts. These federal officials granted only rare allowance for state individualism, a pattern in keeping with other New Deal initiatives. The demise of the WPA in 1943 removed one of the more visible arms of the welfare state, the arm that had allegedly subsidized boondogglers and coddled communists. When federal support for writers returned in 1965 with the national endowment for the arts and humanities, the underlying concept was similar to the FWP, although the execution was considerably different, since the government largess came in the form of grants instead of wages. The controversies and criticism that resulted from the programs were reminiscent of those that had greeted the FWP thirty years earlier. Disagreements over federal rules, individual taste, and taxpayers' money all had a familiar sound. Missing from this later debate, however, was the charge of radicalism. That concept had apparently faded as a threat to the status quo as the New Deal legacy merged increasingly into mainstream America.

As mentioned in the introduction, almost fifty years after the publication of the famous American Guide series, historian Bernard A. Weisberger referred to the books as an "immensely valuable" treasure for students of American civilization. Their aggregate effect was that of "national self-portraiture."[23] The guides provided a brief trek back into the nation's past and an extended journey across the contemporary landscape of the 1930s. America's self-portrait was the composite work of thousands of FWP fieldworkers subsidized by the federal government to portray their country firsthand. The resulting picture was surprisingly upbeat, considering that the fieldworkers were relief workers, victims of the Great Depression. Their portrayal was a positive one without hero worship, heavier on folklore than muckraking, quicker to amuse than to reproach. Weisberger's analogy of self-portrait certainly holds true for the Indiana guide. It renders a miniature of the Hoosier past and an expansive mural of the contemporary scene. And typical of portraitists, the FWP personnel injected their attitudes and interpretations into the finished product. The result, as published in 1941, was an ambivalent portrait of a white male of western European stock, reading James Whitcomb Riley's poetry while standing on a bridge built by the WPA. The other Indiana FWP publications, whether books, stories, or newspaper columns, offer this same gently conflicted portrait, a state and a people clinging to rural traditions while giving grudging thanks for New Deal innovations.

Ross Lockridge, Gordon Briggs, and Rebecca Pitts are probably more responsible than anyone else for the Hoosier self-portrait that emerged from the FWP. Lockridge was a native who loved his home state and developed a version of its past and character that was heroic, dramatic, romantic, and nostalgic. He was a living personification of that vision, and his two years of leadership influenced much of the final product even after he left as director. Briggs's years in New York and Washington shaped his intellect more than did his recent residency in Indiana. Consequently he was unable to see the state as urban or ethnically diverse; his Indiana in the 1930s was still rural and homogeneous. Likewise, Briggs's abiding love for folklore probably diverted the FWP research and publications away from Lockridge's heroic pioneers to his more ephemeral stories and legends. The left-wing activism that Pitts brought to the editorial office sometimes tinted the self-portrait ideologically, simply because she wrote or rewrote so much of the copy for the state guide. The essay on New Harmony was a subtle argument for communal goals, women's rights, and a classless society that Marx and Lenin might have applauded. And Eugene V. Debs's gentle socialism appears far too many times to be coincidental. With these three individuals in charge, there should be little wonder that the resulting self-portrait was ambivalent and conflicted.

Three collections of FWP papers flesh out this official published portrait and give a fuller picture of Indiana in the 1930s. They are located in the Library of Congress, National Archives, and Cunningham Library at Indiana State University. These repositories contain the raw research, unfinished manuscripts, interviews, and administrative correspondence that reveal the background materials for the finished products. These three archival windows offer a view of Indiana that is far more urban, female, multiracial, and multiethnic than the published works portray. The heretofore unused public memories present more local, personal, and idiosyncratic versions of the Hoosier past and character than do the officially approved ones. By combining the published accounts and unpublished records, an Indiana of the Depression decade emerges that is more complex and less nostalgic than that found in the FWP books and articles.

Jerre Mangione served as one of the FWP editors in Washington and wrote a memoir of the experience thirty years after its demise. He described the confusion that accompanied the Depression and some of the New Deal programs, but recalled that he and some of his associates "felt we had never done anything of more value in our lifetime. . . . We had the sense of being part of a significant historical event. . . . For nothing like the Writers' Project or the other three federal arts projects had ever been tried by any nation anywhere."[24] Mangione admitted that many other FWP employees disagreed and regarded their unemployment and government subsidies as a "secret shame" not to be mentioned in their personal résumés.[25]

This ambivalence also appears among Hoosiers who participated in the program. Emery Turner displayed an attitude similar to Mangione's in a guest editorial for the *Indianapolis Star* on May 8, 1940. He said he felt no shame about being on relief and that he was proud to be a fieldworker with the FWP because it involved "honest, worth-while work." For several of the full-time administrators and editors, there was no attempt to conceal their stint with the project. Résumés published during their lifetimes and obituaries prepared later by family or friends mentioned the FWP for Ross Lockridge, Rebecca Pitts, Dickson J. Preston, and Bessie Roberts. But for many of the fieldworkers, this time and work rarely surfaces. Even some of the more successful and prolific employees have no coverage of the FWP in their death notices. For example, obituaries of Emery Turner, Iris Cook, William Tuttle, Clarence Godfroy, and Albert Strope make no reference to this chapter in their lives. Granted, this chapter was a brief one, and they were largely anonymous individuals at the time. So this ambivalence about unemployment and relief work is understandable for the FWP employees, but there need be neither silence nor shame about their legacy. The publications they researched and wrote provided a valuable self-portrait of Indiana and a mirror to the Depression decade. More important, they compiled an even larger body of unpublished materials that is slowly proving invaluable to current scholars. Emery Turner was right: their job of exhuming and preserving large portions of the Hoosier past was truly "worth-while work."

NOTES

Introduction

1. Alfred Kazin, *On Native Grounds* (New York: Harcourt, Brace and World, 1942), 489.

2. Bernard A. Weisberger, *WPA Guide to America: The Best of 1930s America as Seen by the Federal Writers' Project* (New York: Pantheon, 1985), xi–xii.

3. Jerre Mangione, *The Dream and the Deal: The Federal Writers' Project, 1935–1943* (Boston, 1972); Monty N. Penkower, *The Federal Writers' Project: A Study in Government Patronage of the Arts* (Urbana: University of Illinois Press, 1977); Paul Sporn, *Against Itself: The Federal Theater and Writers' Projects in the Midwest* (Detroit: Wayne State University Press, 1995); Jerrold Hirsch, *Portrait of America: A Cultural History of the Federal Writers' Project* (Chapel Hill, 2003).

4. John Bodnar, *Remaking America: Public Memory, Commemoration, and Patriotism in the Twentieth Century* (Princeton, N.J.: Princeton University Press, 1992), 114.

1. The National Context

1. Bureau of the Census, *Historical Statistics of the United States* (Washington, D.C., 1975), 135.

2. See Alan Brinkley, *Voices of Protest: Huey Long, Father Coughlin, and the Great Depression* (New York: Alfred A. Knopf, 1982); David M. Kennedy, *Freedom from Fear: The American People in Depression and War, 1929–1945* (New York: Oxford University Press, 1999), chap. 8; George H. Gallup, *The Gallup Poll, 1935–1971* (New York, 1972), 1:5.

3. Richard Hofstadter, *The Age of Reform* (New York: Vintage Press, 1955), 97.

4. Richard B. Morris, *Encyclopedia of American History,* rev. ed. (New York: Harper, 1961), 337, 340.

5. Kennedy, *Freedom from Fear,* chap. 8; and William E. Leuchtenburg, *Franklin D. Roosevelt and the New Deal* (New York: Harper and Row, 1963), chap. 5.

6. Lincoln Steffens, *The Letters of Lincoln Steffens* (New York: Harcourt, Brace, 1938), 1:463.

7. See Kennedy, *Freedom from Fear*, 226; Daniel Aaron, *Writers on the Left: Episodes in American Literary Communism* (New York: Columbia University Press, 1992).

8. Leo Gurko, *The Angry Decade: American Literature and Thought from 1929 to Pearl Harbor* (New York: Harper, 1968) 180.

9. Works Projects Administration, *Final Report on the WPA Program, 1935–1943* (Washington, D.C., 1946), 30 and 124.

10. Robert E. Sherwood, *Roosevelt and Hopkins: An Intimate History* (New York: Harper, 1948), 57.

11. Hallie Flanagan, *Arena: The Story of the Federal Theatre* (New York: Duell, Sloan and Pearce, 1940), 435.

12. See Jane D. Mathews, *The Federal Theatre, 1935–1939: Plays, Relief, and Politics* (Princeton, N.J.: Princeton University Press, 1967).

13. See Kenneth J. Bindas, *All of This Music Belongs to the Nation: The WPA's Federal Music Project and American Society* (Knoxville: University of Tennessee Press, 1995).

14. See Richard D. McKinzie, *The New Deal for Artists* (Princeton, N.J.: Princeton University Press, 1973).

15. Kathleen O'Conner McKinzie, "Writers on Relief, 1935–1942" (Ph.D. diss., Indiana University, 1970); Mangione, *The Dream and the Deal;* Penkower, *Federal Writers' Project.*

16. Robert E. Spiller et al., eds., *Literary History of the United States* (New York: Macmillan, 1949), 2:1264; McKinzie, "Writers on Relief," 3–4.

17. Edward Weeks, "Hard Times and the Author," *Atlantic Monthly,* May 1935, 554–57.

18. Penkower, *Federal Writers' Project,* 4.

19. Charles E. Rush, "The Book Buyer Speaks Out," *Saturday Review of Literature,* January 30, 1932, 485.

20. Spiller, *Literary History of the United States,* 2:1265.

21. William F. McDonald, *Federal Relief Administration and the Arts* (Columbus: Ohio State University Press, 1969), 650–52.

22. Mangione, *The Dream and the Deal,* 34.

23. McKinzie, "Writers on Relief," 9–12.

24. Harry L. Hopkins, "Food for the Hungry," *Colliers,* December 7, 1935, 62.

25. "Unemployed Arts," *Fortune* 15 (May 1937): 172.

26. Penkower, *Federal Writers' Project,* 62.

27. Mangione, *The Dream and the Deal,* 9.

28. McKinzie, "Writers on Relief," 256.

29. Mangione, *The Dream and the Deal*, 369.

30. Blair Bolles, "The Federal Writers' Project," *Saturday Review of Literature* 18 (July 9, 1938): 4.

31. Penkower, *Federal Writers' Project*, 238.

32. Matthew Josephson, *Infidel in the Temple: A Memoir of the Nineteen-Thirties* (New York: Alfred A. Knopf, 1967), 377.

33. Mangione, *The Dream and the Deal*, 9 and 119.

34. McKinzie, "Writers on Relief," 20–21; Mangione, *The Dream and the Deal*, 53–58; Penkower, *Federal Writers' Project*, 18–20.

35. McDonald, *Federal Relief Administration and the Arts*, 665.

36. Malcom Cowley, "Federal Writers' Project," *New Republic*, October 21, 1972, 24.

37. Mangione, *The Dream and the Deal*, 331.

38. *Time*, August 12, 1940, 64.

39. McDonald, *Federal Relief Administration and the Arts*, 687.

40. Penkower, *Federal Writers' Project*, 33.

41. Ray Allen Billington, "Government and the Arts: The WPA Experience," *American Quarterly* 13 (Winter 1961): 477.

42. McKinzie, "Writers on Relief," 247.

43. "WPAccounting," *Time*, February 15, 1943, 95–96.

44. Robert Cantwell, "America and the Writers' Project," *New Republic* 98 (April 26, 1939): 323.

45. Penkower, *Federal Writers' Project*, 227.

46. Henry G. Alsberg, ed., *The American Guide: A Source Book and Complete Travel Guide for the United States* (New York: Hastings House, 1949).

47. John Steinbeck, *Travels with Charley: In Search of America* (New York: Bantam, 1962), 134.

48. Geoffrey O'Gara, *A Long Road Home* (New York: Norton, 1989), xv.

49. Archie Hobson, ed., *Remembering America: A Sampler of the WPA American Guide Series* (New York: Columbia University Press, 1985).

50. Mangione, *The Dream and the Deal*, 352; Penkower, *Federal Writers' Project*, 234.

51. Penkower, *Federal Writers' Project*, 154.

52. Mangione, *The Dream and the Deal*, 268.

53. W. T. Couch, *These Are Our Lives* (Chapel Hill: University of North Carolina Press, 1939), 420.

54. Ibid., xi.

55. Benjamin Botkin, ed., *A Treasury of American Folklore* (New York: Crown, 1944); Tom E. Terrill and Jerrold Hirsch, *Such as Us: Southern Voices of the Thirties* (Chapel Hill: University of North Carolina Press, 1978); Ann Banks, *First-Person America* (New York: Alfred A. Knopf, 1980); Nancy J.

Martin-Perdue and Charles L. Perdue Jr., *Talk about Trouble: A New Deal Portrait of Virginians in the Great Depression* (Chapel Hill: University of North Carolina Press, 1996).

56. McDonald, *Federal Relief Administration and the Arts,* 720.

57. Ibid., 721.

58. Charles L. Perdue Jr. et al., eds., *Weevils in the Wheat: Interviews with Virginia Ex-Slaves* (Charlottesville: University of Virginia Press, 1976).

59. C. Vann Woodward, "History from Slave Sources," *American Historical Review* 79 (April 1974): 470–81; John Blassingame, "Using the Testimony of Ex-Slaves," *Journal of Southern History,* November 1975, 473–92.

60. Benjamin A. Botkin, *Lay My Burden Down: A Folk History of Slavery* (Chicago: University of Chicago Press, 1945), ix.

61. James W. Davidson and Mark H. Lytle, *After the Fact: The Art of Historical Detection,* 2nd ed. (New York: Alfred A. Knopf, 1986), 201–02.

62. Woodward, "History from Slave Sources," 475.

63. McDonald, *Federal Relief Administration and the Arts,* 701.

64. Mangione, *The Dream and the Deal,* 244–47.

65. *New York Times Book Review,* August 29, 1937, 2.

66. McKinzie, "Writers on Relief," chap. 7.

67. *Washington Post,* December 11, 1938, III, 1.

68. Mangione, *The Dream and the Deal,* 308.

69. Penkower, *Federal Writers' Project,* 197.

70. Mangione, *The Dream and the Deal,* 308.

71. Mathews, *The Federal Theatre,* 222 and 226.

72. *Nation,* August, 19, 1939, 23–24; Hirsch, *Portrait of America,* 212.

73. McDonald, *Federal Relief Administration and the Arts,* 306–07.

74. Penkower, *Federal Writers' Project,* 229.

75. Mangione, *The Dream and the Deal,* 48.

76. McDonald, *Federal Relief Administration and the Arts,* 747.

77. *New York Times,* September 14, 1938, 27.

2. The Hoosier Situation

1. Bureau of the Census, *Statistical Abstracts of the United States, 1938* (Washington, D.C., 1939), 90–96.

2. Indiana, *Yearbook,* 1930–33, pp. 352, 820, 604, 803.

3. Indiana, *Yearbook,* 1931–34, pp. 575, 201, 282, 475.

4. Bureau of the Census, *Financial Statistics of Cities, 1929–1932,* pp. 90–91.

5. Indiana, *Report of Study Commission for Indiana Financial Institutions* (Indianapolis, 1932), 54; Indiana Bankers Association, *Report of the Research Committee* (Indianapolis, 1937), 103; Indiana, *Yearbook,* 1932, p. 41.

6. Indiana, *Yearbook of the Governor's Commission on Unemployment Relief, 1933–1935* (Indianapolis, 1935), 19 and 36.

7. James B. Lane, *City of the Century: A History of Gary, Indiana* (Bloomington: Indiana University Press, 1978), 162.

8. *Recovery in Indiana*, official bulletin of the Governor's Commission on Unemployment Relief, December 1934, 22–24.

9. Harold Barger and Hans Landsberg, *American Agriculture, 1899–1939: A Study of Output, Employment, and Productivity* (New York: National Bureau of Economic Research, 1942), 348; Bureau of the Census, *Statistical Abstracts, 1938*, 8.

10. Raymond Mohl and Neil Betten, *Steel City: Urban and Ethnic Patterns in Gary, Indiana, 1906–1950* (New York: Holmes and Meier, 1986), 104.

11. Robert S. Lynd and Helen M. Lynd, *Middletown in Transition: A Study in Cultural Conflicts* (New York: Harcourt, Brace, 1937), 105, 113, and 199.

12. Edward A. Leary, *Indianapolis: The Story of a City* (Indianapolis: Bobbs-Merrill, 1971), 208.

13. Anonymous interview by author, fall 1974.

14. Theodore Whiting, ed., *Final Statistical Report of the Federal Emergency Relief Administration* (Washington, D.C., 1942), 145.

15. *Recovery in Indiana*, May 3, 1934, 7.

16. Bureau of the Census, *Statistical Abstracts, 1938*, 264, and *Recovery in Indiana*, November 1934, 9.

17. Indiana, *Yearbook*, 1933, p. 379, and 1934, p. 591.

18. See I. George Blake, *Paul V. McNutt: Portrait of a Hoosier Statesman* (Indianapolis: Central, 1966) and Robert R. Neff, "The Early Career and Governorship of Paul V. McNutt" (Ph.D. diss., Indiana University, 1963).

19. *Indianapolis Star*, May 29, 1932 and Indiana, *Yearbook*, 1932, p 1479.

20. *Indianapolis News*, September 16, 1935, and *Indianapolis Times*, September 16, 1935.

21. *Indianapolis News*, February 7, 1935, and Brinkley, *Voices of Protest*, 285.

22. "Wayne Coy," Indiana Biography Series, 36:17; *Who Was Who in America*, vol. 3: *1951–1961* (Chicago: Marquis, 1960), 190.

23. *Indianapolis Star*, September 30, 1972; *Indianapolis News*, March 30, 1937.

24. WPA, *Final Report*, 111 and 120.

25. *Recovery in Indiana*, May 1936, p. 6.

26. Iwan Morgan, "Fort Wayne and the Great Depression: The New Deal Years, 1933–1940," *Indiana Magazine of History* 80 (December 1984): 361.

27. Glenn A. Black, *Angel Site: An Archaeological, Historical, and Ethnological Study* (Indianapolis: Indiana Historical Society, 1967), 1:20–26.

28. WPA of Indiana, "Monthly Narrative Report," January 20 to February 20, 1937, Works Projects Administration Papers, National Archives, RG 69

(hereafter called WPA Records), Press Information and Publicity Material, 1936–1942, box 16.

29. WPA, *Final Report,* 136.

30. James T. Patterson, *Congressional Conservatism and the New Deal: The Growth of the Conservative Coalition in Congress, 1933–1939* (Lexington: University Press of Kentucky, 1967), 293; George T. Blakey, *Hard Times and New Deal in Kentucky, 1929–1939* (Lexington: University Press of Kentucky, 1986), 186.

31. See Iwan Morgan, "Factional Conflict in Indiana Politics during the Later New Deal Years, 1936–1940," *Indiana Magazine of History* 79 (March 1983).

32. *New York Times,* June 12, 1938, IV, 6; *Indianapolis Star,* April 19, 1939.

33. See George T. Blakey, "Battling the Great Depression on Stage in Indiana," *Indiana Magazine of History* 90 (March 1994): 1–25; Dorothy Webb, "Betty Kessler Lyman and the Indiana Federal Children's Theatre," *Youth Theatre Journal* 9 (1995): 68–78.

34. *Indianapolis Star,* July 31, 1938; *Indianapolis News,* July 18, 1939; WPA, *Indiana: A Guide to the Hoosier State* (New York: Oxford University Press, 1941), 136.

35. Florence Kerr to Beatrice D'enbeau, July 19, 1939, WPA, Correspondence with State Officers, 1938–1940, box 48. This WPA official explains to an Indiana artist that the FAP has been unable to set up a unit in Indiana. See also Clarence P. Hornung, *Treasury of American Design* (New York: Harry N. Abrams, 1972). Indiana is missing from the listings of states and artists that participated in the Index of American Design activities.

36. *Indianapolis Star,* July 4, 1937, and January 8, 1939; *Indianapolis Times,* January 20, 1937.

37. Bureau of the Census, *Statistical Abstracts, 1938,* 43.

38. Harold Rosenberg, "Anybody Who Could Write English," *New Yorker,* January 20, 1973, 99–102.

39. N. W. Ayer and Sons, *American Newspaper Annual and Directory* (Philadelphia: N. W. Ayer and Sons, 1929 and 1935), 302 and 252.

40. Lynd and Lynd, *Middletown in Transition,* 572 and 569; Gary Public Library, annual reports, 1929–35; Irene R. McDonough, *History of the Public Library in Vigo County, 1816–1975* (Terre Haute: Vigo County Public Library, 1977), 77–79; Marian McFadden, *Biography of a Town: Shelbyville, Indiana, 1822–1962* (Shelbyville: Tippecanoe Press, 1968), 304–05.

41. The best biographical account is written by his grandson, Larry Lockridge, a professor of English. See chapters 2 and 3 of Lockridge's *Shade of the Raintree: The Life and Death of Ross Lockridge Jr.* (New York: Viking Press, 1994). See also obituaries in Indianapolis *Star, News,* and *Times,* January 14, 1952.

42. Lockridge, *Shade of the Raintree,* 48.

43. Ibid., 47.

44. *Recovery in Indiana,* August 1935, 14; "Report of Special Project Series (Morgan Raid Pilgrimage, July 8–13, 1935), Ross Lockridge Papers, box 3, History Education file, Indiana State University Library.

45. Joseph Gaer to Henry Alsberg, November 1, 1935, WPA Records, Central Office Field Reports, box 2.

46. Ross Lockridge to Henry Alsberg, November 16, 1936, WPA Records, Central Office Administrative Correspondence, box 13; Lockridge, *Shade of the Raintree,* 161.

47. "Indiana—State and District Projects," December 15, 1936, WPA Records, Central Office Field Reports, box 2; and McDonald, *Federal Relief Administration and the Arts,* 680.

48. *Indianapolis Star,* May 24, 1954; Indianapolis city directory, 1935.

49. George Cronyn to Wayne Coy, October 11, 1935; and Henry Alsberg to Rebecca Pitts, December 18, 1937, WPA Records, Central Office Administrative Correspondence, box 13; Rebecca Pitts, "Women and the New Masses," *New Masses* 21 (December 1, 1936): 15.

50. Clay Stearley to Henry Alsberg, December 11, 1935, WPA Records, Central Office Administrative Correspondence, box 13.

51. Ellen Woodward to Paul King, July 7, 1937, WPA Records, Central Office Administrative Correspondence, box 13. The 1935 file is filled with requests for employment in the Indiana FWP.

52. Ross Lockridge to Henry Alsberg, August 20, 1936, WPA Records, Central Office Administrative Correspondence, box 13.

53. Ross Lockridge to Henry Alsberg, November 30, 1935, WPA Records, Central Office Administrative Correspondence, box 13.

54. Indiana Field Report, December 1, 1936, WPA Records, Central Office Field Reports, box 2.

55. "Notes on Negro Material, August 11, 1936"; and William Myers to Sterling Brown, February 5, 1937, WPA Records, Central Office Reports: Negro Studies Reports, box 1.

56. "Indiana—State and District Projects," December 15, 1936, WPA Records, Central Office Field Reports, box 2. See Mangione, *The Dream and the Deal,* 100.

57. "Autobiography of Albert Strope," Indiana Federal Writers' Project Papers, Indiana State University Library, microfilm reel 22, exposure 2295.

58. Donald E. Thompson, *Indiana Authors and Their Books,* 2 vols. (Crawfordsville: Wabash College, 1974, 1981), 1:236; and *Wabash Plain Dealer,* October 8, 1962.

59. *New Albany Ledger-Tribune,* December 27, 1992; New Albany city directory, 1923–42.

60. Evansville city directory, 1930–42; Bureau of the Census, 1930, Vanderburgh County, roll 63.

61. Emery C. Turner, "I, Too, Am on Relief" (guest editorial), *Indianapolis Star*, March 8, 1940.

62. *Muncie Star*, September 29, 1945; *Muncie Evening Press*, September 24, 1945.

63. *Indianapolis Star*, March 5, 1978.

64. *Muncie Evening Press*, September 24, 1945.

65. Doyle Joyce to Ross Lockridge, February 16, 1937, Lawrence County file, Lockridge Papers.

66. Lockridge to Alsberg, July 1, 1937, WPA Records, American Stuff file.; Alsberg to Briggs, October 6, 1937, ibid.

67. Poems by Tuttle, Indiana Poetry file; poems by Turner, Lawrence County file; poems by Kargacos, Knox County file, Lockridge Papers.

68. Ross Lockridge to Henry Alsberg, December 21, 1936 and Alsberg to Lockridge, January 8, 1937, WPA Records Central Office Administrative Correspondence, box 13.

69. Lockridge to Alsberg, March 4, 1937 and Alsberg to Lockridge, March 10, 1937, WPA Records, Central Office Editorial Correspondence, box 13.

70. James Dunton, "Field Report," September 3, 1936, WPA Records, Central Office Field Reports, box 2.

71. Lockridge to Alsberg, December 16, 1935, WPA Records, Central Office Administrative Correspondence, box 13, and *Indianapolis Star*, December 15, 1935.

72. Joseph Gaer to Henry Alsberg, January 30, 1936, WPA Records, Central Office Field Reports, box 2; "Harrison Trail" Program, October 3–4, 1936, Lockridge Papers, box 2; *Indianapolis Star*, December 12, 1935.

73. James G. Dunton, Field Report, September 3, 1936, WPA Records, Central Office Field Reports, box 2; Wayne Coy to Henry Alsberg, September 2, 1936, WPA Records, Central Office Administrative Correspondence, box 13.

74. Ross Lockridge to Henry Alsberg, July 16, 1937, WPA Records, Central Office Administrative Correspondence, box 13.

75. Mangione, *The Dream and the Deal*, 79–80.

76. See William B. Pickett, *Homer E. Capehart: A Senator's Life, 1897–1979* (Indianapolis: Indiana Historical Society, 1990), chap. 4.

77. Dunton, "Field Report on Indiana," August 4, 1936, Central Office Field Reports, box 2.

78. Turner, "Why I Am a Socialist," Lockridge Papers, box 1, Lawrence County file; Pitts, "Something to Believe In," "Women and Communism,"

and "Women and the New Masses," all in *New Masses,* March 13, 1934; February 19, 1935, and December 1, 1936.

79. *Indianapolis Star,* June 6, 1940, and June 17, 1940.

80. *Indianapolis Times,* April 15, 1942.

81. Robert K. O'Neill, "The Federal Writers' Project Files for Indiana," *Indiana Magazine of History* 76 (June 1980).

3. The Indiana Guide

1. Press release, Indiana FWP Papers, reel 30, exposure 947.

2. McKinzie, "Writers on Relief," 61–62.

3. McDonald, *Federal Relief Administration and the Arts,* 668.

4. Penkower, *Federal Writers' Project,* 23.

5. Mangione, *The Dream and the Deal,* 338–39 and Penkower, *Federal Writers' Project,* 31–33.

6. Indiana Monthly Narrative Report, December 15, 1935–January 20, 1936, WPA Records, Press Information and Publicity Materials, box 16.

7. K. McKinzie, "Writers on Relief," 73.

8. Blair Bolles, "The Federal Writers' Project," *Saturday Review of Literature* 18 (July 9, 1938): 3.

9. *Indianapolis Star,* November 5, 1935, p. 4.

10. Supplementary Instructions #2, "Collection of Data," December 10, 1935, Indiana FWP Papers, reel 30, exposure 971.

11. Indiana FWP Papers, reel 26, exposure 1280.

12. Indiana FWP Papers, reel 22, exposure 345.

13. *Fort Wayne News-Sentinel,* September 19, 1936.

14. Indiana FWP Papers, Administrative Material, reel 29, exposure 2305.

15. Reed Harris to Jacob Baker, April 24, 1936, WPA Records, Central Office, Consultants and References, box 1.

16. Indiana FWP Papers, reel 23, exposures 896–1038, passim.

17. Alsberg to Briggs, November 8, 1937, FWP Papers, Library of Congress, box A-132; and Briggs to Alsberg, November 11, 1937, WPA Records, Central Office Editorial Correspondence, box 13.

18. WPA, *Indiana: A Guide,* 4.

19. Briggs to Clair Laning, April 22, 1938, WPA Records, Central Office Administrative Correspondence, box 13.

20. Rebecca Pitts to Alsberg, April 24, 1937, ibid.

21. Mildred Schmitt to Florence Kerr, July 8, 1940, Indiana FWP Papers, reel 29, exposure 181.

22. Federal Writers' Project, "A Brief History of the FWP," typescript, p. 9, FWP Papers, Library of Congress, box A-1081.

23. Briggs to Stella Hanau, November 12, 1940, FWP Papers, Library of Congress, box A-130; Mildred Schmitt to Florence Kerr, November 28, 1940, Indiana FWP Papers, reel 29, exposure 206.

24. Briggs to Hanau, October 14, 1940, FWP Papers, Library of Congress, box A-130.

25. Briggs to Alsberg, October 11, 1937, WPA Records, Central Office Administrative Correspondence, box 13.

26. Briggs to Hanau, October 30, [1940], FWP Papers, Library of Congress, box A-130.

27. Mangione, *The Dream and the Deal*, 84; Penkower, *Federal Writers' Project*, 45–46.

28. Mangione, *The Dream and the Deal*, 228 and 337.

29. Ibid., 59; Penkower, *Federal Writers' Project*, 128.

30. Lockridge to Edward Kennard, May 14, 1936, WPA Records, Central Office, Indians/Archeology, box 2.

31. Lockridge to Cronyn, February 23, 1937, ibid.

32. Crawford critique, June 16, 1936, WPA Records, Central Office Editorial Correspondence, box 13.

33. Briggs to Alsberg, August 16, 1937, and Cronyn to Briggs, August 19, 1937, WPA Records, Central Office, Indians/Archaelogy, box 2.

34. Rebecca Pitts, editor's notes, "Indians," Indiana FWP Papers, reel 30, exposure 838.

35. J. C. Godfroy, "Witch Lore of the Miamis," FWP Papers, box A-605.

36. "A Reflection of Indiana Folklore in the Form of a Memorial Tribute to Mrs. Elsie Durre," typescript in Lockridge Papers, box 3.

37. John Lomax to William Myers, June 30, 1938, WPA Records, Central Office Correspondence, Folklore, box 1.

38. Alsberg to Briggs, May 17, 1938, WPA Records, Central Office Editorial Correspondence, box 13.

39. Indiana FWP Papers, reel 2, exposures 730–72.

40. Ibid., reel 12, exposures 601–27.

41. Ibid., reel 2, exposure 72.

42. *Indiana: A Guide*, 125.

43. Crawford critique, June 16, 1936, WPA Records, Central Office Editorial Correspondence, box 13.

44. Seidenberg critique, March 22, 1937, WPA Records, Central Office Correspondence, Architecture Studies, box 2; *Indiana: A Guide*, 131.

45. Pitts's response to Seidenberg critique, n.d., WPA Records, Central Office Correspondence, Architecture Studies, box 2; Ibid., and Pitts to

Cronyn, October 11, 1937, WPA Records, Central Office Editorial Correspondence, box 13.

46. Cronyn to Lockridge, March 29, 1937, ibid.

47. Cronyn to Briggs, October 14, 1937, ibid.

48. McKinzie, "Writers on Relief," 92; Billington, "Government and the Arts," 472–73.

49. History critique, August 28, 1936, FWP Papers, box A-131.

50. Agriculture file, ibid., box A-127.

51. Cronyn to Lockridge, June 14, 1937, WPA Records, Central Office Editorial Correspondence, box 13.

52. The Negro: editorial comments, FWP Papers, box A-130.

53. Literature file, critique, January 18, 1938, ibid., box A-131.

54. *Indiana: A Guide,* 148.

55. Indiana editorial comments, 1940, FWP Papers, box A-130.

56. Cronyn to Briggs, September 11, 1937, ibid., box A-131.

57. Lockridge to Cronyn, December 11, 1936, WPA Records, Central Office Editorial Correspondence, box 13.

58. French Lick critique, March 15, 1937, FWP Papers, box A-128.

59. Alsberg to Briggs, October 3, 1938, WPA Records, Central Office Editorial Correspondence, box 13.

60. Anderson critique, March 3, 1937; Cronyn to Briggs, August 25, 1937; Anderson critique, October 31, 1938, FWP Papers, box A-128.

61. Indiana Status Report, May 15, 1939, FWP Papers, box A-5.

62. Indiana FWP Papers, reel 27, exposure 2093.

63. Ibid., exposure 2592.

64. Briggs to Alsberg, November 2, 1937, WPA Records, Central Office Editorial Correspondence, box 13.

65. *Indiana: A Guide,* 339.

66. Cronyn to Briggs, October 13, 1937, FWP Papers, box A-128.

67. *Indiana: A Guide,* 207.

68. Ibid., 163–64.

69. Cronyn to Briggs, September 23, 1937, FWP Papers, box A-128.

70. Terre Haute critique, Indiana FWP Papers, reel 26, exposure 1554.

71. New Harmony file, FWP Papers, box A-129.

72. Paul Yoder, "Contemporary Scene," Indiana FWP Papers, reel 22, exposure 2199.

73. *Indiana: A Guide,* 250.

74. Elizabeth Vickery to Mildred Schmitt, April 26, 1941, Indiana FWP Papers, reel 22, exposure 1970.

75. South Bend critique, FWP Papers, box A-129.

76. Penkower, *Federal Writers' Project,* 25 and McDonald, *Federal Relief Administration and the Arts,* 658.

77. "A Brief History of the FWP," 4.

78. Indiana FWP Papers, reel 20, exposures 651 and 1073; Alsberg to Briggs, January 4, 1938, WPA Records, Central Office Editorial Correspondence, box 13.

79. Iris Cook, Tours, Floyd County file, Lockridge Papers, box 1.

80. Briggs to Bess Ehrman, August 29, 1938, Indiana FWP Papers, reel 23, exposures 1001–02.

81. Ibid., reel 12, exposure 1872; *Indiana: A Guide*, 307.

82. Mangione, *The Dream and the Deal*, 202.

83. *Indianapolis News*, February 4, 1938.

84. Briggs to Alsberg, November 10, 1937, WPA Records, Central Office Editorial Correspondence, box 13.

85. Indiana Tour Draft, November 29, 1937, FWP Papers, box A-132.

86. Kellock critique, December 17, 1937, ibid.

87. McKinzie, "Writers on Relief," 69.

88. Alsberg to Briggs, November 8, 1937, and January 4, 1938, WPA Records, Central Office Editorial Correspondence, box 13.

89. Cronyn to Briggs, July 30, 1937, FWP Papers, box A-128.

90. Alsberg to Briggs, January 4, 1938, WPA Records, Central Office Editorial Correspondence, box 13.

91. Briggs to Alsberg, July 20, 1938, ibid.; *Indianapolis News*, September 24, 1941.

92. Frederick Gutheim, "America in Guide Books," *Saturday Review of Literature* 24 (June 14, 1941): 3–5; Bernard De Voto, "The Writers' Project," *Harper's Magazine* 184 (January 1942): 222.

93. *Indiana: A Guide*, 445.

94. Ibid., 476.

95. Ibid., 325.

96. Ibid., 377.

97. Ibid., 436–37.

98. Indiana Chronology file, 1936–40, FWP Papers, box A-128.

99. Indiana FWP Papers, reel 23, exposure 173 and reel 29, exposure 266.

100. Alsberg to Briggs, March 27, 1939, WPA Records, Central Office Editorial Correspondence, box 13; and Alsberg to Briggs, April 4, 1939, FWP Papers, box A-4.

101. Editorial Report (Photos), September 16, 1940, Indiana FWP Papers, reel 30, exposures 891–94.

102. Indiana Editorial Comments, October 13, 1940, FWP Papers, box A-130.

103. Briggs to Alsberg, September 6, 1938, WPA Records, Central Office Editorial Correspondence, box 13.

104. Frederick to Alsberg, February 14, 1939, ibid.; *Indianapolis News,* March 3, 1939.

105. Robert K. O'Neill, "The Federal Writers' Project Files for Indiana," *Indiana Magazine of History* 76 (June 1980): 90; Errol Wayne Stevens, "The Federal Writers' Project Revisited: The Indiana Historical Society's New Guide to the State of Indiana," ibid., 100.

106. D. L. Chambers to Alsberg, May 31, 1938, WPA Records, Central Office Editorial Correspondence, box 13.

107. Penkower, *Federal Writers' Project,* 135.

108. D. W. Hufford to John Sembower, April 24, 1941, and Sembower to Faculty, memo, n.d., Indiana FWP Papers, reel 29, exposure 360.

109. *Indiana: A Guide,* v.

110. *New York Herald Tribune,* April 12, 1942; *Christian Science Monitor,* October 29, 1941.

111. *Indianapolis News,* February 27, 1941; *Indianapolis Times,* September 30, 1941; *Indianapolis Recorder,* January 31, 1942; Briggs to Mildred Schmitt, October 10, 1941, Indiana FWP Papers, reel 30, exposure 842.

112. *Fort Wayne News-Sentinel,* November 4, 1941; *South Bend Tribune,* October 16, 1941; *Elkhart Truth,* September 30, 1941; *Vincennes Sun-Commercial,* September 30, 1941.

113. Royalty Accounts, Indiana FWP Papers, reel 29, exposures 434–39.

114. Errol Wayne Stevens, "The FWP Revisited," 102.

4. Other Publications

1. Penkower, *Federal Writers' Project,* 140.

2. Alsberg to Lockridge, April 13 and August 12, 1936, WPA Records, Central Office, Folklore, box 1.

3. Lockridge to George Cronyn, December 15, 1936, ibid.; *Women of Indiana,* ed. Mrs. Blanche Foster Boruff (Indianapolis: Matthew Farson, 1941), 225.

4. "Some Tall Tales," Mss, September 29, 1936, FWP Papers, box A-785.

5. Penkower, *Federal Writers' Project,* 149.

6. Indiana FWP Papers, reel 6, exposure 175; *Hoosier Tall Stories,* 7–8.

7. Indiana FWP Papers, reel 8, exposure 2052; *Hoosier Tall Stories,* 11–12.

8. Indiana FWP Papers, reel 27, exposure 1009; *Hoosier Tall Stories,* 28.

9. *Hoosier Tall Stories,* 24.

10. Alsberg to Lockridge, September 8, 1936, WPA Records, Central Office, Folklore, box 1.

11. Lomax critique, n.d., ibid.

12. Lockridge to Alsberg, September 22, 1936, ibid.

13. Cronyn to Lockridge, December 8, 1936, Lockridge to Alsberg, December 15, 1936, and Lockridge to Alsberg, January 28, 1937, ibid.

14. Alsberg to Briggs, March 31, 1939, FWP Papers, box A-4; Alsberg to Daniel Kidney, n.d., WPA Records, Central Office Administrative Correspondence, box 13.

15. Lockridge to Alsberg, January 28, 1937, WPA Records, Central Office Correspondence, Folklore, box 1.

16. "Report of Work Accomplished," Indiana FWP Papers, reel 29, exposure 92.

17. Lockridge to George Cronyn, December 15, 1936, WPA Records, Central Office Correspondence, Folklore, box 1.

18. Alsberg to Lockridge, September 19, 1936, ibid.

19. Ronald L. Baker, *Hoosier Folk Legends* (Bloomington: Indiana University Press, 1982).

20. Penkower, *Federal Writers' Project,* 137; McKinzie, "Writers on Relief," 131.

21. Indiana Writers' Program, *Calumet Region Historical Guide* (Gary, 1939), ix. Hereinafter referred to as *Calumet Guide.*

22. Ibid., 272.

23. Ibid., xi.

24. *Gary Post-Tribune,* January 25, 1940; Briggs to Clair Lanning, April 22, 1938, and John Frederick to Alsberg, February 14, 1939, WPA Records, Central Office Administrative Correspondence, box 13.

25. *Gary Post-Tribune,* January 25, 1940; Briggs to Clair Lanning, April 22, 1938, ibid.

26. Alsberg to John Frederick, April 18, 1939, FWP Papers, box A-4.

27. *Calumet Guide,* x.

28. Ibid., 179

29. Ibid., 135.

30. Indiana FWP Papers, reel 13, passim.

31. *Calumet Guide,* 4.

32. Ibid., 58.

33. Ibid., 93.

34. Ibid., 97.

35. Ibid., 114.

36. Ibid., 162.

37. Ibid., 225.

38. Ibid., 230.

39. Ibid., 233.

40. Ibid., 59.

41. Ibid., 60–61; Indiana FWP Papers, reel 13, exposure 1280.

42. *Calumet Guide,* 63; Indiana FWP Papers, reel 13, exposure 1264.

43. *Indiana: A Guide,* 3–4.

44. *Calumet Guide,* 222 and 233.

45. Bureau of the Census, *Historical Statistics of the United States,* 27.

46. *Calumet Guide,* 233.

47. Ibid., 53.

48. Indiana FWP Papers, reel 13, exposure 539.

49. *Calumet Guide,* 55.

50. Ibid., x.

51. Ibid., 3.

52. Ibid., 33.

53. Ibid., 49.

54. Ibid., 196.

55. Ibid., 67

56. *Gary Post-Tribune,* January 25, 1940.

57. *Calumet News,* January 25 and February 1, 1940.

58. *Chesterton Tribune,* January 25, 1940.

59. See Richard J. Meister, "A History of Gary, Indiana: 1930–1940" (Ph.D. diss., University of Notre Dame, 1967); Lance Trusty, "Afterword," in Powell A. Moore, ed., *The Calumet Region: Indiana's Last Frontier* (Indianapolis: Indiana Historical Bureau, 1977); Lane, *City of the Century;* Polly Smith, ed., *Times Capsule: The Times' History of the Calumet during the Twentieth Century* (Crown Point: Northwest Indiana Newspapers, 1999).

60. "Request for Writers' Project Activity, February 5, 1940, Indiana FWP Papers, reel 29, exposure 40.

61. See chapter 2.

62. Indiana FWP Papers, reel 29, exposure 90, and reel 30, exposure 843.

63. Ibid., reel 29, exposure 90.

64. *Muncie Evening Press,* June 12, 1940.

65. *Princeton Clarion-News,* July 25, 1940.

66. *Muncie Evening Press,* March 21, 1941.

67. *Princeton Clarion-News,* June 6, 1940.

68. *Muncie Evening Press,* October 12, 1940.

69. Ibid., April 28, 1941.

70. Ibid., August 4, 1941.

71. Ibid., September 22, 1941.

72. Ibid., March 2, 1942.

73. Ibid., January 12, 1942.

74. Indiana FWP Papers, reel 9, exposure 955.

75. Ibid., reel 27, exposure 417.

76. Ibid., reel 12, exposures 1797–1800.

77. Mangione, *The Dream and the Deal,* 345.

78. Alsberg to Briggs, March 31, 1939, FWP Papers, box A-4; Carl Malmberg to Alsberg, August 3, 1939, WPA Records, Central Office, Special Publications, box 3.

79. Indiana Writers' Program, *Indiana: Facts, Events, Places, Tours* (New York, 1941).

80. *Indiana: A Guide,* xxi; *Indiana: Facts,* 11.

81. *Indiana: A Guide,* xxii; *Indiana: Facts,* 9.

82. *Indiana: A Guide,* 380; *Indiana: Facts,* 22.

83. *Indiana: A Guide,* 486; *Indiana: Facts,* 24.

84. Connecticut Writers' Program, *Connecticut: Facts, Events, Places, Tours* (New York: Bacon and Wieck, 1940); Arizona Writers' Program, *Arizona: Facts, Events, Places, Tours* (New York: Bacon and Wieck, 1940).

85. *Indiana: Facts,* 15.

86. *Indiana: A Guide,* 386–87 and *Indiana: Facts,* 27.

87. *Indiana: Facts,* 20–21.

88. Ibid., 3–4.

89. Ibid., 9.

90. Mildred Schmitt to S. W. Hufford, Ray Thurman, et al., July 3, 1941, Indiana FWP Papers, reel 29, exposure 155.

91. Mangione, *The Dream and the Deal,* 345.

92. *Indiana: Facts,* 6.

93. WPA, *Final Report,* 134.

94. "Linebarger," Indiana State Library clippings file; *Indianapolis Star,* February 28, 1928.

95. *Indianapolis Star,* June 10, 1942.

96. "WPA Supervision," Indiana FWP files, reel 29, exposure 71.

97. Ibid., reel 29, exposures 1793–1850. An additional eight-page manuscript covered county and township governments. See exposures 1853–61.

98. Ibid., exposures 1793 and 1809 and 1807 and 1836.

99. Mildred Schmitt to Donald Hufford, March 30, 1942, ibid., exposure 5; *Indianapolis Star,* June 10, 1942.

5. Oral History

1. Ronald L. Baker, *Homeless, Friendless, and Penniless: The WPA Interviews with Former Slaves Living in Indiana* (Bloomington: Indiana University Press, 2000), 6 and 285.

2. McDonald, *Federal Relief Administration and the Arts,* 720.

3. Henry Alsberg to State Directors, July 30 and September 8, 1937,

WPA Records, Central Office Correspondence, Ex-Slaves, box 1; McDonald, *Federal Relief Administration and the Arts,* 721.

4. Baker, *Homeless,* 12.

5. See Woodward, "History from Slave Sources," and Blassingame, "Using the Testimony of Ex-Slaves."

6. Baker, *Homeless,* 6.

7. Alsberg to Briggs, September 9, 1937, and Wharton to Botkin, February 25, 1941, WPA Records, Central Office Correspondence, Ex-Slaves, box 1.

8. Baker, *Homeless,* 10.

9. Indiana FWP Collection, reel 15.

10. Ibid., exposures 340–42.

11. George Rawick, ed., *The American Slave: A Composite Autobiography* (Westport, Conn.: Greenwood Press, 1972, 1977, and 1979), 6:8–10.

12. Baker, *Homeless,* 113–14.

13. Bureau of the Census, 1930, Indiana, Vanderburgh County; Evansville city directory, 1930–40.

14. Briggs to Alsberg, September 17, 1937, WPA Records, Central Office Correspondence, Ex-Slaves, box 1.

15. John Lomax to William Meyers, June 30, 1938, WPA Records, Central Office Editorial Correspondence, Folklore, box 1.

16. Indiana FWP Collection, reel 25, exposures 720–23.

17. Ibid., exposure 673.

18. Wharton to Botkin, February 25, 1941, WPA Records, Central Office Correspondence, Ex-Slaves, box 1.

19. Indiana FWP Collection, reel 5, exposures 1092–95.

20. Ibid., exposure 1092.

21. Ibid., exposure 1094.

22. Indiana FWP Collection, reel 16, exposures 1017–18.

23. Indianapolis city directory, 1933–40; *Indianapolis Recorder,* August 21, 1937.

24. Indiana FWP Collection, reel 16, exposures 1022–24 and 1052–53.

25. Rawick, *American Slave,* supplement 1, 5:lx.

26. Lester V. Horwitz, *The Longest Raid of the Civil War* (Cincinnati: Farmcourt, 1999); Arville L. Funk, *The Morgan Raid in Indiana and Ohio* (Corydon: ALFCO, 1971). Horwitz lists fifteen direct deaths from the raid, 387; Funk adds five more from indirect causes, 61.

27. W. H. H. Terrell, *Indiana in the War of the Rebellion: Report of the Adjutant General* (Indianapolis: Indiana Historical Bureau, 1960), 224.

28. GCUR, History Education file, July 3, 1935, Lockridge Papers.

29. Morgan Pilgrimage Flier, Dearborn County file, Lockridge Papers; and *Versailles Republican,* July 11, 1935.

30. Report of Special Project Series, 5, History Education file, Lockridge Papers; and *North Vernon Sun,* July 18, 1935.

31. Report of Special Project Series, 1, History Education file, Lockridge Papers.

32. Addendum to "Report of Special Project Series," July 16, 1935, ibid.

33. See enclosures from Carrie Stark, Ripley County file, A. M. Pender, Jefferson County file, and Lois Taylor, Dearborn County file in Lockridge Papers.

34. Horwitz cites four memoirs from the Library of Congress.

35. Greenville Johnson memoir, Indiana FWP Papers, reel 11, exposures 782–84; Melvin Marling memoir, ibid., exposures 778–79, Charles Dome memoir, ibid., reel 9, exposures 1453–54; Maston Harris memoir, ibid., reel 11, exposures 1225–26; Eliza Lawrence memoir, ibid., exposures 791–92.

36. G. R. Burdsal memoir, ibid., reel 11, exposures 816–17; Charles Burdsall memoir, ibid., reel 11, exposures 774–75; Elizabeth Swan memoir, Lockridge Papers, Dearborn County file; Harry McGrain memoir, Indiana FWP Papers, New Albany Public Library, Harrison County file.

37. E. A. Gladden memoir, ibid., reel 23, exposure 30; Pirene Vallile memoir, ibid., reel 11, exposures 763–64; James C. Bland memoir, ibid., reel 11, exposures 787–90.

38. Report of Special Project Series, 6, in History Education file, Lockridge Papers.

39. See Louis B. Ewbank, "Morgan's Raid in Indiana," *Indiana Historical Society* 7, no. 2 (1917): 146; and Middleton Robertson memoir, Indiana FWP Papers, reel 11, exposures 767–73. A revised version of this memoir appeared as "Recollections of Morgan's Raid," *Indiana Magazine of History* 34 (June 1938).

40. New Albany city directory, 1921–42; *New Albany Ledger-Tribune,* December 27, 1992.

41. William Haughey memoir, Indiana FWP Papers, reel 7, exposures 178–79.

42. E. A. Gladden memoir, ibid., reel 23, exposure 30.

43. Bureau of the Census, 1930, Indiana, Jefferson County.

44. Maston Harris memoir, Indiana FWP Papers, reel 11, exposures 1225–26.

45. G. R. Burdsal memoir, ibid., exposures 816–17.

46. *Indianapolis News,* September 14, 1957; *Wabash Plain-Dealer,* October 8, 1962; Thompson, *Indiana Authors,*1:236.

47. James Clarence Godfroy, *Miami Indian Stories* (Winona Lake, Ind.: Light and Life Press, 1961).

48. Indiana FWP Papers, reel 17, exposures 1424–25.

49. Ibid., reel 27, exposures 60–66.

50. Ibid., reel 27, exposure 285; reel 17, exposures 1482–85.

51. Ibid., reel 27, exposure 255, exposure 162.

52. Ibid., reel 17, exposure 1435.

53. Ibid., reel 29, exposure 1009.

54. Ibid., reel 27, exposures 260–65.

55. John Bodnar, ed., *Bonds of Affection: Americans Define Their Patriotism* (Princeton, N.J.: Princeton University Press, 1996), 302.

6. Almost Finished Projects

1. FWP, South Bend guide, Lockridge Papers, St. Joseph County file.

2. FWP, Fort Wayne guide, copy in Indiana Historical Society Library.

3. FWP, city guides, copies in Indiana Historical Society Library; "Progress Report," November 18, 1936, WPA Records, Central Office Editorial Correspondence, box 13.

4. Lockridge to Alsberg, January 28, 1937, WPA Records, Central Office Editorial Correspondence, box 13.

5. Briggs to Alsberg, June 7, 1938, ibid.

6. Ray Thurmond to Briggs, June 6, 1938, ibid.; Application for "An Abridged History and Guide for Each County in Indiana," February 14, 1940, Indiana FWP Papers, reel 29, exposure 42.

7. Author's interview with Margaret Schricker Robbins, August 21, 2002.

8. FWP, Fayette County guide, copy in Indiana Historical Society Library, pp. 7–8.

9. FWP, Howard County guide, copy in Indiana Historical Society Library, chapter 6, p. 5.

10. FWP, Warren County guide, copy in Indiana Historical Society Library, chapter 6, n.p.

11. FWP, Franklin County guide, copy in Indiana Historical Society Library, p. 4.

12. FWP, Crawford County guide, copy in Indiana Historical Society Library, chapter 3, p. 3.

13. Briggs to Alsberg, July 8, 1938, WPA Records, Central Office, Reports: Activities and Plans, box 1; *Indianapolis Star,* July 17, 1938.

14. John Frederick report, February 14, 1939, WPA Records, Central Office Editorial Correspondence, box 13; Alsberg to Frederick, March 27, 1939, FWP Collection, box A-4.

15. Robbins interview.

16. *Indianapolis News,* February 27, 1941; *Muncie Evening Press,* November 18, 1941.

17. Mildred Schmitt to Florence Kerr, January 7, 1942, Indiana FWP Papers, reel 29, exposure 160.

18. John Sembower to Mildred Schmitt, January 8, 1942, ibid., exposure 158.

19. McDonald, *Federal Relief Administration and the Arts,* 690.

20. Alsberg to Lockridge, September 19, 1936, WPA Records, Central Office Correspondence, box 1.

21. Lockridge to Alsberg, October 31, 1936, ibid.

22. "Pricking Thumbs," Indiana FWP Papers, reel 29, exposures 2570–71.

23. Ibid., exposure 2573.

24. Ibid., exposure 2582; Wallace Brown, "The Antics of a Witch," Indiana FWP Papers, reel 23, exposures 417–18.

25. "Pricking Thumbs," Indiana FWP Papers, reel 29, exposure 2574; Flora Mae Harris, "Story of a Witch," ibid., reel 11, exposures 116–17.

26. "Pricking Thumbs," Indiana FWP Papers, reel 29, exposure 2583; Velsie Tyler, "Superstitions," Indiana FWP Papers, reel 7, exposure 405.

27. Ronald L. Baker, *Hoosier Folk Legends* (Bloomington: Indiana University Press, 1982).

28. McDonald, *Federal Relief Administration and the Arts,* 689.

29. Penkower, *Federal Writers' Project,* 228; Mangione, *The Dream and the Deal,* 375–96, state listings.

30. Cynthia R. Fadool, ed., *Contemporary Authors* (Detroit, 1976), 61–64: 432.

31. "Indiana: The Hoosier State in Pictures," Indiana FWP Papers, reel 30, exposure 10.

32. Ibid., draft 1, exposures 12–24.

33. Ibid., exposures 25–27.

34. Ibid., draft 1, exposures 30–34; draft 2, exposure 87.

35. Ibid., draft 1, exposures 35–40.

36. Ibid., exposures 40–51.

37. Ibid., exposures 54–59.

38. Ibid., exposure 7.

39. Ibid., draft 2, exposures 115–19.

40. Mildred Schmitt to Florence Kerr, January 7, 1942, Indiana FWP Papers, reel 29, exposure 160.

41. "Indiana: The Hoosier State in Pictures," Indiana FWP Papers, reel 30, draft 1, exposure 11.

42. Ibid., draft 1, exposures 33, 40, 59; draft 2, exposure 102.

43. Introduction to Cecelia Ray Berry, *Folk Songs of Old Vincennes* (Chicago: H. T. FitzSimons, 1946), 9.

44. Bessie K. Roberts, "The Trail of Song," manuscript, FWP Collection, box A-603.

45. Lockridge to Gino A. Ratti, December 9, 1936, Indiana FWP Papers, reel 29, exposure 166.

46. Ratti to Lockridge, December 15, 1936, ibid., exposure 170.

47. "The Creole (French) Pioneers at Old Post Vincennes," manuscript, ibid., reel 12, exposures 757–1034.

48. M. W. Royse to Alsberg, March 21, 1939, WPA Records, Central Office Reports: Ethnic Studies, box 1; Briggs to Paul [King], July 2 [1940], Indiana FWP Papers, reel 12, exposure 1201.

49. Foreword to "Creole (French) Pioneers," Indiana FWP Papers, reel 12, exposures 760–67.

50. Title page, ibid., exposure 757.

51. George Cronyn to Briggs, August 13, 1937; Briggs to Cronyn, October 27, 1937, WPA Records, Central Office Editorial Correspondence, box 13.

52. Botkin critique, May 16, 1940, Indiana FWP Papers, reel 12, exposures 1202–03.

53. "Development," draft 2, ibid., exposures 1075–90.

54. Botkin critique, ibid., exposures 1202–03.

55. Briggs to Paul [King], July 2 [1940], ibid., exposure 1201.

56. In addition to the two manuscripts in the Indiana FWP Papers, there is a shorter version in the Library of Congress, box A-746, and an incomplete manuscript in the Lockridge Papers. Paul Sporn has located another draft of a different length that he discusses in *Against Itself.*

57. Ronald L. Baker, *French Folklife in Old Vincennes* (Terre Haute: Hoosier Folklore Society, 1989).

58. McDonald, *Federal Relief Administration and the Arts,* 727; Mangione, *The Dream and the Deal,* 281.

59. Emery C. Turner to Briggs, April 17, 1939, Indiana FWP Papers, reel 15, exposure 475.

60. *Bedford Daily Times-Mail,* September 17, 1956.

61. Turner to Briggs, n.d., ibid., exposure 677; E. C. Turner, "The Limestone Industry of Lawrence and Monroe Counties," ibid., exposure 56.

62. Alsberg to Frederick, April 24, 1939, FWP Collection, box A-4.

63. *Indianapolis Star,* November 3, 1935 and June 6, 1938.

64. Royse to Alsberg, March 21, 1939, WPA Records, Central Office Reports: Ethnic Studies, box 1.

65. The Millholland interviews are scattered throughout the Lawrence County files of the Indiana FWP Papers, reel 15, exposures 292–1099.

66. "Limestone Town" manuscript, ibid., exposures 663–72.

67. Frederick to Briggs, July 25, 1939, ibid., reel 29, exposure 282.

68. *Indianapolis Star,* April 21, 1940.

7. Incomplete Projects

1. "Riley—Hoosier Monograph," Lockridge Papers, box 3.

2. Ibid.

3. Murphy interview, March 4, 1937, Indiana FWP Papers, reel 31, exposures 588–93.

4. Lockridge to Murphy, November 21, 1936, ibid., exposure 760.

5. Dickey interview, n.d., ibid., exposures 167–85.

6. Sweenie interview, November 6, 1936, ibid., exposures 837–43.

7. Brumfield interview, n.d., ibid., exposure 29.

8. McCulloch interview, November 10, 1936, ibid., exposure 711.

9. McCutcheon reminiscence, November 12, 1936, ibid., exposures 125–26.

10. Rabb reminiscence, n.d., ibid., exposures 136–37.

11. Nicholson reminiscence, n.d., ibid., exposures 130–35.

12. Tarkington reminiscence, November 13, 1936, ibid., exposures 141–42.

13. Indiana FWP Papers, reel 31, exposures 3, 456, 466.

14. Ibid., exposures 688–97.

15. Ibid., exposures 763–812.

16. Lockridge to E. F. Murphy, January 13, 1937 and February 24, 1937, ibid., exposures 761–62.

17. Note of transmittal, November 27, 1940, ibid., exposure 594.

18. Indiana FWP Papers, reel 3, Clark County Flood file; reel 7; Floyd County Flood file.

19. Lockridge to Alsberg, January 28, 1937, WPA Records, Central Office Editorial Correspondence, box 13.

20. Fieldworker manuscripts from both Spencer and Vanderburgh counties mention the flood scrapbooks in their bibliographies. Indiana FWP Papers, reel 23, Spencer County Flood file and reel 25, Vanderburgh County Flood file.

21. Indiana WPA, monthly narrative report, January/February 1937, WPA Records, press information and publicity material, 1936–42, box 16.

22. Indiana FWP Papers, reel 11, exposure 575.

23. Ibid., reel 25, exposure 36.

24. Ibid., reel 7, exposures 42–45.

25. Ibid., reel 7, exposure 49.

26. Ibid., reel 4, exposures 931–39.

27. Ibid., reel 27, exposure 1282.

28. Ibid., reel 19, exposure 442.

29. Ibid., reel 3, exposure 28.

30. Ibid., reel 23, exposure 920.

31. Ibid., reel 4, exposure 67; reel 19, exposures 104–09; reel 25, exposure 69.

32. Ibid., reel 4, exposure 74.

33. Indiana WPA, "Supplement to Monthly Narrative Report on Emergency Flood Activities," WPA Records, press information and publicity material, 1936–42, box 16.

34. "Kankakee Marsh" prospectus, Lockridge Papers, box 1.

35. "Kankakee River Monograph," prospectus, Indiana FWP Papers, reel 30, exposures 1091–94. The Kankakee monograph materials are clearly labeled but are scattered among the administrative files and those of seven counties in the Indiana FWP Papers (Lake, Porter, LaPorte, St. Joseph, Starke, Jasper, and Newton).

36. Ibid., exposures 1045–55.

37. Ibid., exposures 1098–1103; reel 14, exposures 351–56.

38. Ibid., reel 30, exposures 1058–83.

39. Kankakee prospectus, Lockridge Papers, box 1.

40. Indiana FWP Papers, reel 22, exposures 793–813.

41. Ibid., reel 14, exposure 98.

42. Ibid., reel 23, exposure 1806.

43. Ibid., reel 14, exposure 81.

44. Ibid., reel 18, exposure 1975.

45. Ibid., reel 14, exposures 84–92; reel 30, exposure 1078.

46. Ibid., reel 30, exposures 1133–51.

47. Ibid., reel 13, exposures 268–72; reel 18, exposures 2043–45.

48. Demmon, "Kankakee Prospectus," ibid., reel 30, exposure 1094.

49. Ibid., reel 14, exposures 68–69.

50. Demmon to Briggs, n.d., ibid., reel 29, exposure 175.

51. Alsberg to FWP State Directors, October 20, 1937, ibid., reel 30, exposure 840.

52. Briggs to Alsberg, November 2, 1937 and November 29, 1937, ibid., reel 29, exposures 132–34.

53. "America Eats," Memorandum #2, ibid., reel 30, exposure 926, and John C. Camp, "America Eats: Toward a Social Definition of American Foodways" (Ph.D. diss., University of Pennsylvania, 1978), 94, 127–51.

54. Indiana FWP Papers, reel 23, exposures 2492 and 1515.

55. Ibid., reel 3, exposure 1123; reel 21, exposure 1467.

56. Ibid., reel 22, exposure 1810; reel 23, exposure 760.

57. Ibid., reel 26, exposures 1969–71; reel 22, exposure 1789; reel 27, exposure 1162.

58. Nelson Algren, *America Eats* (Iowa City: University of Iowa Press, 1992), xvii–xviii; Mangione, *The Dream and the Deal*, 121.

59. Schmitt to Kerr, January 7, 1942, Indiana FWP Papers, reel 29, exposure 160.

60. Algren, *America Eats,* 35–37; "Family Reunion," Indiana FWP Papers, reel 29, exposures 1713–17.

61. Indiana FWP Papers, reel 29, exposure 1717.

62. A copy of Algren's manuscript is in the FWP Collection in the Library of Congress. Sporn, *Against Itself,* 271; Camp, "America Eats," 144.

63. Algren, *America Eats,* xiii.

64. Camp lists submissions from the states, "America Eats," 127–60.

65. Mangione, *The Dream and the Deal,* 277; Penkower, *Federal Writers' Project,* 149–50.

66. Cronyn to Lockridge, June 29, 1937, WPA Records, Central Office, Special Publications, box 2.

67. Cronyn to Briggs, September 30, 1937, ibid.

68. Indiana FWP Papers, reel 22, exposures 846–71.

69. "Pockets," WPA Records, Central Office, Special Publications, box 2; Penkower, *Federal Writers' Project,* 150.

70. Mangione, *The Dream and the Deal,* 284–85.

71. Newsom to Jennings, January 13, 1942, Indiana FWP Papers, reel 29, exposure 13; Mangione, *The Dream and the Deal,* 346; Penkower, *Federal Writers' Project,* 229.

72. Mangione, *The Dream and the Deal,* 346; Penkower, *Federal Writers' Project,* 229; Newsom, Indiana FWP Papers, reel 29, exposure 14.

73. "Indiana Factbook," Prospectus, July 26, 1940, ibid., reel 29, exposure 74; *Indianapolis News,* January 30, 1941; Mangione, *The Dream and the Deal,* 345; Penkower, *Federal Writers' Project,* 228.

74. Briggs, Preston and Thurman to Sembower, n.d., Indiana FWP Papers, reel 30, exposures 921–23.

75. "Education Moves Forward," prospectus, July 26, 1940, ibid., reel 29, exposure 35; Newsom to Jennings, January 13, 1942, ibid., reel 29, exposure 13.

76. "Sociological Studies," prospectus, July 26, 1940, and Questionnaires, ibid., reel 29, exposures 75–90.

77. Sembower to Schmidt, January 8, 1942, ibid., reel 29, exposures 158–59.

78. Penkower, *Federal Writers' Project,* 234.

79. Schmidt to Kerr, January 7, 1942, Indiana FWP Papers, reel 29, exposures 160–61.

80. *Indianapolis Times,* April 15, 1942.

8. Research Inventories

1. Indiana FWP Papers, reel 12, exposure 535.
2. Ibid., exposures 542–43.
3. Ibid., reel 5, exposure 745.
4. Ibid., reel 18, exposures 171–74.
5. Ibid., reel 13, exposures 223–25.
6. Ibid., reel 25, exposure 1163.
7. Ibid., reel 21, exposure 1437.
8. Ibid., reel 22, exposure 1619.
9. Ibid., reel 1, exposure 1311.
10. Ibid., reel 16, exposures 2329–35.
11. Ibid., reel 25, exposures 1147–75.
12. Ibid., reel 16, exposure 1740.
13. Ibid., reel 23, exposure 2001.
14. Ibid., reel 3, exposure 997.
15. Ibid., reel 16, exposure 1800.
16. Ibid., reel 11, exposure 1446.
17. Ibid., reel 24, exposure 1665.
18. Ibid., reel 27, exposure 1850.
19. Ibid., reel 23, exposure 1365.
20. Ibid., reel 16, exposure 1757.
21. Ibid., reel 22, exposure 1317.
22. Ibid., reel 16, exposures 1775, 1777, 1780, 1838, and 1848.
23. Ibid., reel 7, exposure 1200; reel 16, exposure 1794.
24. Ibid., reel 19, exposure 639.
25. Ibid., reel 24, exposure 1095.
26. Ibid., reel 7, exposure 607.
27. Ibid., reel 3, exposure 724.
28. Ibid., exposure 734.
29. Ibid., reel 25, exposure 724.
30. Ibid., reel 4, exposure 1001.
31. Ibid., reel 9, exposure 872.
32. Ibid., reel 27, exposure 2211.
33. Ibid., exposures 2214–16.
34. Ibid., reel 9, exposure 1908 and reel 25, exposure 629.
35. Ibid., reel 27, exposure 2216.
36. Ibid., reel 6, exposure 372.
37. Ibid., reel 12, exposure 1522.
38. Ibid., exposure 1516.
39. Ibid., reel 9, exposures 1236–40.
40. Ibid., reel 6, exposures 1160–73.

41. Ibid., reel 11, exposures 1400–1435.

42. Ibid., reel 19, exposures 635–36.

43. Ibid., reel 12, exposure 1523. Telephone interview with Richard Day, Vincennes, March 21, 2003, and Richard Day to George Blakey, March 25, 2003.

44. Indiana FWP Papers, reel 15, exposures 260–63.

45. Ibid., reel 27, exposures 290–91.

46. Sporn, *Against Itself,* 248; McDonald, *Federal Relief Administration and the Arts,* 711; Penkower, *Federal Writers' Project,* 148 and 229.

47. Indiana FWP Papers, reel 18, exposures 238–39.

48. Ibid., reel 3, exposures 1648–49.

49. Ibid., reel 5, exposures 938–42.

50. Ibid., reel 22, exposures 722 and 740.

51. Ibid., reel 16, exposures 462–63; reel 17, exposure 1501.

52. Ibid., reel 27, exposure 1020.

53. Ibid., reel 22, exposure 734; reel 27, exposures 1019–20.

54. *Indiana: A Guide,* 3.

55. Indiana FWP Papers, reel 5, exposures 1834–36.

56. Ibid., reel 27, exposures 103–85.

57. Ibid., reel 16, exposures 961–1007; reel 13, exposures 524–54.

58. Ibid., reel 8, exposures 2075–78.

59. Ibid., reel 1, exposures 779–86; reel 25, exposures 613–19; reel 16, exposures 824–28.

60. Ibid., reel 8, exposures 436–41.

61. Ibid., reel 7, exposures 564–71.

62. Ibid., reel 11, exposures 1157–66.

63. Ibid., reel 23, exposures 1959–60.

64. Ibid., reel 7, exposure 413.

65. Ibid., reel 19, exposures 138–39.

66. Ibid., reel 25, exposures 505–07. See also *Evansville Courier,* September 13, 1936.

67. Indiana FWP Papers, reel 19, exposures 2211–12.

9. Conclusions and Legacy

1. WPA, *Final Report,* 30 and 124; *Indianapolis Star,* February 2, 1943.

2. *Indianapolis News,* May 8, 1943.

3. McKinzie, "Writers on Relief," 264.

4. Mangione, *The Dream and the Deal,* 369.

5. WPA Records, Central Office Field Reports, December 15, 1936, box 2.

6. Emery C. Turner, "I, Too, Am on Relief," *Indianapolis Star,* March 8, 1940.

7. Larry Lockridge, *Shade of the Raintree,* 26–27; Thompson, *Indiana Authors,* 1:375; *Indianapolis Star,* January 14, 1952.

8. *Indianapolis News,* May 24, 1954.

9. Thompson, *Indiana Authors,* 2:310; Cynthia R. Fadool, ed., *Contemporary Authors* (Detroit, 1985), 114:369.

10. Thompson, *Indiana Authors,* 1:516–17.

11. *Indianapolis News,* October 15, 1983; Debra White, "My Life Had Stood: A Loaded Gun—The Dissent of Rebecca Pitts, Indianapolis Poet and Philosopher" (graduate research paper, Emory University, April 22, 1997), 33; author's interview with Diane Prenatt, June 24, 2003; Rebecca Pitts, *Brief Authority: Fragments of One Woman's Testament* (New York: Vantage Press, 1986). Although Pitts's recollection of the Red Scare in Indiana in 1948 is accurate, her departure from the Butler University English Department coincided with the replacement of several female staff members who did not hold doctorate degrees by new male professors who did. Author's interview with Werner Beyer, July 11, 2003.

12. *Indianapolis Star,* March 5, 1978.

13. Bedford city directory, 1943–1956; *Bedford Daily Times-Mail,* September 17, 1956.

14. *Muncie Evening Press,* September 24, 1945; *Muncie Star,* September 25, 1945.

15. *New Albany Ledger-Tribune,* December 27, 1992.

16. Evansville city directory, 1942–1948.

17. South Bend city directory, 1942–1963; *South Bend Tribune,* May 29, 1969.

18. *New York Herald Tribune,* April 12, 1942.

19. See Terre Haute Critique, Indiana FWP Papers, reel 26, exposure 1554.

20. *Indiana: A Guide,* 86.

21. Allen County Public Library, *A Brief Guide to Fort Wayne* (Fort Wayne: Allen County Public Library, 1957).

22. Ira Berlin et al., *Remembering Slavery: African Americans Talk About Their Personal Experiences of Slavery and Freedom* (New York: New Press, 1998); Henry Louis Gates Jr. et al., *Unchained Memories: Readings from the Slave Narratives* (Boston: Bulfinch, 2002).

23. Weisberger, *WPA Guide to America,* xi–xii.

24. Mangione, *The Dream and the Deal,* 9.

25. Ibid., 119.

BIBLIOGRAPHY

Manuscript Collections

Federal Writers' Project (FWP) Records. Library of Congress, Manuscript Division.

Gary Public Library. Annual Reports, 1928–35. Gary, Ind.

Indiana Federal Writers' Project Papers. Indiana State University Library, Terre Haute (also available on microfilm).

Indiana Federal Writers' Project Papers. New Albany Public Library (manuscripts for Clark, Floyd, Harrison, and Jefferson counties).

Lockridge, Ross, Papers. Indiana State University Library, Terre Haute (housed with the Indiana FWP Papers, but separately and not indexed or microfilmed).

Work Projects Administration (WPA) Records. RG69, National Archives.

Oral History Interviews Recorded by George T. Blakey

Beyer, Werner. July 11, 2003. (Werner taught English at Butler University beginning in 1948.)

Day, Richard. March 21, 2003. (Day is an official with the Indiana Department of Natural Resources in Vincennes.)

Prenatt, Diane. June 24, 2003. (Prenatt was a student and friend of Rebecca Pitts, Indiana FWP editor from 1935 to 1938.)

Robbins, Margaret Schricker. August 21, 2002. (Robbins was an Indiana FWP editor in 1939.)

Federal Writers' Project Publications for Indiana

Calumet Region Historical Guide. Gary: Garman Printing, 1939.

Hoosier Tall Stories. Indianapolis, 1937, 1939.

Indiana: A Guide to the Hoosier State. New York: Oxford University Press, 1941.

Indiana: Facts, Events, Places, Tours. New York: Oxford University Press, 1941.

"It Happened in Indiana." Newspaper columns, 1940–42.

Bibliography

Cited from *Muncie Evening Press.*
Cited from *Princeton Clarion-News.*
"Text for Americanization and Naturalization Classes."
Located in Indiana FWP Papers.

Federal Publications

Bureau of the Census. *Financial Statistics of Cities Having a Population over 30,000,* 1929–32.
————. *Historical Statistics of the United States,* 1975.
————. *Statistical Abstracts of the United States,* 1939.
————. Census for 1930, Indiana.
Whiting, Theodore, ed., *Final Statistical Report of the Federal Emergency Relief Administration,* 1942.
Works Projects Administration, *Final Report on the WPA Program, 1935–1943,* 1946.

State of Indiana Publications

Recovery in Indiana. Official bulletin of Governor's Commission on Unemployment Relief, 1934–36.
Report of Study Commission for Indiana Financial Institutions, 1932.
Yearbook, 1928–35.
Yearbook of the Governor's Commission on Unemployment Relief, 1933–35.

Unpublished Materials

Camp, John C. "America Eats: Toward a Social Definition of American Foodways." Ph.D. dissertation, University of Pennsylvania, 1978.
McKinzie, Kathleen O. "Writers on Relief, 1935–1942." Ph.D. dissertation, Indiana University, 1970.
Meister, Richard J. "A History of Gary, Indiana: 1930–1940." Ph.D. dissertation, University of Notre Dame, 1967.
Neff, Robert R. "The Early Career and Governorship of Paul V. McNutt." Ph.D. dissertation, Indiana University, 1963.
White, Debra. "My Life Had Stood: A Loaded Gun—The Dissent of Rebecca Pitts, Indianapolis Poet and Philosopher." Graduate research paper, Emory University, April 22, 1997.

Bibliography

Newspapers

Bedford Daily Times-Mail
Calumet News
Chesterton Tribune
Christian Science Monitor
Elkhart Truth
Evansville Courier
Fort Wayne News-Sentinel
Gary Post-Tribune
Indianapolis News
Indianapolis Recorder
Indianapolis Star
Indianapolis Times
Muncie Evening Press
Muncie Star
New Albany Ledger Tribune
New York Herald Tribune
New York Times
Peru Daily Tribune
Princeton Clarion News
South Bend Tribune
Vincennes Sun-Commercial
Wabash Plain Dealer

Research Aids

Bloxom, Marguerite D. *Pickaxe and Pencil: References for the Study of the WPA.* Washington, D.C.: Library of Congress, 1982.

Brewer, Jeutonne P. *The Federal Writers' Project: A Bibliography.* Metuchen, N.J.: Scarecrow Press, 1994.

Carter, Robert L., and David E. Vancil. *Indiana Federal Writers' Project/Program Papers: Guide to the Microfilm Edition at Indiana State University.* Terre Haute: Friends of the Cunningham Memorial Library, 1992.

Books

Aaron, Daniel. *Writers on the Left: Episodes in American Literary Communism.* New York: Columbia University Press, 1992.

Algren, Nelson. *America Eats.* Iowa City: University of Iowa Press, 1992.

Bibliography

Alsberg, Henry G., ed. *The American Guide: A Source Book and Complete Travel Guide for the United States.* New York: Hastings House, 1949.

Arizona Writers' Program. *Arizona: Facts, Events, Places, Tours.* New York: Bacon and Wieck, 1940.

Ayer, N. W., and Sons. *American Newspaper Annual and Directory.* Philadelphia: N. W. Ayer and Sons, 1929, 1935.

Baker, Ronald L. *French Folklife in Old Vincennes.* Terre Haute: Hoosier Folklore Society, 1989.

———. *Homeless, Friendless, and Penniless: The WPA Interviews with Former Slaves Living in Indiana.* Bloomington: Indiana University Press, 2000.

———. *Hoosier Folk Legends.* Bloomington: Indiana University Press, 1982.

Banks, Ann. *First-Person America.* New York: Alfred A. Knopf, 1980.

Barger, Harold, and Hans Landsberg. *American Agriculture, 1899–1939: A Study of Output, Employment, and Productivity.* New York: National Bureau of Economic Research, 1942.

Berlin, Ira, et al. *Remembering Slavery: African Americans Talk about Their Personal Experiences of Slavery and Freedom.* New York: New Press, 1998.

Berry, Cecelia Ray, ed. *Folk Songs of Old Vincennes.* Chicago: H. T. Fitz-Simons, 1946.

Bindas, Kenneth J. *All of This Music Belongs to the Nation: The WPA's Federal Music Project and American Society, 1935–1939.* Knoxville: University of Tennessee Press, 1995.

Black, Glenn A. *Angel Site: An Archaeological, Historical, and Ethnological Study.* Vol. 1. Indianapolis: Indiana Historical Society, 1967.

Blake, I. George. *Paul V. McNutt: Portrait of a Hoosier Statesman.* Indianapolis: Central, 1966.

Blakey, George T. *Hard Times and New Deal in Kentucky, 1929–1939.* Lexington: University Press of Kentucky, 1986.

Bodnar, John. *Remaking America: Public Memory, Commemoration, and Patriotism in the Twentieth Century.* Princeton, N.J.: Princeton University Press, 1992.

———, ed. *Bonds of Affection: Americans Define Their Patriotism.* Princeton, N.J.: Princeton University Press, 1996.

Bold, Christine. *The WPA Guides: Mapping of America.* Jackson: University Press of Mississippi, 1999.

Botkin, Benjamin A. *Lay My Burden Down: A Folk History of Slavery.* Chicago: University of Chicago Press, 1945.

———, ed. *A Treasury of American Folklore.* New York: Crown, 1944.

Brinkley, Alan. *Voices of Protest: Huey Long, Father Coughlin, and the Great Depression.* New York: Alfred A. Knopf, 1982.

Bibliography

Browder, Laura. *Rousing the Nation: Radical Culture in Depression America.* Amherst: University of Massachusetts Press, 1998.

Connecticut Writers' Program. *Connecticut: Facts, Events, Places, Tours.* New York: Bacon and Wieck, 1940.

Couch, W. T., ed. *These Are Our Lives.* Chapel Hill: University of North Carolina Press, 1939.

Davidson, James W., and Mark H. Lytle. *After the Fact: The Art of Historical Detection.* 2nd ed. New York: Alfred A. Knopf, 1986.

Davis, Charles T., and Henry Louis Gates Jr., eds. *The Slave's Narrative.* New York: Oxford University Press, 1985.

Flanagan, Hallie. *Arena: The Story of the Federal Theatre.* New York: Duell, Sloan and Pearce, 1940.

Gallup, George H. *The Gallup Poll, 1935–1971.* Vol. 1. New York, 1972.

Gates, Henry Louis, Jr. *Unchained Memories: Readings from the Slave Narratives.* Boston: Bulfinch, 2002.

Godfroy, Clarence. *Miami Indian Stories.* Winona Lake, Ind.: Light and Life Press, 1961.

Goodall, Hurley C. *Underground Railroad: The Invisible Road to Freedom through Indiana as Recorded by the WPA Writers' Project.* Indianapolis: Department of Natural Resources, 2001.

Gurko, Leo. *The Angry Decade: American Literature and Thought from 1929 to Pearl Harbor.* New York: Harper, 1968.

Hirsch, Jerrold. *Portrait of America: A Cultural History of the Federal Writers' Project.* Chapel Hill: University of North Carolina Press, 2003.

Hobson, Archie, ed. *Remembering America: A Sampler of the WPA American Guide Series.* New York: Columbia University Press, 1985.

Hofstadter, Richard. *The Age of Reform.* New York: Vintage Press, 1955.

Holtzman, Abraham. *The Townsend Movement: A Political Study.* New York: Octagon Press, 1975.

Hornung, Clarence P. *Treasury of American Design.* 2 vols. New York: Harry N. Abrams, 1972.

Horvitz, Lester V. *The Longest Raid of the Civil War.* Cincinnati: Farmcourt, 1999.

Indiana Bankers Association. *Report of the Research Committee.* Indianapolis: Indiana Bankers Association, 1937.

Josephson, Matthew. *Infidel in the Temple: A Memoir of the Nineteen-Thirties.* New York: Alfred A. Knopf, 1967.

Kazin, Alfred. *On Native Grounds.* New York: Harcourt, Brace and World, 1942.

Kennedy, David M. *Freedom from Fear: The American People in Depression and War, 1929–1945.* New York: Oxford University Press, 1999.

Bibliography

Lane, James B. *City of the Century: A History of Gary, Indiana.* Bloomington: Indiana University Press, 1978.

Leary, Edward A. *Indianapolis: The Story of a City.* Indianapolis: Bobbs-Merrill, 1971.

Leuchtenburg, William E. *Franklin D. Roosevelt and the New Deal.* New York: Harper and Row, 1963.

Lockridge, Larry. *Shade of the Raintree: The Life and Death of Ross Lockridge Jr.* New York: Viking Press, 1994.

Lynd, Robert, and Helen Lynd. *Middletown in Transition: A Study in Cultural Conflicts.* New York: Harcourt, Brace, 1937.

Madison, James H. *Indiana through Tradition and Change: A History of the Hoosier State and Its People, 1920–1945.* Indianapolis: Indiana Historical Society, 1982.

Mangione, Jerre. *The Dream and the Deal: The Federal Writers' Project, 1935–1943.* Boston: Little, Brown, 1972.

Martin-Perdue, Nancy J., and Charles L. Perdue Jr., eds. *Talk about Trouble: A New Deal Portrait of Virginians in the Great Depression.* Chapel Hill: University of North Carolina Press, 1996.

Mathews, Jane DeHart. *The Federal Theatre, 1935–1939: Plays, Relief, and Politics.* Princeton, N.J.: Princeton University Press, 1967.

McDonald, William F. *Federal Relief Administration and the Arts.* Columbus: Ohio State University Press, 1969.

McDonough, Irene R. *History of the Public Library in Vigo County, 1816–1975.* Terre Haute: Vigo County Public Library, 1977.

McFadden Marian. *Biography of a Town: Shelbyville, Indiana, 1822–1962.* Shelbyville: Tippecanoe Press, 1968.

McKinzie, Richard D. *The New Deal for Artists.* Princeton, N.J.: Princeton University Press, 1973.

Meltzer, Milton. *Violins and Shovels: The WPA Arts Projects.* New York: Delacorte, 1976.

Mohl, Raymond, and Neil Betten. *Steel City: Urban and Ethnic Patterns in Gary, Indiana, 1906–1950.* New York: Holmes and Meier, 1986.

Moore, Powell A., ed. *The Calumet Region: Indiana's Last Frontier.* Indianapolis: Indiana Historical Bureau, 1977.

Morris, Richard B. *Encyclopedia of American History.* Rev. ed. New York: Harper, 1961.

O'Gara, Geoffrey. *A Long Road Home.* New York: Norton, 1989.

Patterson, James T. *Congressional Conservatism and the New Deal: The Growth of the Conservative Coalition in Congress, 1933–1939.* Lexington: University Press of Kentucky, 1967.

Penkower, Monty N. *The Federal Writers' Project : A Study in Government Patronage of the Arts.* Urbana: University of Illinois Press, 1977.

Perdue, Charles L., Jr., et al., eds. *Weevils in the Wheat: Interviews with Virginia Ex-Slaves.* Charlottesville: University of Virginia Press, 1976.

Pickett, William B. *Homer E. Capehart: A Senator's Life, 1897–1979.* Indianapolis: Indiana Historical Society, 1990.

Pitts, Rebecca. *Brief Authority: Fragments of One Woman's Testament.* New York: Vantage Press, 1986.

Rafert, Stewart. *The Miami Indians of Indiana: A Persistent People, 1654–1994.* Indianapolis: Indiana Historical Society, 1996.

Rawick, George, ed. *The American Slave: A Composite Autobiography.* Westport, Conn.: Greenwood Press, 1972, 1977, and 1979.

Sherwood, Robert E. *Roosevelt and Hopkins: An Intimate History.* New York: Harper, 1948.

Smith, Polly, ed. *Times Capsule: The Times' History of the Calumet during the Twentieth Century.* Crown Point: Northwest Indiana Newspapers, 1999.

Spiller, Robert E., et al., ed. *Literary History of the United States.* Vol. 2. New York: Macmillan, 1949.

Sporn, Paul. *Against Itself: The Federal Theater and Writers' Projects in the Midwest.* Detroit: Wayne State University Press, 1995.

Steffens, Lincoln. *The Letters of Lincoln Steffens.* Vol. 1. New York: Harcourt, Brace, 1938.

Steinbeck, John. *Travels with Charley: In Search of America.* New York: Bantam, 1962.

Swados, Harvey, ed. *The American Writer and the Great Depression.* Indianapolis: Bobbs-Merrill, 1966.

Taylor, Robert M. Jr., et al. *Indiana: A New Historical Guide.* Indianapolis: Indiana Historical Society, 1989.

Terrill, Tom E., and Jerrold Hirsch, eds. *Such as Us: Southern Voices of the Thirties.* Chapel Hill: University of North Carolina Press, 1978.

Thompson, Donald E. *Indiana Authors and Their Books.* 2 vols. Crawfordsville: Wabash College, 1974, 1981.

Weisberger, Barnard A. *WPA Guide to America: The Best of 1930s America as Seen by the Federal Writers' Project.* New York: Pantheon, 1985.

Women of Indiana. Ed. Mrs. Blanche Foster Boruff. Indianapolis: Indiana Women's Biography Association, Matthew Farson, Publisher.

Articles

Adams, Grace. "The White Collar Chokes." *Harper's* 177 (October 1938): 474–84.

Alsberg, Henry. "Writers and the Government." *Saturday Review of Literature,* January 4, 1936, 9 and 23.

Billington, Ray Allen. "Government and the Arts: The WPA Experience." *American Quarterly* 13 (Winter 1961): 466–79.

Blakey, George T. "Battling the Great Depression on Stage in Indiana." *Indiana Magazine of History* 90 (March 1994): 1–25.

Blassingame, John. "Using the Testimony of Ex-Slaves." *Journal of Southern History* 41 (November 1975): 473–92.

Bolles, Blair. "The Federal Writers' Project." *Saturday Review of Literature* 18 (July 9, 1938): 3–4, 18–19.

Boyer, Margrette. "Morgan's Raid in Indiana." *Indiana Magazine of History*, December 1912, 149–65.

Cantwell, Robert. "America and the Writers' Project." *New Republic* 98 (April 26, 1939): 323–25.

Cowley, Malcom. "Federal Writers' Project." *New Republic*, October 21, 1972, 23–26.

DeVoto, Bernard. "The Writer's Project." *Harper's Magazine* 184 (January 1942): 221–24.

Ewbank, Louis B. "Morgan's Raid in Indiana." *Indiana Historical Society* 7, no. 2 (1917): 131–83.

"Federal Poets: An Anthology." *New Republic*, May 11, 1938, 10–12.

"Federal Poets Number." *Poetry*, July 1938.

Fox, Daniel M. "The Achievements of the Federal Writers' Project." *American Quarterly* 13 (Spring 1961): 3–19.

Gutheim, Frederick. "America in Guide Books." *Saturday Review of Literature* 24 (June 14, 1941): 3–5, 15.

Hopkins, Harry L. "Food for the Hungry." *Colliers* 96 (December 7, 1935): 10–11, 61–62.

"Mirror to America." *Time*, January 3, 1938, 55–56.

Morgan, Iwan. "Factional Conflict in Indiana Politics during the Later New Deal Years, 1936–1940." *Indiana Magazine of History* 79 (March 1983): 29–60.

———. "Fort Wayne and the Great Depression: The Early Years, 1929–1933." *Indiana Magazine of History* 80 (June 1984): 122–45.

———. "Fort Wayne and the Great Depression: The New Deal Years, 1933–1940." *Indiana Magazine of History* 80 (December 1984): 348–78.

O'Neill, Robert K. "The Federal Writers' Project Files for Indiana." *Indiana Magazine of History* 76 (June 1980): 85–96.

Oppenheimer, George. "What Is the Answer?" *Saturday Review of Literature*, December 19, 1931, 395.

Pitts, Rebecca. "Something to Believe In." *New Masses*, no. 10 (March 13, 1934): 14–17.

———. "Women and Communism." *New Masses*, no. 14 (February 19, 1935): 14–18.

―――. "Women and the New Masses." *New Masses,* no. 21 (December 1, 1936): 15.

Rosenberg, Harold. "Anybody Who Could Write English." *New Yorker,* January 20, 1973, 99–102.

Rush, Charles. "The Book Buyer Speaks Out." *Saturday Review of Literature,* January 30, 1932, 485–87.

"Unemployed Arts." *Fortune* 15 (May 1937): 109–17, 168, 171–72.

Webb, Dorothy. "Betty Kessler Lyman and the Indiana Federal Children's Theatre." *Youth Theatre Journal* 9 (1995): 68–78.

Weeks, Edward. "Hard Times and the Author." *Atlantic Monthly* 155 (May 1935): 551–62.

"What the Writers Wrote." *New Republic* 92 (September 1, 1937): 89–90.

Wilson, William L. "Thunderbolt of the Confederacy, or King of the Horse Thieves." *Indiana Magazine of History* 54 (June 1958): 119–30.

Woodward, C. Vann. "History from Slave Sources" *American Historical Review* 79 (April 1974): 470–81.

"WPAccounting." *Time,* February 15, 1943, 95–96.

INDEX

abolitionists, 183–186

Abraham Lincoln, 38

Adams, John Q., 37

Adams, Mildred, 153

Adams County, Ind., 134

Ade, George, 37, 167, 170

African Americans, 42, 62, 78, 88, 92–94, 107–117, 121–122, 183–186, 192–194, 204, 207–208

Against Itself, 3

agriculture, 28, 30, 55, 57, 58, 62, 63, 69, 75, 103, 133, 140, 160, 163, 191, 205

Aiken, Conrad, 15

Akron, Ohio, 146

Alabama, 43, 165

"Alabama Health Almanac," 20

Albania, 193, 194

Algren, Nelson, 16, 26, 166–168, 208

Allen, Joseph, 115

Allen County, Ind., 60, 135, 174, 177, 194

Alsberg, Henry, 16, 17, 19, 24–26, 41, 46, 50, 52, 58, 60, 75, 77, 80, 81, 83–85, 112, 132, 135, 146, 147, 164, 165

America Eats, 26, 164–168, 208

American Association for State and Local History, 201

American Federation of Labor, 90

American Guide, The, 19

American Guide Series, 1, 12, 17–20, 27, 40, 41, 45, 46, 48–50, 55, 61, 63, 69, 72, 205

American Legion, 32

American Pictorial History Guide Series, 139

American Recreation Series, 81, 100, 102

American Slave, The, 22, 110, 112

American Stuff, 24, 25, 44, 47

American Tragedy, An, 9

Americanization, 104–106, 142, 207

Amish, 54, 91

Anderson, C. A., 100

Anderson, Ind., 58, 64, 169

Anderson College, 64

A'Neals, Clyde, 161

Angel Mounds State Park, 35

Angola, Ind., 71

Anthony, William, 128

antiques, 53, 174–176, 196, 209

"Appeal to the Great Spirit," 45

Appleseed, Johnny, 60, 172

archeology, 57

Architectural Record, 35

architecture, 53, 55, 57, 58, 64, 66, 71, 75, 100, 143, 177, 186–189, 196

Arizona, 56, 102, 165, 170

Arkansas, 111

Armenians in Massachusetts, The, 168

Arnold, Eleanor, 108

Arsenal Tech, 141

art, 55, 57, 60–61, 69, 103

Ash, Thomas, 113–114

Associate Volunteers, 54–55

Atlantic Monthly, 14, 164

(Aurora) *Dearborn Independent,* 38

Aveline, Lewis and Frank, 127

Awake and Sing, 10

Baedeker guides, 50

Baker, Ronald L., 85, 112–117, 139, 145–146, 196, 208

Ball brothers, 190

Ball State Teacher's College, 134

banking, 6, 29

Banks, Ann, 21–22

Barnett, Inez, 55

Bauerley, Charles, 37

Beatty, Clive, 88, 162, 176

Beaty, Elizabeth, 176

Bedford, Ind., 46, 76, 146–149, 202, 208

Belgians, 91, 169–171, 208

Bellow, Saul, 16

Ben Hur, 162

Benton, Thomas Hart, 61
Benton County, Ind., 60
Berlin, Ira, 207
Berry, Cecilia, 145
Beveridge, Albert, 74
Bicknell, Ind., 45, 175
Bierce, Ambrose, 71
Big Four Railroad, 182
Billington, Ray A., 62
Binz, Fred, 182
Black, Glenn, 35, 57
Blackford, Edgar, 131
Bland, James, 123
Bloomington, Ind., 39, 40, 58, 176
Bobbs-Merrill Company, 40–41, 77
Bodnar, John, 5, 129
Bondy, Comilius, 127
Book of the Month Club, 19
book publishing, 13
book sales, 13
Borden, Ind., 184
Bossley, Eva, 127
Botkin, Benjamin, 20–22, 59, 110, 112,
    144, 145, 168, 171, 195
Boulder, Utah, 171
Bowen, Ephrain Hale, 138
Bowers, Claude, 37
Bowles, William, 188
Bowman, Julia, 116
Braun, John Paul, 180
Bridge Junction, Ind., 53
Brief Authority, 201
Briggs, Gordon F., 40, 46, 47, 55, 56, 58–
    60, 63, 67, 68, 70–72, 75, 77, 85, 87,
    93, 96, 98, 101, 103, 105, 106, 112,
    114, 132, 135, 140, 144, 145, 147, 148,
    163, 164, 165, 167, 169–173, 192, 195,
    200, 208, 210, 211
Broederenkring, 170
Brouillette, Mary, 175
Brown, Sterling, 110
Brown, Wallace, 138
Brown County, Ind., 76, 82, 102, 140
Bruceville, Ind., 187
Bulgarians, 194
Burdsall, Charles, 122
Burns, George T., 114, 184
Burns, Lee, 57, 58
Burns Statutes, 105
Burnworth, Cornet, 187
Bursts and Duds, 146

Butler, Belle, 116
Butler, Raymond, 181
Butler University, 40, 143, 201

California, 7, 8, 14, 24, 51, 56, 176
Calumet News, 95
Calumet region, 2, 30, 64, 67, 85–95, 132,
    155, 176, 192, 206
Calumet Region Historical Guide, 80, 85–95,
    163, 206
Camp Morton, 123
Canada, 142, 183, 184
canals, 39, 66, 73, 76, 97, 100
Caney, Josephine, T., 144–145
Cannelton, Ind., 196
Capehart, Homer, 46
Carmichael, Hoagy, 62
Carnegie-Illinois Corporation, 94
Carriere, Joseph M., 143
Carroll County, Ind., 153
Cedar Lake, Ind., 88
cemeteries, 45, 52, 60, 98, 99, 175, 179–
    182, 196
Chapman, John, 60
Charles, Samuel, 185
Chautauqua, 70, 105
Chesterton Tribune, 95
Chicago, Ill., 41, 44, 57, 58, 61, 65, 71, 72,
    75, 86, 87, 147, 148, 166, 167
Chicago Tribune, 154
Choir Chopin, 91
Choir Karogeorge, 91
Christian Science Monitor, 78, 86
Cincinnati, Ohio, 117, 183–185
circus, 191
Civil War, 22, 32, 39, 69, 72, 73, 99, 107,
    109, 110, 113, 114, 117–125, 129, 152,
    154, 176, 177, 183, 188, 192, 207
Civil Works Administration (CWA), 6, 14,
    31, 43, 186
Civilian Conservation Corps (CCC), 6, 21,
    26, 31, 76, 94, 119, 134, 159
Clark, George Rogers, 45, 65, 69, 72
Clark, Helen, 180, 196
Clark County, Ind., 165, 178, 183
Clay, Henry, 65
Clay County, Ind., 190
Clemens, Homer Oscar Louis, 31
Cleveland Press, 201
Clifty Falls State Park, 101
Clinton, Ed, 191

Index

Cockrum, William, 161
Coffin, Levi and Katharine, 73, 185
Coleman, Christopher B., 57
college enrollments, 28
Columbia City, Ind., 178
Columbia University, 16
Columbian Exposition, 72
communism, 8, 9, 25, 47, 201, 209
Congress of Industrial Organizations, 90
Connecticut, 14, 50, 102
Connersville, Ind., 187, 189
Cook, Iris, 4, 43, 70, 75, 123, 124, 157, 158, 183, 195, 203–204, 212
Corydon, Ind., 64, 73, 76, 117, 119, 122, 131, 205
Corydon Democrat, 119
Couch, W. T., 21
Coy, Wayne, 34, 35, 46
Crandall, Andrew W., 57
Crane, Mary, 113–114
Crawford, Ruth, 58, 59, 61
Crawford County, Ind., 135, 158
Creel, Lauana, 43, 60, 114, 115, 158, 184, 203
Creole, 60, 130, 142–146, 149, 208
"Creole (French) Pioneers at Old Post Vincennes, The," 144
Creole King Ball, 101
Croatians, 91
Cronyn, George, 51, 58, 61, 83, 144, 169
Crown Point, Ind., 72
Cudahy Packing Company, 89
Culver Military Academy, 75
Cunningham Library, 211
Cypress Beach Dance Hall, 158
Czechs, 194

Dearborn County, Ind., 122, 125, 157, 184
Dearborn Independent (Aurora), 38
Debs, Eugene V., 8, 9, 33, 45, 47, 74, 149, 211
Decatur County, Ind., 33
"Defense Reporter, The," 173
Delaware County, Ind., 115, 134, 176, 185
Delaware Indians, 172
Delphi, Ind., 153, 156
Demmon, Alice, 160, 161, 163
Democratic Party, 7–9, 29, 32, 36, 39, 105, 188

DePauw University, 57, 105, 140, 141
Deputy, Ind., 123
Deshee Farms, 76
Diana of the Dunes, 70, 73, 85, 206
Dickey, Marcus, 153, 156
Dickinson, Arline, 82
Dies, Martin, 24
Dies Committee, 24–26, 46, 209
Dillinger, John, 72
Dixon, Samuel, 157, 158, 184
Dodson, Estelle, 147, 176, 190
Dome, Charles, 121
Dos Passos, John, 9, 41
Dream and the Deal, The, 3
Dreiser, Theodore, 9, 14, 37
Dresser, Paul, 67
DuBois County, Ind., 193
dunes, 70, 86, 88, 93, 94
Dunker, Henry, 161
Dunn, Jacob P., 59
Dunton, James, 47, 84
Dupont, Ind., 122, 123
Durre, Elsie, 59, 81

Earlham College, 65, 141
East Chicago, Ind., 64, 86, 88, 89, 91, 95, 142
Edinburg, Ind., 98, 178
education, 55, 57, 65, 73, 75, 88, 116, 131, 133, 139, 141, 172–173
"Education Moves Forward," 172
Eggleston, Edward, 63
Elbel, Richard, 53
elections: 1928, 8, 137; 1932, 8, 9, 32, 33; 1934, 8, 9; 1936, 7, 33; 1938, 26, 36; 1940, 33, 47, 74
Eli Lilly Company, 31
Elkhart, Ind., 64, 71, 76, 206
Elkhart County, Ind., 82, 91, 187
Elkhart Truth, 79
Ellison, Ralph, 16
Elmhurst, 187, 189
Elwood, Ind., 167
End Poverty in California (EPIC), 9
England, 17, 42, 72, 161, 196
English Hotel, 40
Esarey, Logan, 59, 161
ethnicity, 2, 26, 62, 91–92, 133, 140, 142–146, 149, 151, 166, 168–171, 190, 192–194, 196, 204, 206, 211
Europe, 140, 141, 210

Evansville, Ind., 29, 34–36, 43, 60, 64, 81, 102, 114, 131, 153, 157, 158, 177, 178, 183, 194, 201, 203
Evansville Courier, 41

Fairbanks, Calvin, 184
Farm Security Administration, 22, 75, 76, 151
Faun, 44
Fauntleroy House, 45, 75
Fayette County, Ind., 134, 187
Federal Arts Project, 11–12, 27, 36, 171
Federal Deposit Insurance Corporation (FDIC), 6, 31
Federal Emergency Relief Administration (FERA), 6, 14, 16, 22, 31, 43, 110
Federal Music Project, 11, 36
Federal One, 10–11, 12, 14, 17, 25, 36, 37
Federal Theater Project, 11, 25, 36, 94, 209
Federal Writers' Project, The, 3
Fields, John W., 208
Filipinos, 178
First Person America, 22
Fisk University, 110
Flanagan, Hallie, 25
Flatbelly, Chief, 98, 100
Fleming Publishers, 139
Florida, 156, 171
Floyd County, Ind., 70, 99, 138, 157, 182, 195
folklore, 2, 20, 21, 27, 37, 40, 43, 45, 52, 56, 58, 59, 69, 80, 81–85, 96, 98, 99, 103, 107, 109, 113, 114, 126, 127, 130, 131, 139, 143, 144, 145, 151, 172, 194–196, 201, 203, 206, 207, 211
Folklore Unit, 20
Folksongs of Old Vincennes, 145
Followell, Loy, 144, 175
food, 2, 164–168, 174
Fort Wayne, Ind., 29, 35, 36, 64, 67, 81, 102, 131, 174, 178, 194, 201, 205
Fort Wayne News Sentinel, 78
Fort Wayne's Family Album, 201
Fortville, Ind., 155
Fountain City, Ind., 185
Fountain County, Ind., 82
France, 17, 42, 91, 142–146, 160, 161, 168
Francoeur, Frances L., 87, 89
Frankfort, Ind., 105
Frankfort, Ky., 22

Franklin County, Ind., 134, 194
Frederick, John, 58, 87, 148
Freeman, Douglas S., 56
Freeman, Martha, 115, 154, 190, 191
French Folklife in Old Vincennes, 146
French Lick, Ind., 63, 102, 188

Gallup Poll, 7, 25
Garfield Park, 67
Gary, Elbert, 90
Gary, Ind., 29, 30, 36, 38, 64, 86, 88, 89, 91, 92, 102, 141, 160, 170, 193, 197
Gary Board of Education, 86, 88
Gary Civic Theater, 94
Gary Commercial Club, 86, 93
Gary Post-Tribune, 86, 95
George Rogers Clark, 38
Germans, 61, 92, 135, 143, 166, 168, 169, 176, 192–194, 196
Gettysburg, Pa., 117, 123
Giffin, William, 194
Giles, Hazel, 195
Gladden, E. A., 122, 124
Gnaw Bone, Ind., 206
Godfroy, Francis, 43, 125
Godfroy, James Clarence, 43, 59, 125–129, 171, 189, 193, 203, 212
Godfroy, Louise, 186
Goldman, Emma, 9
Goodall, Hurley, 186, 208
Goshen, Ind., 187
Gospel Messenger, 13
Governor's Commission on Unemployment Relief (GCUR), 32, 34, 39, 54, 118, 119
Grand Calumet River, 85, 89
Grant County, Ind., 82, 193
Graubman, Henrietta, 160, 162, 163
gravestones, 2, 60, 179–182
Greeks, 91, 170, 194
Greencastle Herald, 38
Greenfield, Ind., 154, 187
Greenwich Village, 16
Gregoire, James M., 57
Grenada Theater, 68
Guhrt family, 179–180

Hagerty, Ruth, 132
Halsted, Micha R., 93
Hamilton, Alice, 67, 205
Hamilton County, Ind., 98, 184

Index

Hammond, Ind., 36, 64, 71, 86–89, 91, 94
Hanau, Stella B., 58
Handbook of American Indians, 59
"Hands That Built America," 26–27, 171
Hanover, Ind., 122, 124, 179
Hard Times, 22
Harding, Ede, 181
Harrington, Francis, 26
Harris, Eliza, 185
Harris, Flora Mae, 65, 66, 138, 185
Harris, Maston, 121, 124
Harris, Walter, 190
Harrison, Benjamin, 69, 162, 177, 187
Harrison, William H., 46, 65, 69, 74
Harrison County, Ind., 121, 125, 157
Harvard University, 16
Hastings Publishers, 18
Haughey, William, 124
Haynes, Elwood, 73, 180
Haynes, Susanna, 180
HBO, 207
Heck, Frederick, 196
Henson, Edward, 184
Henspeter, Ruth, 131
Herodotus, 108
Herron Art Institute, 57, 60
Hewett, Alexander, 179
Hickey, Andrew, 40
Hill, E. G., 65–66
Hill Floral Products, 65–66
Hirsch, Jerrold, 3, 21, 26
Historic American Building Survey
    (HABS), 186, 187
historic site pilgrimages, 39, 45, 59, 73,
    118–119, 152–153, 200
Historic Sites Act, 186
Hobart, Ind., 176
Hobson, Archie, 19
Hobson, Edward, 118
Hofstadter, Richard, 8
Holliday, Simeon and Rachel, 185
Home Owners Loan Corporation
    (HOLC), 6, 31
Homeless, Friendless, and Penniless, 112,
    208
Hoosier Folk Legends, 85, 139, 196
Hoosier Group, 60
Hoosier Historical Institute, 200
Hoosier Salon, 60
Hoosier Tall Stories, 80–85, 136–139, 143,
    174, 195, 206

Hoover, Herbert, 33, 137
Hopkins, Harry, 11, 14, 16, 25–27, 31, 34,
    110, 199
House Committee on Un-American Activi-
    ties, 24
Howard County, Ind., 134
Howard University, 110
Huggard, William, 58
Humphrey, Ina Mae, 180
Hungarians, 91
Huntington, Ind., 127
Hurston, Zora Neale, 16, 37
Hyde Park, 49

Idaho, 18
"If You're Irish, It Don't Matter Where
    You Are," 44
Illinois, 46, 58, 86, 159, 166
"Immigrant Settlements in Connecticut,"
    20
Index of American Design, 12, 27, 36, 171
Indiana: Facts, Events, Places, Tours, 100–
    104, 206
Indiana: A Guide to the Hoosier State, 46, 49–
    79, 204–205
"Indiana: The Hoosier State in Pictures,"
    139–142, 200
Indiana: A New Historical Guide, 79, 205
Indiana Board of Charities and Correc-
    tions, 32
Indiana character, 56, 63, 103, 175, 205
Indiana Defense Council, 173
Indiana Department of Conservation, 75,
    106, 186, 189, 208
Indiana Department of Public Welfare,
    32, 34
Indiana Gladiolus Society, 99
Indiana Historical Society, 45, 79, 136,
    194, 205, 208
Indiana State Fair, 30–31, 141
Indiana State Library, 57
Indiana State Teachers College. *See* Indi-
    ana State University
Indiana State University, 4, 41, 47, 77, 78,
    85, 95, 96, 105, 112, 113, 120, 132,
    135, 136, 139, 140, 149, 172–174, 194,
    211
Indiana University, 32, 35, 36, 38, 39, 43,
    44, 57, 116, 141, 144, 200, 201
Indiana Yearbook, 105
Indianapolis, 28–201, passim

255

Index

Indianapolis Board of Park Commissioners, 200
Indianapolis Chamber of Commerce, 40
Indianapolis Children's Museum, 37, 178
Indianapolis Civic Theater, 44
Indianapolis Federal Orchestra, 36
Indianapolis Naval Armory, 37
Indianapolis News, 78, 136, 197, 200
Indianapolis Recorder, 78
Indianapolis Star, 52, 78, 135, 154, 199, 212
Indianapolis Times, 41, 74, 78, 140, 200
"Indians of North America," 171
industrial jargon, 174
industry, 28, 30, 55, 65, 69, 75, 76, 85, 87, 89, 93, 103, 131, 133, 141, 146–149, 206
Inland Steel Corporation, 89
Iowa, 59
Irish, 168, 192, 194
Irvin, Robert C., 99, 184, 187
"It Happened in Indiana," 80, 95–100, 174, 195, 206–207
Italians, 194
Italians of New York, The, 168

Jamison, Olis, 106
Japan, 98, 99
jargon. *See* Linguistics
Jasper County, Ind., 164
Jay County, Ind., 138, 185
Jefferson County, Ind., 122, 124, 157, 180, 187, 194
Jeffersonville, Ind., 64, 132, 156, 158, 179, 184
Jennings, John K., 34–36
Jewish Symphony Orchestra, 91
Jews, 91, 166
Johanni, Joe, 161
Johnson, Greenville, 121
Johnson, William R., 180
Jokelore, 196
Jordan Conservatory, 153
Jordan River Revue, 44
Joyce, Doyle, 144
Jungle, The, 8

Kaeser, William, 37
Kankakee River, 141, 155, 159–164, 208
Kansas, 56, 111
Kargacos, Elizabeth, 45, 144, 187, 189

Kazin, Alfred, 1, 2, 5
Keith Theater, 36
Kellams, Nellie, 158
Kellock, Katherine, 50, 71, 164
Kentucky, 10, 43, 51, 56, 72, 85, 113, 117, 123, 165, 183, 184
Kentucky Commission for Handicapped Children, 203
Kentucky State College, 22, 110
Kerr, Delight, 184
Kerrigan Theater, 43
Kilmer, Joyce, 18
King, Paul, 144
Kirk, Jerry, 52–53
Knight, Sudie, 177–178
Knights of the Golden Circle, 188
Knowles, Merton, 45, 155, 166
Knox, Ind., 179
Knox County, Ind., 60, 98, 175, 187, 189
Kokomo, Ind., 73, 134, 178
Kokomo Dispatch, 38
Koritz, Archie, 70, 89, 90, 161
Kosciusko County, Ind., 70, 98, 100
Ku Klux Klan, 74

La Follette, Robert, 18
La Porte, Ind., 40, 99, 131
La Porte County, Ind., 161
labor unions, 26, 89–91, 94, 149, 209
Lach, John, 91
Lafayette, Ind., 173, 182, 208
Lafayette Soldiers Home, 99
LaGrange, Ind., 71
Lake County, Ind., 30, 86, 89, 135, 176, 190, 193
Lake Michigan, 86, 93
Lake Wawasee, 98, 100
Lanier House, 75, 140, 188
LaSalle, 38
LaSalle, 161, 178
Laube, Audrey, 89, 90
Lavouncher, Robert, 127
Lawrence, Eliza, 122
Lawrence County, Ind., 43, 113, 146, 147, 149, 189, 197
Lawrenceburg, Ind., 158
Lay My Burden Down, 22, 110
Leavenworth, Ind., 158, 183
Lee, Robert E., 123
Lend Lease, 99
Lenin, Vladimir, 47, 211

Index

Levering, Julia, 161
Lewis, Sinclair, 14
Lexington, Ind., 118
Lexington and the Bluegrass Country, 85
liars' bench, 81, 82
Liberty, Ind., 178
Liberty Party, 8
libraries, 13, 38, 39, 49, 52, 59, 72, 105, 154, 205, 206
Library of Congress, 4, 12, 21, 22, 27, 75, 110, 111, 114, 116, 120, 167, 207, 211
Life History Series, 21, 27, 109
Life magazine, 75
limestone, 146–149, 190
"Limestone Industry of Lawrence and Monroe Counties, The," 147
"Limestone Town," 146–149
Lincoln, Abraham, 69, 70, 72, 76, 165, 178, 187
Lincoln, Nancy Hanks, 55
Lincoln National Bank, 29
Lindley, William, 188
Lindsay, William, 175
Linebarger, John A., 105
linguistics, 189–192, 196
literature, 37, 55, 58, 63, 103
Lithuania, 193
Little Calumet River, 85
Little Turtle, 59, 177
Living Theater, The, 11
Lochry, Archibald, 97
Lockefield Gardens, 76
Lockridge, Elsie, 39
Lockridge, Ross, 4, 38–42, 45, 46, 50, 51, 54–56, 59, 63, 64, 67, 71, 72, 74, 75, 77, 80–85, 96, 118, 119, 121, 123, 125, 131, 132, 136–138, 143, 144, 152–157, 159–161, 163, 164, 169, 178, 195, 200, 201, 209, 210, 212
Lockridge, Ross, Jr., 39, 45, 200
Logansport Pharos, 155
Lomax, John, 20, 22, 59, 81, 83, 85, 110, 137, 138
London Daily Journal, 16
Long, Huey, 7, 33, 47
Long Road Home, A, 19
Louisiana, 56, 85, 110, 142
Louisville, Ky., 117, 183
Louisville Courier-Journal, 138
Louisville Herald-Post, 43, 113, 202
Louisville Orchestra, 203

Loup-Garou, 146
Lynd, Robert and Helen, 30

Macbeth, 11, 85, 137
Madison, Ind., 64, 75, 101, 122, 140, 183, 184, 188, 189, 194
Madison County, Ind., 134
magazines, 13
Manchester College, 42, 57
Mangione, Jerre, 3, 16, 24, 211
Marion, Ind., 193
Marion County, Ind., 42, 112, 116, 179, 181, 182, 193
Marling, Melvin, 121
Marmon Motor Car Company, 40
Marshall, John, 74
Marshall, William, 124
Martin, Abe, 102
Martin-Perdue, Nancy, 22
Marx, Karl, 211
Marxism, 3
Masonic Lodge, 183
Massachusetts, 15, 18, 25, 62
Mauckport, Ind., 117
McCutcheon, John T., 154
McDonald, William, 27
McGrain, Harry, 122
McNutt, Paul V., 29, 32, 34, 39, 48, 118
Meharry, Floyd, 160, 162
Memories of Hoosier Homemakers, 108
Memories of White Oak School Days, 44
Mennonites, 54
Metamora, Ind., 76
Mexicans, 30
Miami County, Ind., 38, 43
Miami Indian Stories, 126, 203
Miami Indians, 59, 125–128, 161, 172, 177, 193, 203
Michigan, 17, 183, 190
Michigan City, Ind., 132, 160
Middletown, 30, 75, 149
Miller, Cecil, 82, 83, 155
Miller, Merle, 108
Miller, Sharlotte, 195
Millholland, Charles Bruce, 44, 147–149, 201–202
Milstead, Lavier, 72
Mineville, N.Y., 146
Mishawaka, Ind., 42, 166, 169–171, 203, 208
Mississinewa River, 82

Mississippi, 15
Mississippi River, 20, 156
Missouri, 51, 72
Mongosa, John, 127
Monroe, Grace, 124, 157, 158, 179, 187–188
Monroe County, Ind., 146, 147, 176, 190
Monrovia, Ind., 15
Montana, 139
Montezuma, Ind., 105
Monticello, Ind., 140
Moore, Marianne, 14
Moore, Perry, 127
Mooresville, Ind., 152
Morgan, John Hunt, 39, 69, 73, 117–125, 152
Morgan County, Ind., 178
Mormons, 171
Morton, Oliver P., 18, 99, 118
Mullings, Willie, 179
Munchausen, Baron, 84
Muncie, Ind., 30, 38, 64, 75, 115, 136, 149, 176, 191, 202
Muncie Star, 44
Munster, Ind., 88
Murphy, Elizabeth F., 153, 156
museums, 39, 52, 65, 69, 176–179, 196
music, 55, 60, 62, 91, 143, 145, 195
Mutchmore, Bernice, 144
Myers, Herman, 176

Napoleon, Ind., 184
Nation, 16, 26
National Archives, 4, 27, 211
National Cathedral, 147
National Endowment for the Arts, 27, 209
National Historic Landmarks, 186, 189
National Industrial Recovery Act, 94
National Labor Relations Act, 94, 209
National Register of Historic Places, 189
National Road, 97
National Youth Administration (NYA), 10, 35, 55, 76, 94, 148
Native Americans, 43, 52, 55, 56, 58, 59, 62, 64, 74, 91, 92, 97, 98, 108, 125–129, 142, 161, 172, 175, 177, 192, 193
Naval Ammunition Depot, 197
Nebeker Opera House, 155
Nebraska, 59, 81
Negro in Virginia, The, 20
Nelson, Oman, 147

Nevada, 63
New Albany, Ind., 43, 64, 123, 183, 194, 202
New Albany Public Library, 120, 157
New Deal, 3, 4, 6, 7, 10, 25, 26, 31, 32, 48, 76, 90, 94, 134, 148, 150, 151, 178, 186, 197, 207, 209–211
New Hampshire, 22, 56
New Harmony, Ind., 33, 45, 64, 65, 67, 74, 140, 169, 172, 205, 211
New Harmony Register, 38
New Masses, 47
New Orleans, La., 20, 165
New Orleans City Guide, 85
New Republic, 19, 24, 41
New York, 15, 24, 25, 40, 95, 101, 139, 210
New York City, 16, 44, 46, 100, 149, 190, 201
New York Evening Post, 16
New York Herald Tribune, 78
New York Times, 24, 27
Newburgh, Ind., 158
Newport, Ind. *See* Fountain City, Ind.
Newsom, John, 17, 26, 171, 172
Newspaper Guild, 14
newspapers, 13, 37–39, 43, 52, 65, 75, 80, 95–97, 103, 119, 123, 138, 147, 157, 159, 162, 163, 185, 207
Newspapers of Maryland's Eastern Shore, 201
Nicholson, Meredith, 37, 56, 77, 154
Noble County, Ind., 73, 195
Noblesville, Ind., 99
North Carolina, 21, 56
Norvelle, Lee, 36
Northwest Territory, 97
Northwestern University, 58

O'Bannon, Lew, 119
Odets, Clifford, 9
O'Flynn, Anna, 144, 145
O'Gara, Geoffrey, 19
Ohio, 46, 71, 73, 84, 118, 183, 190
Ohio County, Ind., 97, 157
Ohio River, 35, 70, 72, 117, 132, 140, 156–159, 163, 183, 184, 194, 202, 208
Oklahoma, 18, 38, 49, 56
Old Dutch Cleanser, 89
Old Fauntleroy Home, The, 200
Old Libby Prison, 72
Oldenburg, Ind., 194

Omaha, Neb., 170
On Native Grounds, 1
Oolitic High School, 43
oral history, 21–24, 107–129, 138, 164, 203
Orange County, Ind., 135, 188
Oregon, 22, 81
Oregon Trail, The, 20
Orpheus Choir, 91
Oxford University Press, 21, 77, 78, 205

Pacific Ocean, 20
Paderewski Choral Society, 91
Paoli, Ind., 188
Parke County, Ind., 97
Patterson, Mae, 88
Pearl Harbor, 15, 78, 98, 99, 104
Peat, Wilbur, 57
Pelz, William, 36
Penkower, Monty, 3
Pennsylvania, 54, 72, 176
Peopling Indiana, 194
Perdue, Charles, Jr., 22
Persian Wars, 108
Peru, Ind., 127, 191
Peru High School, 38
Peru Republican, 155
Pfrimmer, Will, 162
Phillips, Naomi P., 86–87
Phoenix, Ariz., 102
Pine Village, Ind., 134
Pitts, Rebecca, 4, 40, 41, 47, 55, 56, 59–61, 65, 66, 68, 72, 201, 209–212
Pittsburgh, Pa., 156
"Pockets in America," 168–170
Poe, Edgar A., 134
Poetry, 24, 44–45
Poland, 165, 166
Poles, 68, 91, 194
Pollock, Jackson, 12
Populist Party, 8
Porter, Cole, 62
Porter County, Ind., 70, 86
Portrait of America, 3
Posey County, Ind., 157
Potawatomi Indians, 74, 161, 172
Powers, Hapgood, 33, 34
Preston, Dickson J., 140–142, 200–201, 208, 212
Price, Wayne, 178
"Pricking Thumbs," 85, 137, 138, 208

Pritchett, Anna, 112, 116–117
Provincetown Playhouse, 16
Public Utility Holding Company Act, 209
Public Welfare Act, 32
Public Works Administration (PWA), 76
Pulaski County, Ind., 164
Pulitzer Prize, 15, 35, 63, 74, 154
Purdue University, 57, 75, 141, 205
Pyle, Ernie, 37

Quakers, 63, 184, 185
Queen Anne Candy Company, 89
Quince, John, 127

Rabb, Kate M., 154
radicalism, 3, 7, 9, 18, 24, 25, 47, 74, 198, 201, 209–210
Rappites, 169, 172
Ratti, Gino, 143
Rawick, George, 22, 110, 112, 116
Reader's Digest, 35
Red Cross, 158, 159
Red Romance, 9
Red Scare, 3, 90, 201
Reddick, Lawrence D., 22, 110
Reddix, Jacob L., 93
religion, 55, 91, 113, 127, 128, 142, 149
Remembering America, 19
"Remembering Slavery," 207
Rensselaer, Ind., 155, 160
Republican Party, 8, 9, 29, 32, 35–36, 46, 54
Revolutionary War, 69, 97, 143, 175
Richmond, Ind., 64–66, 153, 185
Richmond Art Association, 65
Ringo, Pete, 123
Riley, James Whitcomb, 2, 45, 77, 79, 103, 134, 140, 152–156, 162, 163, 177, 187, 208, 210
Ripley County, Ind., 165, 178
Rising Sun, Ind., 158
Roberts, Bessie, 81, 82, 85, 137, 138, 143, 201, 208, 212
Roberts, Pearl M., 100, 187
Robertson, Middleton, 123
Robinson, Joe, 116
Rockefeller Center, 147
Rockefeller family, 186
Rockport, Ind., 55, 76, 158
Rockville, Ind., 105
Roll, Charles, 106

Index

Roman Catholicism, 91, 142, 170
Rome City, Ind., 102
Roosevelt, Eleanor, 41
Roosevelt, Franklin D., 1, 3, 6, 32, 33, 45, 49, 99, 151, 209
Roosevelt High School, 93, 94
Royse, Morton, 20, 144, 146, 147, 168, 171
Rural Electrification Administration (REA), 76
Rushville American, 38
Russia, 9, 16

Sacco and Vanzetti, 18
Salem, Ind., 118, 119, 183
Salm, Odie, 196
Santa Claus, Ind., 206
Saturday Evening Post, 13
Saturday Review of Literature, 13, 52
Saxon, Lyle, 165
Schmitt, Mildred, 57
Schricker, Henry, 32, 35, 48
Schumann, William, 11
Schwartz, Rudolph, 61
Scotland, 196
Scott County, Ind., 121, 122
Scripps-Howard newspapers, 84, 201
Scudder, Janet, 61, 205
Seagram's distillery, 158
Sembower, John, 96, 97, 173
Shahn, Ben, 12
Shame of the Cities, The, 9
Shand, Cora, 60
Shawnee Stone Company, 190
Sheehan, Bess J., 88
Shelby County, Ind., 76, 138, 165
Shelbyville, Ind., 38
Shrewsbury House, 189
Sinclair, Upton, 8, 9
slave narratives, 12, 22–24, 27, 45, 100, 107, 109–117, 129, 198, 207–208
Slavs, 92
Slocum, Frances, 43, 125, 193
Slovaks, 91
Smith, Alfred, 134, 194
Smithsonian Institution, 207
Social-Ethnic Studies Unit, 20, 146
Social Security, 3, 10, 32, 76, 134, 209
socialism, 3, 8, 33, 39, 47, 74, 197, 209, 211
Soldiers and Sailors Monument, 61

Somerset Publishers, 79, 205
South Bend, Ind., 29, 31, 36, 53, 64, 67–68, 76, 102, 131, 160, 161, 166, 178, 181, 191
South Bend Tribune, 78
South Carolina, 23
Southern University, 110
Spain, 161
Spencer County, Ind., 55, 70, 82, 158, 165, 180
Spencer County Historical Society, 55
Sporn, Paul, 3
sports, 55, 69, 102, 141, 205
Spring Mill Village, 169
St. Joseph County, Ind., 42, 53, 91, 135, 161, 165, 169, 193
St. Meinrad, Ind., 169
St. Paul, Ind., 119
Stalcup, Clyde, 98
Standard Oil, 71, 88–90, 94
Standard Steel Car Company, 89
Starke County, Ind., 72, 161, 195
Stearley, Clay, 41, 66, 68
Steffens, Lincoln, 9
Steinbeck, John, 19
Stephenson, D. C., 74
Steuben County, Ind., 71, 165, 185
Story of Indiana, The, 200
Stout, Elihu, 189
Stranz, Allen, 54, 71
Stratton-Porter, Gene, 102
Strope, Albert, 42–43, 68, 82, 131, 166, 169–171, 191, 203, 212
Studebaker Company, 76, 191
Such as Us, 21
suicides, 28
Sulphur, Ind., 72
Sunday, Billy, 70
Sutton, Katie, 114
Swan, Elizabeth, 122
Sweenie, Ida Belle, 153
Switzerland County, Ind., 133, 157
Sylvan Lake, 73, 102
Symphonic Boys' Band, 91

Talk about Trouble, 22
Tarkington, Booth, 14, 37, 56, 63, 154
Tarpon Springs, Fla., 170–171
Tecumseh, 59
Tell City, Ind., 158
Tennessee, 3, 76, 110

Index

Tennessee Valley Authority (TVA), 76
Terkel, Studs, 15, 22
Terre Haute, Ind., 33, 36, 38, 47, 52, 58, 61, 64, 67, 96, 97, 105, 131, 133, 136, 172, 173, 208
Terre Haute Auto Club, 99
Terre Haute Post, 38, 41
Terrill, Tom, 21
Texas, 62
"Text for Americanization and Naturalization Classes, A," 106
theater, 55
These Are Our Lives, 21
Thomas, Norman, 39
Thompson, Maurice, 162
Thompson, Stith, 58, 60, 144
Thompson, Virgil, 11
Three Soldiers, 9
Thurman, Ray, 105–106
Time magazine, 17
Tippecanoe battleground, 46
Tippecanoe County, Ind., 173
Tirey, Ralph N., 78, 140, 142
Townsend, Clifford, 32, 34, 35, 77, 119
Townsend, Francis, 7, 33–34, 48
Tragic America, 9
"Trail of Song, The," 143
Travels with Charley, 19
Treasury of American Folklore, 21, 195
Treaty of Greenville, 127
Truman, Harry S, 108
Tucson, Ariz., 102
Turkey Run State Park, 101
Turner, Emery C., 4, 43–45, 47, 113, 114, 146–148, 182, 188, 189, 199, 202, 212
Tuttle, William W., 44, 45, 115, 176, 190–191, 202, 212
Twentieth Century, 44, 147, 202
Tyler, Velsie, 138

Ulery, Val, 98
"Unchained Memories," 208
Uncle Tom's Cabin, 185
Underground Railroad, 73, 100, 172, 174, 183–186, 196, 208
Underwood, Howard, 87
unemployment, 7, 11, 30, 31, 34, 36, 38, 41, 43, 85, 139, 166
Union City, Ind., 155
Union County, Ind., 178, 180

United Press International, 40
University of Chicago, 40
University of Iowa, 168
University of Notre Dame, 68, 69, 102, 131, 141
University of Pennsylvania, 16
urbanization, 28, 63, 72, 87, 102–104, 142, 204, 205, 210
U.S. Steel, 75, 89, 94
U.S.A., 9

Vallile, Pirene, 123
Valparaiso, Ind., 88, 160
Van Meter, Beulah, 158, 183
Vanderburgh County, Ind., 133, 157, 178, 196
Vanderwalker, Alvin, 132
Vermont, 139
Vernon, Ind., 118, 119
Versailles, Ind., 118, 119, 178
Vevay, Ind., 72
Vicksburg, Miss., 117
Vienna, Ind., 124
Vigo, Francis, 189
Vigo County, Ind., 52, 165, 173
Viking Press, 18, 24
Vincennes, Ind., 45, 53, 57, 60, 64, 65, 69, 101, 130, 142–146, 153, 168, 175, 187, 208
Vincennes Sun-Commercial, 79
Virginia, 22, 23, 56, 72, 139, 176
Virginia Conservation Commission, 100
Voeglin, Erminie and John, 58
Voelker, Philip, 196
Vonnegut, Kurt, 57

Wabash, Ind., 53, 100
Wabash and Erie Canal, 39, 172, 196
Wabash College, 141
Wabash County, Ind., 82, 125, 190
Wabash Gazette, 97, 100
Wabash River, 97, 142
Waiter, Elizabeth, 155
Waiting for Lefty, 10
Wakarusa, Ind., 82
Wallace, Lew, 63, 162
Walli, Emile, 179
Warren County, Ind., 45, 82, 134, 166
Warren Republican, 155
Warrick County, Ind., 137, 157
Warsaw, Ind., 155

Index

Washington, D.C., 6–211, passim
Washington County, Ind., 180
Wayne, Anthony, 127
Wayne County, Ind., 31, 73, 184, 185
Weevils in the Wheat, 23
Weisberger, Bernard, 1, 2, 206, 210
welfare state, 3, 29, 32, 33, 76, 209
Welles, Orson, 11
West Baden Springs, Ind., 188, 189
West Harrison, Ind., 117
Westfield, Ind., 184
Wettengel, Louis, 176
White, Albert, 182
White, William A., 56
White House, 49
Whiting, Ind., 64, 71, 88, 90, 92, 94
Willem, Charles, 165
Williams, James, 175
Williamsburg, Va., 186
Willkie, Wendell, 32, 74
Wills, Carl, 154
Wilson, Gilbert, 61
Wilson, Vivian, 178
Winchester, Ind., 154
Winger, Hallie, 193

Winger, Otho, 57
Winona Lake, Ind., 70
Winter, Mrs. Paul, 175
Wirt, William A., 88
Wisconsin, 18
Wise, George, 98, 99
witchcraft, 2, 59, 137–139, 149, 195
Witt, James, 128
Women's Army Corps, 124, 203
Woodward, C. Vann, 24
Woodworth, Dorothy, 180, 187
Working, 22
Works Progress Administration (WPA), 1–210, passim
World War I, 9, 16, 40, 42, 94, 99, 193
World War II, 17, 26, 68, 104, 106, 130, 140, 142, 164, 186, 197, 203
World's Fair (1933), 61
Wright, Richard, 24, 25, 37

Yaqui Indians, 170
Yoder, Paul, 53, 67, 170, 171, 178, 191
Young Frederick Douglass, 201
Young Men's Christian Association, 193
Yugoslavia, 209

Following residencies in Kentucky and Virginia, **George T. Blakey** became a Hoosier in 1964. He was professor of American and Indiana history until his retirement from Indiana University East in 2001. This is his third book, the second dealing with the Great Depression. He owns and operates a bookstore in Richmond, Indiana.

FRIENDS FREE LIBRARY
GERMANTOWN FRIENDS LIBRARY
5418 Germantown Avenue
Philadelphia, PA 19144
215-951-2355

Each borrower is responsible for all items
checked out on his/her library card, for
fines on materials kept overtime, and
replacing any lost or damaged materials.